Issues of Gender

Other readers featured in the "Longman Topics" series include:

Language and Prejudice
Tamara Valentine

Translating Tradition
Karen E. Beardslee

The Counterculture Reader
E. A. Swingrover

Citizenship Now
Jon Ford and Marjorie Ford

Considering Cultural Difference
Pauline Uchmanowicz

A Longman Topics Reader

Issues of Gender

ELLEN G. FRIEDMAN
The College of New Jersey

JENNIFER D. MARSHALL
Lehigh University

PEARSON
Longman

New York   San Francisco   Boston
London   Toronto   Sydney   Tokyo   Singapore   Madrid
Mexico City   Munich   Paris   Cape Town   Hong Kong   Montreal

Senior Vice President and Publisher: Joseph Opiela
Acquisitions Editor: Susan Kunchandy
Marketing Manager: Deborah Murphy
Managing Editor: Bob Ginsberg
Project Coordination, Text Design, and Electronic Page Makeup:
    Sunflower Publishing Services, Inc.
Cover Design Manager: Nancy Danahy
Cover Image: © Getty Images, Inc./Stone
Manufacturing Manager: Dennis J. Para
Printer and Binder: RR Donnelley & Sons Company
Cover Printer: Lehigh Press, Inc.

For permission to use copyrighted material, grateful acknowledg-
ment is made to the copyright holders on pp. 259–260, which are
hereby made part of this copyright page.

Library of Congress Cataloging-in-Publication Data

 Issues of gender/[edited by] Ellen G. Friedman, Jennifer D. Marshall.
    p. cm. — (Longman topics)
  Includes bibliographical references.
  ISBN 0-321-10879-5
   1. Sex role. 2. Gender identity. I. Friedman, Ellen G., 1944-
II. Marshall, Jennifer D. III. Series.

HQ1075.I77 2004
305.3—dc22   2003061135

Please visit our website at http://www.ablongman.com

ISBN 0-321-10879-5

  45678910—DOH—06

CONTENTS

PREFACE

Gender has become an increasingly important category in the understanding and analysis of society and its intellectual productions in such fields as literature, history, law, psychology, and sociology. It is a major topic of theory-making and in inquiries dealing with knowledge and methodology across disciplines. The scholarship that has come out of women's and gender studies has radically altered the way we define identity and the way we perceive ourselves in relation to culture. In the last twenty years, gender scholars have also played a significant role in advancing understanding across cultures.

The Women's Liberation Movement and "second-wave feminism" at the end of the 1960s gave rise to heightened consciousness about the position of women in society and raised women's expectations for self-development and political and economic equality. Although second-wave feminism is connected to the growth in women's education in the 1960s and the resulting high hopes women had, real progress in wages and social advancement was small. However, second-wave feminists did make significant progress in the academy where they applied their feminist analytical perspectives to the various fields of study, particularly transforming what counts as knowledge. From the early to mid-1970s, in feminist journals such as *Signs*, the disciplines were criticized for their masculinist assumptions and biases. These journals demanded new research concerned with women.

One of the concepts that the new feminist scholarship found particularly useful from the very beginning was that of gender. In his book *Sex and Gender* (1968), Robert J. Stoller developed a distinction between sex and gender: gender identity is the product of psychological and social, not biological, influences, although gender identity and biological sex can conflict, as in the case of transsexuals. Since Stoller made this distinction, sex is defined as the biological foundation of male-female differences, while gender is defined as a social construction. This distinction between biological sex and culturally constructed gender roles provided a basis for rejecting biological determinism; men and women were no longer frozen in their assigned cultural roles. The sex/gender distinction allowed the possibility of moving towards more equitable social and cultural gender roles. In the words of historian Ann Curthoys, this distinction "was what made it possible to think of a future different from the past and the present, a future where men and women had equal opportunities, mutual respect, shared childcaring and rearing, and equal cultural value. Where 'sex' was inescapable, gender was malleable; sex was destiny, gender was free will" ("Gender Studies in Australia: a History," *Australian Feminist Studies*, March 2000: p. 21).

The new understanding of the sex/gender system inspired an outpouring of scholarship about patriarchy and masculinist domination of culture and academic disciplines. In the academic arena, projects to transform curricula to expose patriarchal bias and substitute perspectives that reflected the new gender scholarship began to affect what professors taught and what students learned. Such transformations required a radical change in the position from which the world and knowledge is understood. For literature professors, it meant not only putting, for instance, slave narratives and women's "sentimental" novels into U.S. literature courses but also asking how these books change our understanding of our history and culture. In the social/cultural arena, it required rethinking the patriarchal underpinnings of social institutions such as family, the healthcare system, religion, and workplaces.

As feminist lenses were used to look at received assumptions, those assumptions crumbled. For instance, Joan Kelly asked the now classic question "Did women have a Renaissance?" in her book *Women, History, and Theory* (1984). This question forever affected how historians approached their subject. Her answer is that women were much better off in the Middle Ages, which traditionally had been understood as a time when European cultural life stagnated. According to Kelly, however, during the Middle Ages, women owned and managed vast estates, the maternal name was commonly used for children, the legitimacy of offspring was not a great issue, and women participated in creating courtly literature. As smaller political units, such as fiefdoms, coalesced into nation-states during the period known as the Renaissance, women lost all of these rights. By defining the Renaissance as an advance over the Middle Ages, the older scholarship revealed that it associated progress with male achievement alone, ignoring women and other powerless groups. Thus, examining a historical period through the feminist gaze transforms how one interprets it. Not only has the smile been wiped off the Renaissance as a result of gender scholarship, but some historians have abandoned it as a meaningful category.

The enormous transformative power of the lens of gender sug-gested other inequities in knowledge and perception. Feminists who went about deconstructing the assumptions and values of traditional perceptions of history and reality paid most attention to white, middle class women and their problems. "Woman" as a uniform category began to come under scrutiny. Who and what is this "woman" of feminist inquiry? Can women of all classes, races, ethnicities, and sexual orientations be lumped together in this category? What's more important in identity formation: gen-der, race, class, ethnicity, or sexual orientation?

Such questions drove gender inquiries during the late 1970s and 1980s. The result of such examinations was an emphasis on differences among women. It was argued that the differences be-tween women have a range that is as large as the differences be-tween women and men. This insight troubled feminist scholar-ship, which became divided over whether one even could talk about women as a social category. It was recognized that, from some points of view, the divisions between white, middle class men and women were not as significant as the divisions between women of different races or classes or sexual orientations. The questions that drove gender studies were applicable to the entire range of identity markers. It became clear that the instabilities in the category of "woman" also appeared in the gamut of identity categories, whether of class, race, ethnicity, or sexuality. A lesbian identity, for instance, is not unitary. Not everyone who claims les-bian identity experiences her identity exactly the same way, pres-ents herself to others in the same way, or has the same relation to the world outside. Judith Butler, in *Gender Trouble: Feminism and the Subversion of Identity* (1990), proposed that all identity cate-gories are "performed" and are the result of imitation—not biol-ogy, not nature. We learn how to act our identities in the same way that an actor learns a part for a play (see "Where Do the Mer-maids Stand?" p. 78).

Indeed, all identity categories are contingent and unstable. In-dividuals have a number of overlapping and conflicting identities. One of the results of this way of looking at identity was scholar-ship that looked at how identities were produced, engendered, or raced by social assumptions, customs, and specific cultures. Scholars began to study not only the effects of engendering on various categories of women, but also on men and ideas of mas-culinity, another aspect of gender studies. Just like femininity, masculinity is under perpetual construction and revision as indi-viduals go about their lives. Thus, by the late 1990s, gender stud-ies concerned not only women, but also men and masculinity of and across various nations, ethnicities, races, sexualities, and classes. Women's studies theorists assume that what is female has been treated in culture as off-center, subordinate, secondary, and requiring explanation (see "Gender and Ritual: Giving Birth the American Way" p. 31). Women's femininity needed an explanation. Just as we have an NBA and a WNBA, what belongs to the male is normative in society; it needs no qualification or explanation, no "W" to discriminate it because it is central and assumed normal. However, the new studies of masculinity and men exploded the idea of a uniform, normal masculinity. Demonstrations of the construction of masculinity and the wide range of behaviors and expectations incorporated by the idea of masculinity in various cultures and contexts put forth a complex picture that was more diverse than assumed by early feminism, which tended to view the male as singular, monolithic, and universal (see "How Men Have (a) Sex" p. 125). Masculinity studies have also helped the feminist cause by reinforcing the idea that gender identities are not natural but made, constructed by cultural forces and fortified by familial, religious, and social institutions and, therefore, variable and vulnerable to the contingencies of culture and history.

As women's studies, men's studies, and gay, lesbian, bi- and transsexual studies developed, they gave rise to yet another field, gender studies, which looks at all gender construction. Taking their cue from Eve Sedgwick's groundbreaking book *Between Men* (1985), gender scholars describe sexuality as a continuum, with homosexuality and heterosexuality as points on that continuum (see "Le Freak, C'Est Chic! Le Fag, Quelle Drag!" p. 154). According to Sedgwick, they can be construed as related. For instance, she describes heterosexual masculinity as constructed partly as a "panic" response to homosexuality and thus, in some ways, inseparable from it. Furthermore, she argues, the male bonding that characterizes patriarchal institutions is always homophilic and thus on a continuum with homosexuality. Gender theory thus emphasizes the fragility of all rigidly held notions of homosexuality and heterosexuality. Gender and sexuality are best represented as a range rather than as fixed points, as various and contingent upon cultural and historical contexts (see "Is There a Muslim Sexuality?" p. 141) rather than polar opposites, and as multiple and protean rather than immutable.

Gender and sexuality as they are represented in popular culture are the foci of the current generation of feminists known as the "third wave" (see "The 3rd WWWave: Who We Are, and Why We

Need to Speak" p. 199). This group of feminists, who are much less identifiable than the second-wave feminists by a set of common concerns, is characterized in part by its commitment to responding and creating alternatives to restrictive, hegemonic norms of femininity and femaleness perpetuated in and by popular culture (see "Putting Ally on Trial: Contesting Postfeminism in Popular Culture" p. 102). In addition, third wavers are decentralized and, for the most part, self-identified. There is no central organization that represents them, but there are many groups and individuals who produce websites, opinion books, and anthologies under the third-wave banner. Although there was considerable disagreement among second wavers, they engaged with one another and attempted to define a unified agenda. This characteristic does not hold for third wavers.

Third-wave feminists can be pro- or antipornography. Not even pro-choice, the one consistently stable position of second-wave feminists, defines them. Although they generally seem to put equality of wages and opportunities on their list of aspirations, they are best described by their resistance to a rigid, imposed identity. Third wavers value freedom of self-determination perhaps above all other goals.

ELLEN G. FRIEDMAN
JENNIFER D. MARSHALL

CHAPTER 1

Gender and Family

OVERVIEW

"Family" from *Morality USA* and "The Transformation of Family Life," the two articles that constitute the Overview for this chapter, highlight two critical notions. First, "family" is a deeply gendered phenomenon. Second, new gender roles for women and men in the twentieth century are changing both the way that families are configured and the way that people understand and define "family." Friedman and Squire in "Family" consider how new social, sexual, economic, and political roles for women position family as a site of legal and cultural ambivalence in contemporary U.S. culture. In "The Transformation of Family Life," Lillian B. Rubin examines the experience of actual U.S. families trying to contend with changing gender roles and the socioeconomic complications they bring to traditional (middle-class, heterosexual, two-parent) family life.

"Family" from *Morality USA*
ELLEN G. FRIEDMAN AND CORINNE SQUIRE

From the wild Irish slums of the nineteenth-century Eastern seaboard, to the riot-torn suburbs of Los Angeles, there is one unmistakable lesson in American history: A community that allows a large number of young men to grow up in broken families, dominated by women, never acquiring any stable relationship to male authority, never acquiring any rational expectations about the future—that community asks for and gets chaos.

SENATOR DANIEL PATRICK MOYNIHAN, *THE NEGRO FAMILY: THE CASE FOR NATIONAL ACTION*

Just because it's your egg, it doesn't make you the mother.

DANNY DEVITO, IN *JUNIOR*

1

BABY M

On 27 March 1986, Mary Beth Whitehead, a New Jersey house-wife and high school dropout, gave birth to a nine-pound two-ounce girl, whom she named Sara. Whitehead had contracted to give up the newborn for $10,000. Instead, she fled with the baby to Florida. Richard, Whitehead's husband, a sanitation worker, was the father of her two older children, but this baby's father was William Stern, a New Jersey biochemist. Stern and his wife, Elizabeth, a pediatrician, had hired Whitehead to be artificially inseminated by Stern. The surrogacy solved certain personal problems for the Sterns: Elizabeth, who had multiple sclerosis, did not have to risk her health further with a pregnancy. And William was able to continue his family line, which, except for him, the Nazis had ended. The Sterns tracked Whitehead to Florida and, with the aid of local police, took the baby and re-named her Melissa. Asserting her natural right to her baby, Whitehead fought back in the New Jersey courts, where the con-test became known as the "Baby M" case.

Uncertainties poured out of the case. Commentators won-dered whether the surrogacy was a womb rental or a baby sale. *Time* asked, "Whose child is this?" (Lacayo, 1987b). Katha Pollitt wrote that the Baby M case bore an "uncanny resemblance to the all-sales-final style of a used-car lot" (1987: 681). Anne Taylor Fleming voiced some of the more emotional uncertainties in a *New York Times Magazine* article: "Always, for women, there are questions: Could I have a baby and give it away? Could I pay someone to have a baby for me? . . . What about her husband who watches her grow large with another man's child? What about the babies themselves who will know they've been 'bought' and there-fore 'sold'?" (1987: 32). *Time* sought biblical precedent, citing Ha-gar, who had Abraham's child when his wife Sarah was past child-bearing age. Hagar was a slave, just as Whitehead, poorer and less powerful than the Sterns, could be construed as a modern-day slave. Yet Baby M lacked the divine sanction of the biblical case. The rights and wrongs of the case seemed undecidable (La-cayo, 1987b: 57). *People* magazine declared, "There are no bad people in this case" (Shaughnessy, 1987: 50).

The Baby M case brought to public consciousness the deeply felt doubts that attend reproductive technology, doubts that mag-nify as the repro-tech bar continues to be raised. In the decade after Baby M hit the news, in vitro fertilization went far beyond the romance of a sperm and an egg in a petri dish to include the precision of moving particular chromosomes from one egg to another (Kolata, 1997b). Whimsical moral speculations about Nobel laureate sperm banks that could produce Einsteinian babies lost their sci-fi resonance when Scottish geneticist Ian Wilmut cloned a sheep named Dolly in his laboratory (*New York Times*, 24 February 1997).

WHO IS THE MOTHER, FATHER, GRANDMOTHER, CHILD?

The Baby M case threw into public debate and further uncertainty the issue of what constitutes a mother. Who is the mother, if not the biological mother? For Whitehead, the simple fact that she had had the baby legitimated her custody. Feminist defenses of Mary Beth Whitehead reduced the rights of the biological father to those of a receiver of a discretionary gift. Psychologists had other criteria for judging motherhood. Those who examined Whitehead for the court said she had an "emotional overinvestment" in her children and criticized her assumption that physically bearing the child gave her a mother's rights (Harrison, 1987: 309). As Barrie Thorne writes, "The same child may now have three different mothers: one who donates the egg, another who nurtures the fetus in her womb and gives birth, and a mother who gives primary care after birth" (1992: 11). Even such enumerations cannot cover all the questions asked about mothers in the unfolding drama of repro-tech, such as whether postmenopausal women have the right to become mothers or, as in cases in which older mothers carried babies for their adult children, whether a woman can be the mother of her own grandchildren.[1]

In addition, the Baby M case pushed to new ground the uncertainty already attached to fatherhood. Outside surrogacy, the identity of the father is a question of faith or of a DNA test. Here, even though the sperm donor was definitively known, his contribution, said Whitehead, did not make him a father. Judge Harvey Sorkow, who ruled on the case in New Jersey Superior Court, took a biological view of fatherhood: "A father cannot buy what is already his" (Lacayo, 1987a; 525 A. 2d N.J. Super. Ct. [1987]).[2]

Baby M's proliferation of possible mothers and fathers illustrated the seemingly new fluidity of moral and emotional claims that men, women, and children may have on one another. Not only does it make more ambiguous the question of who we are to one another, but it also complicates concomitant rights and responsibilities. By becoming a point at which discourses of family, morality, feminism, child custody, and new reproductive technologies collided, Baby M revealed the plasticity of definitions of family and the precarious status of morality within those definitions. Baby M, notes ethicist Arthur Caplan, "takes away a reference point" (qtd. in Hartouni, 1991: 49).[3]

If renting a stranger for surrogacy exacerbates moral uncertainty and explodes icons of parenthood, what does using your mother for the same purpose do? Cases of grandmother surrogates such as those in South Dakota and New York throw notions of family into chaos, violating the normal sense of generational progression, and evoke the specter of incest, the sin against which, according to Freud and Lévi-Strauss, the family is constructed. Debates surrounding these cases concerned who's who in the family: is the grandmother also the mother, and what is her new relationship to her child and to her or his partner? In fact, the Mayo Clinic in Minnesota turned down Arlette Schweitzer, the South Dakota woman who eventually became the surrogate for her daughter, because Minnesota law stipulates that the birth mother is the mother (*New York Times*, 11 August 1991).

Surrogate motherhood is not the only reproductive technology to hurl muddled family ethics into hyperdrive. Does a man have rights over his ex-wife's ova? Does *ex utero* fertilization enhance these rights or lessen them? And is the embryo property owned by the parents or an autonomous person with its own rights? In the Tennessee Supreme Court in 1992, a man won a suit preventing his ex-wife from implanting eggs he had fertilized. The seven embryos, the perplexed judge wrote, are neither "'persons' nor 'property,' but occupy an interim category" (*New York Times*, 2 June 1992). Even when, as often happens, such cases are rescripted in the morally simpler universe of television fiction, the issues still seem terminally tangled. In an episode of the television drama *Picket Fences* (broadcast 5 February 1993), based on a real Long Island case, the parameters of family, as well as of life and death, were indecipherable or simply up to you: A doctor moves into town with his wife, who is on life-support equipment. Although she is legally dead, he wants to keep her organs alive for six more months to bring her pregnancy to term.[4] The wife's mother sues to have the tubes pulled, because her daughter's living will calls for it. The judge decides that because the wife had an organ donor card, her organs, as well as the body that supports them, should be used to continue the life of the fetus. Who has more right over the woman's body, the husband or the mother? Should the woman's wishes supersede the father's right to a child?

Disturbances in supposedly natural ties of affection between parents and children found extreme expression in the first custody case brought by a child, that of Gregory Kingsley, a Florida twelve-year-old who divorced his parents in 1992 to live with his foster parents. Because the case followed the paradigm of a divorce procedure, it suggested, more emphatically than ever before, that children should have choices concerning their family. Just as adults choose their marriage partners, this child wanted to choose his parents (*New York Times*, 8 July and 26 September 1992).[5] The child's claiming of the right to divorce his parents makes ambiguous profoundly entrenched patterns of family hierarchy. In addition, criteria for parenthood are again in question. Here, the foster parents claimed to be Kingsley's "psychological parents," while the mother's claim was the more traditional one of flesh and blood.

THE PRIVATE, THE PUBLIC, AND THE FAMILY

One effect of new reproductive technologies is that the law and professionals have a more visible role in defining good families. The court's intrusion on what felt like private moral terrain in the matter of Baby M, transplanting into the legal realm what had seemed firmly biological, meant that it was brokering definitions of parenthood. In the debate about mothers and fathers that ensued, parenthood seemed suddenly elusive, turning on love, labor, and personal deservedness, as much as on ovum and sperm.

The court's encroachment on a realm that we generally regard as private, bounded at most by religious, moral protocols, involves it in decisions with little basis in legal precedent. As a result of Judge Sorkow's decision that Whitehead was not the mother of Baby M, the court OK'd the rewriting of Baby M's birth certificate to reflect Stern's paternity, a move that flouted the biological mother's conventional right to decide who else is listed on the birth certificate (525 A.2d 1175–76).[6] In the wake of the Baby M case, public interventions in definitions of parenthood proliferated. Twenty-seven state legislatures proposed regulating contract parenthood in what opponents of surrogacy called "bucks for baby" bills (Pollitt, 1987: 682).

The state's participation in family not only crosses the public/private divide in ways that feel transgressive but may also give the blessing of law to bias. In explaining why the private is political and should be state regulated, Catharine MacKinnon writes that for women, unlike men, the private is not a place of personal freedom but the domain of subordination without recourse to police or law (1989: 168). When the courts intervene in the private sphere, they often take their patriarchal assumptions with them. For feminists, Judge Sorkow's decision that Elizabeth Stern was Baby M's mother reduced women to their marital status: whoever is married to the sperm donor is the mother (Ehrenreich, 1989: 71). In this ruling Whitehead became a mere tool of production. Whitehead herself said, "It was like I was a breeder and they were just interested in what I could produce" (1986: 47). Although in an appeal a New Jersey Supreme Court judge ordered that Whitehead's parental status be restored, she still did not get custody, just visitation privileges (537 A. 2d N.J. 1227 [1988]).

Like reproductive technology, child abuse has helped move family discourse onto the couch and into the courts, from where it returns, professionalized, to talk shows and public discussion. The proliferation of therapies, laws, and talk about child abuse lessens the family as a moral body, blurring the boundaries of family responsibility for morality. Definitions of abuse are themselves murky: legal and psychological experts disagree about what constitutes child abuse and who should decide whether a child has been abused. The president of the National Coalition for Child Protection Reform, Elizabeth Vorenberg, makes the point that child protection agencies do not always distinguish between an abused child and a child living in poverty. She tells the story of James Norman of Illinois, whose children were put in foster care in 1993 while he was temporarily unemployed. With the electricity off and the food spoiling in the fridge, a social worker assumed the worst and took the kids. The professionals and the law dragged their feet, and Norman died of a heart attack before the court could rule to restore the children to their father (Vorenberg, 1993: A16).

In cases such as those of Baby M and James Norman, what feels like a violation of a clearly private, biological terrain is perhaps no more than a new sign of the fact that the family has always been a hybrid of the public and the private (Deleuze, 1979: x). Jacques Donzelot argues that the state traditionally defines family functions. In the nineteenth century, it made the family responsible for moral problems in order to deal with indigence, unemployment, and crime that it had difficulty managing (1979: 53–58). Although how you raise children seems your parental prerogative, you do it within a strict, state-mandated set of rules. The nuclear family has always been "permeable" to public institutions (Minson, 1985: 183). The state determines when and for how long your children go to school and what they learn. In August 1994, the United States Congress voted to cut funds to school districts that teach children that homosexuality is an alternative lifestyle (*New York Times*, 2 August 1994). If your method of discipline is corporal punishment, the state may define it as child abuse. It expects you to clean, dress, and feed your children according to its implicit standard. And it frowns on leaving children in the street, in the care of other children, or alone. Unlike the Christmas vacation in the 1990 Hollywood movie *Home Alone*, during which a clever kid, accidentally left home, frustrates the efforts of would-be burglars, a 1993 Acapulco vacation ended in arrest at the Mexican border for David and Sharon Schoo, of suburban Chicago, because they had left their two daughters, aged five and nine, home alone (*New York Times*, 12 July 1993). The family and the roles within it, although experienced privately, are "policed" by the culture to forward its aims of an educated citizenry that is healthy, sexually regulated, and whose members are responsible for one another. The family fulfills public objectives having to do with social control that range from disease to dissidence, and when families violate social norms, the state can walk into the family sphere to deal with those violations (Minson, 1985: 183).

Such policing depends on professionals and courts, the standards and guidelines of which are often slippery and ambiguous, leaving judgments to fall to individual feeling. ABC's *Nightline* repro-tech show on 7 April 1989 put it this way: "With new technologies peering into the womb, women have been forced to peer into their hearts" (qtd. in Hartouni, 1991: 39)—as have psychologists, gynecologists, lawyers, and judges. Inadequate as a moral blueprint, decisions such as the one regarding Baby M are good barometers of emotivist confusion. In the absence of convincing criteria for good parents and surrogacy, the experts filled the vacuum with emotivism—the felt rightness or wrongness of a particular course of action—dressed as psychological, legal, and feminist opinion. Because it was fraught with such emotivism, the Baby M case never seemed definitively morally decided.

Class and gender also complicate lawyers' and psychologists' emotivism in their policing of families. Although court officials and the experts they hired spoke in terms of the "best interests of

15

the child," their judgments regarding the Baby M case seemed to turn more on emotionally determined class differentials. When Whitehead said she wanted to "give the gift of life," a court-appointed psychologist interpreted this phrase as evidence of "a deep seated narcissistic need" and concluded she had a mixed personality disorder. The Sterns, who had greater familiarity with psychological discourse, did not alienate the experts by using such quasi-religious terminology. Michelle Harrison points out that Whitehead's play with the baby was also subject to classed judgments: "Mary Beth Whitehead was said to have 'failed patty-cake' by saying 'Hooray!' to the baby instead of 'pattycake' "(Harrison, 1987: 307). Whitehead herself describes one expert who condemned the stuffed panda she bought for the baby and said that ordinary "pots and pans or spoons" would be more developmentally appropriate (Whitehead, with Schwarz-Noble, 1989: 143). Judge Sorkow and the experts equated the best interests of the child with the heftier salary and academic degrees that the Sterns brought to child rearing. His Superior Court opinion dwells on Whitehead's poverty, the fact that she received public assistance, the two mortgages on her house that went into default, and her filing for bankruptcy in 1983 (525 A. 2d 1128, N.J. Super. Ch. [1987]: 1140–41). On the Sterns' side, the opinion pointed out the opportunities for music lessons and athletics for Baby M at the Sterns (1148). The judge discounted Whitehead's biological connection and her experience in already raising two children, and dismissed the nonbinding nature of the surrogacy contract she had signed. The Superior Court opinion on Baby M reads like the court's and experts' middle-class biases put forward as if they were the law. . . .

NOSTALGIA

Nostalgia is the primary means by which felt absences [are filled] in contemporary configurations of family. The increasing instability in the family constellation and its consequent moral ambiguity closely parallels the enormous attention paid to the ideal of the "traditional family" in U.S. culture. The gestures that nostalgically recall family . . . are countered by transgressive moves on the traditional family constellation. For instance, in awarding custody to the Sterns, parents by contract, Judge Sorkow cited the fact that Elizabeth Stern "will not work full time because she is aware of the infant's needs that will require her presence" (1148).

Family is treated as a basic and universal social unit, the place where morality is modeled and produced. The expectation that it is the primary center for the inculcation of values and the ethical life is heard throughout the culture. Interpersonal family relationships, relying on nostalgic emotions rather than on religious doctrine or rational argument, are used as the template for morality. Across national discourses, whether in sociology texts or in political speeches, one repeatedly hears "the family" yearningly invoked as the fulcrum of the U.S. moral economy. In 1913, Bronislaw Malinowski's *The Family Among the Australian Aborigines* set the terms of family discourse. The family, he argued, fills a universal human need and has three defining features: clear boundaries that distinguish insiders from outsiders, a location where family members can be together, and a connection solidified by the feelings of love and warmth that family members have for one another (see Collier, Rosaldo, and Yanagisako, 1992: 33). In addition to these criteria, most Americans take "family" to mean nuclear, heterosexual, with children, and for life. This configuration is equated with fundamental morality.

But in a demographic sense, this family is unreal. In 1987, only 7% of households fit the pattern of breadwinning father, full-time mother, and at least one child under the age of eighteen (Thorne, 1992: 9).[7] Although we think of a family as protecting children, 20% of U.S. children live in poverty, the majority of these living in female-headed households. Even the bare bones of the nuclear family—a married couple living with their own children—represents only about 17% of U.S. families (*New York Times*, 20 October 1992). Children with divorced parents who themselves get divorced as adults may live with six or seven "families" during their lifetimes. Moreover, the Murphy Brown phenomenon that former Vice President Dan Quayle complained about is growing: although single motherhood is still much more common among poor women and members of minority groups, the percentage of single professional women who became mothers tripled from 1983 to 1993 ("Week in Review," *New York Times*, 18 July 1993). Even [conservative] Newt Gingrich has a lesbian half-sister, whom he says he loves and whom he points to as an exemplar of the American family's diversity (Udovitch, 1995: 158).

Economic necessity and social movements have sufficiently interrogated the rhetoric of stay-home nurturing mothers and breadwinning authoritative fathers, so that, although this rhetoric is still used to manipulate emotions for political purposes, we recognize   20 that the "happy family" paradigm promoted in the popular textbook *The Happy Family*, by John Levy and Ruth Munroe, first printed in 1938 and reprinted nineteen times by 1964, has gone. The U.S. Census Bureau definition of a family—a household of two or more individuals related by blood or law—excludes many informally constituted families . . . but jettisons the patriarchal moral assumptions of *The Happy Family* and may soon include gay married couples in some states. Even Robert Frost's definition of home as "The place where, when you have to go there, / they have to take you in" ("The Death of the Hired Man") seems superannuated, assuming loyalties and commitments that are far from universal. Because the family seems like such an uncertain institution in the present, people seek out a surer model in the past. In idealizing this past, they intensify the uncertainty of the present. They distance themselves from contemporary problems to luxuriate in the stasis of looking back. . . .

[F]amily, despite its infinite variations of form, is less contested in its ethical essence of nurturance, responsibility, altruism, and interdependence. Across ideologies, it is described as having an essential morality . . . (Okin, 1989: 27–29). The nostalgia of this view, in which the family is internally just, goes unacknowledged. Susan Moller Okin summarizes this thinking: "The family is not characterized by the circumstances of justice, which operate only when interests differ and goods being distributed are scarce. An intimate group, held together by love and identity of interests, the family is characterized by nobler virtues" (25–26). Such a view recapitulates Rousseau's and Hume's argument that justice is not pertinent to the family because, unlike the state, it is governed by affection for its members (Okin, 1989: 26–27). Even feminist accounts reiterate these notions. The authors of *Families in Flux* offer a "modern" definition, which nevertheless maintains the family's emotional and moral power: "a unit of intimate, transacting and interdependent persons sharing resources, responsibility, and commitment over time" (Swerdlow et al., 1989: xii). The virtues of love and self-sacrifice that, in this idealized view, drive family relationships put the family's morality on a plane higher than the practical negotiations between self-interest and state interest that mark justice. This characterization makes the politics of family either irrelevant, endless, or endlessly disappointing. It is also the strategy by which patriarchal culture has segmented the family off from the general culture, creating a special zone, even within a democracy, in which democratic processes are partially suspended for the higher authority, the law of the Father. Traditionally, when the state polices the family, it has to have special cause and justification to question a particular familial government—although a family headed by a woman loses much of that immunity.

The entire national enterprise—the economy, crime rates, education, social policy is tied to a similar nostalgic, idealized notion of family. The Reagan administration even imaged defense as a matter of the government paternally protecting children from outside harm when it used a child's drawing of a stick figure family perched on a globe over which arched the Star Wars defense shield. "Star Wars," said Reagan, would protect the United States "just as a roof protects a family from rain" (*New York Times*, 18 August 1983). The shield metaphor from medieval romance literature is, of course, masculine, and in these family metaphors, the speaker implies a patriarch on whose protection and authority the safety of other family members is supposed to depend. Indeed, it is around the absence of this figure that the welfare debate revolves. When Paul Robeson Jr. and Mel Williamson attributed the crimes of the youths indicted for the Central Park jogger assault to the failures of *family* to deal with the "surroundings of drugs and violence [and] with what is seen on TV and in the movies," what they meant by the failures of family was the absence or weakness of fathers. Like many observers of the African American family, Robeson and Williamson extol the extended family paradigm that they say characterizes it. They suggest that African Americans can overcome the difficulties that families face in "trying to instill humane values" by the community's (doctors, lawyers, teachers, ministers, writers, journalists, athletes) taking on this "struggle for our children" (1989). They project the oedipal moment onto a "father" written into every figure of cultural authority.

All images of family, whether in politics, professional discourse, self-help literature, religion, or other grand narratives, hark back to an ideal past. This ideal becomes what is missing in families today. Yet the fantasy of, say, the 1950s family ignores problems that did not enter public consciousness until later and masks the public controversies that beset the real thing. Divorce rates dropped in the 1950s and marriages and childbearing went up, but the stable, happy nuclear family as perfect moral classroom never really existed. As Stephanie Coontz writes, "The reality of these families was far more painful and complex than the expurgated memories of the nostalgic would suggest" (1992: 29). Although homosexuality, children's rights, and incest and other domestic violence had not yet emerged into academic research on the family, abortion, divorce, sexuality, women's work, child discipline, the generation gap, and father or mother absence were hot topics (see, for example, Barber

[1953]). The fragility of 1950s nostalgia is also evident from a quick glance at popular culture of the time, which was obsessed with, as one commentator put it, "the family and its discontent" (Dieckmann, 1987). Adultery is the central theme in movies such as *Peyton Place, East of Eden, Cat on a Hot Tin Roof,* and *The Seven Year Itch.* Popular women's magazines spelled out an agenda of family concern similar to today's. A June 1959 issue of *True Confessions* tackles adultery and incest ("Not Mine to Love"), children and divorce ("Why Cry—Nobody Cares"), irresponsible teenage motherhood ("She Was a Menace"), unloving parents ("Starved for a Father's Affection"), and children's abandonment and poverty ("Forced to Beg in the Streets"). Even the notion of divorce as a modern moral disease—spread, according to the political Right, by women's liberation—is debatable. Divorce, according to sociologist Glenda Riley, is an American tradition dating back to the Puritans. Even in the Victorian era, one in every fourteen marriages ended up broken. Part of the U.S. way of life, writes Riley, is to split up and, like the pioneers, go west to solve problems (1991: 124).

Although the Malinowski "Honey, I'm home" family—and the apple pie, picket-fence, all-American emblem of it—is nowhere, it is, at the same time, everywhere. In Jennie Livingston's film *Paris Is Burning* (1991), the Harlem vogueing community is shown as constituted of "families" of biologically and legally unrelated gay men of color. One "mother," Pepper Labeija, describes the value of these self-generated families, which provide younger members with emotional and material nurturing and support, sometimes even homes. "Mothers" are idealized in traditional ways. For instance, Willi Ninja, mother to another "family," says, "The mother is the strongest one." Yet, also in the traditional pattern, the mother is a figure of which you can make fun. In one scene of sardonic humor, the "children" of Angie Xtravaganza brag about buying her tits for Christmas, pretend to nurse at them, and crow, "My mommy is a drag queen."

25   The idea that the ideal family is intrinsically benign obviously conflicts with family realities. To deal with the resulting confusion, the culture exhibits an obsessive nostalgia for reclaiming a nurturing, altruistic family in which all positions are stable and proper. This unexamined nostalgia is itself a stabilizing, though paralyzing, state. The family is a notion to which we obsessively return. In the words of Jacques Donzelot, "It has become an essential ritual of our societies to scrutinize the countenance of the family at regular intervals in order to decipher our destiny, glimpsing in the death of the family an impending return to barbarism, the letting go of our

reasons for living; or indeed, in order to reassure ourselves at the sight of its inexhaustible capacity for survival" (1979: 4). . . .

Relationships within the family have changed from the hierar-chical to the individual. Each person has rights within the family and has a separate relationship with the state, rather than having access to the state only through the father or the mother. In this explosion of children's, women's, and family rights legislation and legal precedents, the notion of a private sphere fades and the au-thoritarian figure in that sphere—the patriarch—loses power. A sphere emerges in which "private" matters are no longer sacred but open to the scrutiny of the courts and society. Such appropria-tion of the private recapitulates Enlightenment ideals and republi-can ethics, "which held that the transformation of private interests into contractual obligations and political compacts represented a higher morality than the expression of such family values as love or personal nurturance" (Coontz, 1992: 96–97). For John Adams, the "positive Passion for the public good" was "Superior to all pri-vate Passions" (qtd. in Coontz, 1992: 97). If we adopt this perspec-tive, the change to more public oversight of family relations not only may protect those previously unprotected by the ideology of the private, but also may offer an alternative to the romantic no-tion that family morality is superior to public morality.

Even within the newly legislated field of the family, however, in-dividuals' rights in relationships with other family members and with the state remain grounded in feeling. This emotivism leaves de-cisions idiosyncratic, not generalizable. Nevertheless, some change can happen within the democratic possibilities offered by the re-newed emphasis on public/private fluidity, especially in its exten-sion of rights. The notion of acting in the child's best interest allows us to expand ideas of what family is, including nontraditional fami-lies less oppressive to women and children than the conventional model. According to Jeffrey Minson, "The socio-legal formula 'in the best interests of the child' does not especially privilege the conjugal family." He argues for "increasing choice in living arrangements along the lines of social norms which were meant to be realised within a nuclear family but do not depend upon that arrangement" (1985: 216–17). Conversely, the rights of, for instance, gay men and lesbians to marry may also allow us to legitimize "deviant" families, a move that, because it interrogates the traditional, can lead to change. A New York City lesbian couple had two children produced through artificial insemination. In 1993 the sperm donor for one child sued to be declared the father and to get visitation rights. Fa-thers in these cases are not on the birth certificates. In other sperm donor cases, the plaintiffs have succeeded in getting father's rights. Here the judge argued that the suit itself was harming the child and the man's claim was making her anxious, giving her nightmares. The judge said that for this child, "a declaration of paternity would be a statement that her family is other than what she knows it to be and needs it to be." Although ostensibly a victory for children's rights, it was also a victory for lesbians, who had not previously had the "best interests of the child" principle applied to them in the case of a sperm donor. In his opinion, the judge sustained the notion of the two-parent family, saying that the child had a "parental bond to her second mother," as if a third parent or one parent were unnatural. For this judge, the litmus test of family was two parents, not heterosexuality (*New York Times*, 16 April 1993).

Of course, we could argue that a regressive "romance" with children's rights and a co-option of gays into nuclear familiarity are really what is at stake here. Also, legal rights for children are not the answer to difficult social and psychological problems. Nevertheless, in the shift to individual rights such as children's rights and to increasing public surveillance of the private, notions of family become pluralistic. Court decisions have the feel of temporary, negotiated solutions: a boy can divorce his parents, and a child can have as parents two lesbian mothers. Although such solutions are provisional and still underpinned with emotivism, competing discourses can center on a new object in a new field— a child. Traditional biological claims yield to claims of children who, as Emmanuel Levinas argues, command our moral responsibility because our relationship to them is the "first shape" that our moral responsibility for the other takes, and thus they provide a powerful moral imperative (1985: 71). . . .

MORAL MULTILINGUALISM

A fluid negotiation between family moralities can be and often is the result of having a number of [family] paradigms in play at the same time. . . . Optimism [about family] gets repeated in popular culture, in lyrics by Coolio, for instance, that attempt to produce a new relation to fatherhood even when a father is not living with his children. Addressing his own child in "Smilin'," Coolio sings, "Even though we're not together like we used to be / D-A-D-D-Y you can count on me." He acknowledges that his family is not *Cosby*-perfect: "This ain't the Huxtables and my name ain't Cliff," but then tells how looking into his children's eyes makes him smile. These hopes of values that will be shared between young

black men in the city are too high. Even within such a circum-
scribed community, the pluralism of a modern democratic society
breaks up common notions of the good. A member of this community may also be a member of several others that have incon-
gruent goals (Mouffe, 1993: 83). Yet such brave forays into the
discourse of family allow various moralities to circulate and, beyond that, allow them to be articulated, albeit locally, across differences. They face the complex problems they can see in family
morality and make moves toward an ethical beyond, toward better possibilities for living together.

In contrast to the oedipal and class metanarratives that di-   30
rected the therapists, social workers, and judges to make decisions in the Baby M case in the name of the "best interests of the
child" but actually in the interests of the middle-class biological
father and adoptive mother, a more pragmatic, pluralistic, and
negotiatory settlement of the case occurred on appeal. Judge
Birger Sween, who reinstated Whitehead's visitation rights in
New Jersey Superior Court, explained that

> Melissa is a resilient child who is no less capable than thousands
> of children of broken marriages who successfully adjust to com-
> plex family relationships when their parents remarry. . . . William
> and Elizabeth Stern must accept and understand that Melissa
> will develop a different and special relationship with her mother,
> stepfather, siblings, and extended family, and that these relation-
> ships need not diminish their parent-child relationship with
> Melissa. (qtd. in Whitehead with Schwarz-Noble, 1989: 217–18)

Here is a judgment that appreciates the contemporary moral complications of family. In Judge Sween's view, the best interests of the
child do not depend on the traditional bases of biology or class.
Neither one parent nor the others, but all three, are factors in the
child's life. Here the "interests of the child"—including those of all
the parents—are taken into account. . . . Under the "best interests"
banner, [Sween] acknowledged the difficult moral context of family life as well as affirming the network of relationships around
Baby M, a recognition that offers a glimpse of an ethical beyond.

Endnotes

1. The former question, posed in a large-type headline, was prompted
   by a fifty-nine-year-old British woman who gave birth to twins after
   receiving fertility treatment (*Toronto Globe and Mail*, 28 December
   1994). See also Linda Wolfe's op-ed piece "And Baby Makes Three,
   Even if You're Gray" (1994).

2. The two Baby M judgments discussed in this chapter were decided in the Superior Court of New Jersey, Bergen County, 31 March 1987, by Judge Sorkow (525 A. 2d, 1128) and the Supreme Court of New Jersey, 3 February 1988, by Judge Wilentz (537 A. 2d, 1227). See Roberts (1993).

3. *Father of the Bride Part II*, about simultaneous mother and daughter pregnancies, depicts Steve Martin attempting to deal with his simultaneous fatherhood- and grandfatherhood-to-be. The movie hit cineplexes in the 1995 Christmas season.

4. This episode is probably a fictionalization of a real case, in which the "brain-dead" Marie Odette Henderson's fetus was brought to term. See Hartouni (1991).

5. A second case replicates some of the complexities in this one: In 1993, Kimberly Mays, a fourteen-year-old Florida girl, went to court to sever all ties with her biological parents. She had been given to the wrong parents at birth, a mistake discovered ten years later by her biological parents, who then sued for custody. The court gave them visitation rights, which Mays successfully thwarted in court. But every case has its own twists. In 1994, as a result of what her lawyer described as typical adolescent problems, Mays moved in with her biological parents (*New York Times*, 23 August 1993 and 10 March 1994). The point is that the child chose her parents—twice.

6. In New Jersey at the time, no laws regulated surrogacy, although prostitution, a more public commerce, was illegal. Katha Pollitt wrote, "It seems that a woman can rent her womb in the state of New Jersey, although not her vagina, and get a check upon turning the product over to its father" (1987: 681).

7. No matter how the statistics are described, the unreality of this pattern emerges. A 1996 Census Bureau study found, for instance, that only 25.5 percent of households comprised married couples with children in 1995 (Kilborn, 1996).

Works Cited

Collier, Jane, Michelle Z. Rosaldo, and Sylvia Yanagisako. 1992. "Is There a Family?" In *Rethinking the Family: Some Feminist Questions*, edited by Barrie Thorne. Boston: Northeastern University Press.

Coontz, Stephanie. 1992. *The Way We Never Were: American Families and the Nostalgia Trap*. New York: Basic Books.

Deleuze, Gilles. 1979. Foreword to *The Policing of Families*, by Jacques Donzelot. Translated by Robert Hurley, Mark Seem, and Helen R. Lane. New York: Viking.

Dieckmann, Katherine. 1987. "The Way We Weren't: Adultery in '50s Films: Exploring the Great Unknown." *Village Voice*. 16 December 92.

Donzelot, Jacques. 1979. *The Policing of Families*. Translated by Robert Hurley, Mark Seem, and Helen R. Lane. New York: Viking.

Ehrenreich, Nancy. 1989. "Wombs for Hire." *Tikkun* 6: 71–74.

Fleming, Anne Taylor. 1987. "Our Fascination with Baby M." *New York Times Magazine* 9 March 32–36+.

Harrison, Michelle. 1987. "Social Construction of Mary Beth Whitehead." *Gender and Society,* 1 September 300–316.

Hartouni, Valerie. 1991. "Containing Women: Reproductive Discourse in the 1980s." In *Technoculture,* edited by Constance Penley and Andrew Ross. Minneapolis: University of Minnesota Press.

Kilborn, Peter T. 1996. "Shifts in Families Reach a Plateau, Study Says." *New York Times,* 27 November, A18.

Kolata, Gina. 1997a. "Childbirth at 63 Says What about Life?" *New York Times* 27 April.

———. 1997b. "Scientists Face New Ethical Quandaries in Baby-Making." *New York Times* 19 August, C1, C8.

Lacayo, Richard. 1987a. "In the Best Interests of the Child." *Time* 13 April 71.

———. 1987b. "Whose Child is This?" *Time* 19 January 56–58.

Levinas, Emmanuel. 1985. *Ethics and Infinity: Conversations with Philippe Nemo.* Translated by Richard A. Cohen. Pittsburgh: Duquesne University Press.

Levy, John, and Ruth Munroe. 1964. *The Happy Family.* New York: Knopf.

MacKinnon, Catharine. 1989. *Toward a Feminist Theory of the State.* Cambridge: Harvard University Press.

Malinowski, Bronislaw. 1913. *The Family Among the Australian Aborigines.* London: University of London Press.

Minson, Jeffrey. 1985. *Genealogies of Morals: Nietzsche, Foucault, Conzelot, and the Eccentricity of Ethics.* New York: St. Martin's.

Mouffe, Chantal. 1993. *The Return of the Political.* London: Verso.

Okin, Susan Moller, 1989. *Justice, Gender, and the Family.* New York: Basic Books.

Pollitt, Katha, 1987. "The Strange Case of Baby M." *Nation* 23 May 681–82.

Riley, Glenda. 1991. *Divorce: An American Tradition.* New York: Oxford University Press.

Roberts, Melinda A. 1993. "Good Intentions and a Great Divide: Having Babies by Intending Them." *Law and Philosophy* 12: 287–317.

Robeson, Paul, Jr., and Mel Williamson. 1989. "Accountability and Higher Morality." *Amsterdam* (N.Y.) *News* 6 June 15.

Shaughnessy, Mary. 1987. "All for Love of a Baby." *People* 23 March 50–52.

Swerdlow, Amy, Renate Bridenthal, Joan Kelly, and Phyllis Vine. 1989. *Families in Flux.* Westbury, New York: The Feminist Press.

Thorne, Barrie. 1992. "Feminism and the Family: Two Decades of Thought." In *Rethinking the Family: Some Feminist Questions,* edited by Barrie Thorne. Boston: Northeastern University Press.

Udovitch, Mim. 1995. "Sister Act." *George* October-November 156–58, 256–58.

Vorenberg, Elizabeth, 1993. Letter to the editor. *New York Times* 28 June A 16.

Whitehead, Mary Beth, with Loretta Schwarz-Noble, 1989. *A Mother's Story.* New York: St. Martin's.

Whitehead, Mary Beth. 1986. "A Surrogate Mother Describes Her Change of Heart—and Her Fight to Keep the Baby Two Families Love." *People* 26 October 46–52.

Questions for Thought and Writing

1. The authors argue that "The Baby M case threw into public debate and further uncertainty the issue of what constitutes a mother." How, specifically, did the case do this? What are the important differences between the ways in which a mother has traditionally been defined in U.S. culture and in the Baby M case? Do you think these changes represented a gain for women or a loss? Explain why.

2. What are some instances of "the enormous attention paid to the ideal of the " 'traditional family' in U.S. culture"? What evidence is provided by the authors to demonstrate that "this family is unreal"? Identify and describe examples from popular culture that defy the model of the traditional family.

3. The authors suggest that the new "in the best interests of the child" formula for deciding the outcome of complicated custody cases provides opportunities to redefine who counts as a parent. How do you think this new formula differs from the one traditionally used by the legal system to determine acceptable childcare situations? How might this change people's sensibilities about what kinds of families are "natural" and "unnatural"?

The Transformation of Family Life
Lillian B. Rubin

I know my wife works all day, just like I do," says Gary Braunswig, a twenty-nine-year-old white drill press operator, "but it's not the same. She doesn't *have* to do it. I mean, she *has* to because we need the money, but it's different. It's not really her job to have to be working; it's mine." He stops, irritated with himself because he can't find exactly the words he wants, and asks, "Know what I mean? I'm not saying it right; I mean, it's the man who's supposed to support his family, so I've got to be responsible for that, not her. And that makes one damn big difference.

"I mean, women complain all the time about how hard they work with the house and the kids and all. I'm not saying it's not hard, but that's her responsibility, just like the finances are mine."

"But she's now sharing that burden with you, isn't she?" I remark.

"Yeah, and I do my share around the house, only she doesn't see it that way. Maybe if you add it all up, I don't do as much as she does, but then she doesn't bring in as much money as I do. And she doesn't always have to be looking for overtime to make an extra buck. I got no complaints about that, so how come she's always complaining about me? I mean, she helps me out financially, and I help her out with the kids and stuff. What's wrong with that? It seems pretty equal to me."

Cast that way, his formulation seems reasonable: They're each responsible for one part of family life; they each help out with the other. But the abstract formula doesn't square with the lived reality. For him, helping her adds relatively little to the burden of household tasks he *must* do each day. A recent study by University of Wisconsin researchers, for example, found that in families where both wife and husband work full-time, the women average over twenty-six hours a week in household labor, while the men do about ten.[1] That's because there's nothing in the family system to force him to accountability or responsibility on a daily basis. He may "help her out with the kids and stuff" one day and be too busy or preoccupied the next.

But for Gary's wife, Irene, helping him means an extra eight hours every working day. Consequently, she wants something more consistent from him than a helping hand with a particular task when he has the time, desire, or feels guilty enough. "Sure, he helps me out," she says, her words tinged with resentment. "He'll give the kids a bath or help with the dishes. But only when I ask him. He doesn't have to *ask* me to go to work every day, does he? Why should I have to ask him?"

"Why should I have to ask him?"—words that suggest a radically different consciousness from the working-class women I met twenty years ago. Then, they counted their blessings. "He's a steady worker; he doesn't drink; he doesn't hit me," they told me by way of explaining why they had "no right to complain."[2] True, these words were reminders to themselves that life could be worse, that they shouldn't take these things for granted—reminders that didn't wholly work to obscure their discontent with other aspects of the marriage. But they were nevertheless meaningful statements of value that put a brake on the kinds of demands they felt they could make of their men, whether about the unequal division of household tasks or about the emotional content of their lives together.

Now, the same women who reminded themselves to be thankful two decades ago speak openly about their dissatisfaction with the role divisions in the family. Some husbands, especially the younger ones, greet their wives' demands sympathetically. "I try to do as much as I can for Sue, and when I can't, I feel bad about it," says twenty-nine-year-old Don Dominguez, a Latino father of three children, who is a construction worker.

Others are more ambivalent. "I don't know, as long as she's got a job, too, I guess it's right that I should help out in the house. But that doesn't mean I've got to like it," says twenty-eight-year-old Joe Kempinski, a white warehouse worker with two children.

10 Some men are hostile, insisting that their wives' complaints are unreasonable, unjust, and oppressive. "I'm damn tired of women griping all the time; it's nothing but nags and complaints," Ralph Danesen, a thirty-six-year-old white factory worker and the father of three children, says indignantly. "It's enough! You'd think they're the only ones who've got it hard. What about me? I'm not living in a bed of roses either.

"Christ, what does a guy have to do to keep a wife quiet these days? What does she want? It's not like I don't do anything to help her out, but it's never enough."

In the past there was a clear understanding about the obligations and entitlements each partner took on when they married. He was obliged to work outside the home; she would take care of life inside. He was entitled to her ministrations, she to his financial support. But this neat division of labor with its clear-cut separation of rights and obligations no longer works. Now, women feel obliged to hold up their share of the family economy—a partnership men welcome. In return, women believe they're entitled to their husband's full participation in domestic labor. And here is the rub. For while men enjoy the fruits of their wives' paid work outside the home, they have been slow to accept the reciprocal responsibilities—that is, to become real partners in the work inside the home.

The women, exhausted from doing two days' work in one, angry at the need to assume obligations without corresponding entitlements, push their men in ways unknown before. The men, battered by economic uncertainty and by the escalating demands of their wives, feel embattled and victimized on two fronts—one outside the home, the other inside. Consequently, when their wives seem not to see the family work they do, when they don't acknowledge and credit it, when they fail to appreciate them, the men feel violated and betrayed. "You come home and you want to be appreciated a little. But it doesn't work that way, leastwise not here anymore," complains Gary Braunswig, his angry words at odds with the sadness in his eyes. "There's no peace, I guess that's the real problem; there's no peace anywhere anymore."

The women often understand what motivates their husbands' sense of victimization and even speak sympathetically about it at times. But to understand and sympathize is not to condone, especially when they feel equally assaulted on both the home and the economic fronts. "I know I complain a lot, but I really don't ask for that much. I just want him to help out a little more," explains Ralph Danesen's wife, Helen, a thirty-five-year-old office worker. "It isn't like I'm asking him to cook the meals or anything like that. I know he can't do that, and I don't expect him to. But every time I try to talk to him, you know, to ask him if I couldn't get a little more help around here, there's a fight."

One of the ways the men excuse their behavior toward family   15
work is by insisting that their responsibility as bread winner burdens them in ways that are alien to their wives. "The plant's laying off people left and right; it could be me tomorrow. Then what'll we do? Isn't it enough I got to worry about that? I'm the one who's got all the worries; she doesn't. How come that doesn't count?" demands Bob Duckworth, a twenty-nine-year-old factory worker.

But, in fact, the women don't take second place to their men in worrying about what will happen to the family if the husband loses his job. True, the burden of finding another one that will pay the bills isn't theirs—not a trivial difference. But the other side of this truth is that women are stuck with the reality that the financial welfare of the family is out of their control, that they're helpless to do anything to prevent its economic collapse or to rectify it should it happen. "He thinks I've got it easy because it's not my job to support the family," says Bob's wife, Ruthanne. "But sometimes I think it's worse for me. I worry all the time that he's going to get laid off, just like he does. But I can't do anything about it. And if I try to talk to him about it, you know, like maybe make a plan in case it happens, he won't even listen. How does he think *that* makes me feel? It's my life, too, and I can't even talk to him about it."

Not surprisingly, there are generational differences in what fuels the conflict around the division of labor in these families. For the older couples—those who grew up in a different time, whose marriages started with another set of ground rules—the struggle is not simply around how much men do or about whether they take responsibility for the daily tasks of living without being pushed, prodded, and reminded. That's the overt manifestation of the discord, the trigger that starts the fight. But the noise of the explosion when it comes serves to conceal the more fundamental issue underlying the dissension: legitimacy. What does she have a *right* to expect? "What do I know about doing stuff around the house?" asks Frank Moreno, a forty-eight-year-old foreman in a warehouse. "I wasn't brought up like that. My pop, he never did one damn thing, and my mother never complained. It was her job; she did it and kept quiet. Besides, I work my ass off every day. Isn't that enough?"

For the younger couples, those under forty, the problem is somewhat different. The men may complain about the expectation that they'll participate more fully in the care and feeding of the family, but talk to them about it quietly and they'll usually admit that it's not really unfair, given that their wives also work outside the home. In these homes, the issue between husband and wife isn't only who does what. That's there, and it's a source of more or less conflict, depending upon what the men actually do and how forceful their wives are in their demands. But in most of these families there's at least a verbal consensus that men *ought* to participate in the tasks of daily life. Which raises the next and perhaps more difficult issue in contest between them: Who feels responsible for getting the tasks done? Who regards them as a duty, and for whom are they an option? On this, tradition rules.

Even in families where husbands now share many of the tasks, their wives still bear full responsibility for the organization of family life. A man may help cook the meal these days, but a woman is most likely to be the one who has planned it. He may take the children to child care, but she virtually always has had to arrange it. It's she also who is accountable for the emotional life of the family, for monitoring the emotional temperature of its members and making the necessary corrections. It's this need to be responsible for it all that often feels as burdensome as the tasks themselves. "It's not just doing all the stuff that needs doing," explains Maria Jankowicz, a white twenty-eight-year-old assembler in an electronics factory. "It's worrying all the time about everything and always having to arrange everything, you know what I mean. It's like I run the whole show. If I don't stay on top of it all, things fall apart because nobody else is going to do it. The kids can't and Nick, well, forget it," she concludes angrily.

20   If, regardless of age, life stage, or verbal consensus, women usually still carry the greatest share of the household burdens, why is it important to notice that younger men grant legitimacy to their wives' demands and older men generally do not? Because men who believe their wives have a right to expect their participation tend to suffer guilt and discomfort when they don't live up to those expectations. And no one lives comfortably with guilt. "I know I don't always help enough, and I feel bad about it, you know, guilty sometimes," explains Bob Beardsley, a thirty-year-old white machine operator, his eyes registering the discomfort he feels as he speaks.

"Does it change anything when you feel guilty?" I ask.

A small smile flits across his face, and he says, "Sometimes. I try to do a little more, but then I get busy with something and forget that she needs me to help out. My wife says I don't pay attention, that's why I forget. But I don't know. Seems like I've just got my mind on other things."

It's possible, of course, that the men who speak of guilt and rights are only trying to impress me by mouthing the politically correct words. But even if true, they display a sensitivity to the issue that's missing from the men who don't speak those words. For words are more than just words. They embody ideas; they are the symbols that give meaning to our thoughts; they shape our consciousness. New ideas come to us on the wings of words. It's words that bring those ideas to life, that allow us to see possibilities unrecognized before we gave them words. Indeed, without words, there is no conscious thought, no possibility for the kind of self-reflection that lights the path of change.[3]

True, there's often a long way between word and deed. But the man who feels guilty when he disappoints his wife's expectations has a different consciousness than the one who doesn't—a difference that usually makes for at least some small change in his behavior. Although the emergence of this changing male consciousness is visible in all the racial groups in this study, there also are differences among them that are worthy of comment.

Virtually all the men do some work inside the family—tending the children, washing dishes, running the vacuum, going to the market. And they generally also remain responsible for those tasks that have always been traditionally male—mowing the lawn, shoveling the snow, fixing the car, cleaning the garage, doing repairs around the house. Among the white families in this study, 16 percent of the men share the family work relatively equally, almost always those who live in families where they and their wives work different shifts or where the men are unemployed. "What choice do I have?" asks Don Bartlett, a thirty-year-old white handyman who works days while his wife is on the swing shift. "I'm the only one here, so I do what's got to be done."

Asian and Latino men of all ages, however, tend to operate more often on the old male model, even when they work different shifts or are unemployed, a finding that puzzled me at first. Why, I wondered, did I find only two Asian men and one Latino who are real partners in the work of the family? Aren't these men subject to the same social and personal pressures others experience?

The answer is both yes and no. The pressures are there, but, depending upon where they live, there's more or less support for re-

sisting them. The Latino and Asian men who live in
borhoods—settings where they are embedded in an
tional community and where the language and culture
country is kept alive by a steady stream of new immig
strong support for clinging to the old ways. Therefore
comes much more slowly in those families. The men who
side the ethnic quarter are freer from the mandates and co
of these often tight-knit communities, and therefore are
sponsive to the winds of change in the larger society.

These distinctions notwithstanding, it's clear that Asia
Latino men generally participate least in the work of the h
hold and are the least likely to believe they have much resp
bility there beyond bringing home a paycheck. "Taking care of
house and kids is my wife's job, that's all," says Joe Gomez fla

"A Chinese man mopping a floor? I've never seen it yet," say
Amy Lee angrily. Her husband, Dennis, trying to make a joke o
the conflict with his wife, says with a smile, "In Chinese families
men don't do floors and windows, I help with the dishes sometimes if she needs me to or," he laughs, "if she screams loud
enough. The rest, well, it's pretty much her job."

The commonly held stereotype about black men abandoning
women and children, however, doesn't square with the families in
this study. In fact, black men are the most likely to be real participants in the daily life of the family and are more intimately involved in raising their children than any of the others. True, the
men's family work load doesn't always match their wives', and the
women are articulate in their complaints about this. Nevertheless, compared to their white, Asian, or Latino counterparts, the
black families look like models of egalitarianism.

Nearly three-quarters of the men in the African-American
families in this study do a substantial amount of the cooking,
cleaning, and child care, sometimes even more than their wives
do. All explain it by saying one version or another of: "I just figure
it's my job, too"—which simply says what is, without explaining
how it came to be that way.

To understand that, we have to look at family histories that
tell the story of generations of African-American women who
could find work and men who could not, and to the family culture
that grew from this difficult and painful reality. "My mother
worked six days a week cleaning other people's houses, and my father was an ordinary laborer, when he could find work, which
wasn't very often," explains thirty-two-year-old Troy Payne, a
black waiter and father of two children. "So he was home a lot
more than she was, and he'd do what he had to do around the

house. The kids all had to do their share, too. It seemed only fair, I guess."

Difficult as the conflict around the division of labor is, it's only one of the many issues that have become flash points in family life since mother went to work. Most important, perhaps, is the question: Who will care for the children? For the lack of decent, affordable facilities for the care of the children creates unbearable problems and tensions for these working-class families.

Endnotes

1. James Sweet, Larry Bumpass, and Vaugn Call, *National Survey of Families and Households* (Madison, Wisc.: Center for Demography and Ecology, University of Wisconsin, 1988). This study featured a probability sample of 5,518 households and included couples with and without children. See also Joseph Pleck, *Working Wives/Working Husbands* (Beverly Hills: Sage Publications, 1985), who summarizes time-budget studies; and Iona Mara-Drita, "The Effects of Power, Ideology, and Experience on Men's Participation in Housework," unpublished paper (1993), whose analysis of Sweet, Bumpass, and Call's data shows that when housework and employment hours are added together, a woman's work week totals 69 hours, compared to 52 hours for a man.
2. Lillian B. Rubin, *Worlds of Pain* (New York: Basic Books, 1992), p. 93.
3. See Daniel Stern, *The Interpersonal World of the Infant* (New York: Basic Books, 1985), who argues that a child's capacity for self-reflection coincides with the development of language.

Questions for Thought and Writing

1. The feminist movement has disrupted the traditional "neat division of labor" that separated women and men into private and public spheres. In what ways have these changes benefited women? In what ways does the new distribution of labor still leave women at a disadvantage?
2. Why do younger men tend to be more sympathetic to their wives' demands for increased help and support than older men? Why do the older men seem to have a sense of what the author calls "victimization"? Does this divide between older and younger men match your experience and observations? Do magazines, TV shows, and films marketed to male audiences (e.g., *The Man Show*, *Maxim* magazine, etc.) support or disprove this divide?
3. How does the author explain her findings that Asian-American and Latin-American men are less likely than their counterparts of other ethnic backgrounds to share household re-

sponsibilities? How do her findings compare to the division of labor between adults in your own household?

ISSUES

This Issues section gives readers opportunities to view central issues and aspects of family life through a gendered lens. For example, in "Witnessing the Death of Love: She Hears Him Tell the Woman That He Will Kill Her . . . ," bell hooks reveals a daughter's struggle to make sense of women's rights and responsibilities as she witnesses her mother's decision to remain loyal to an abusive husband and father. Robbie E. Davis-Floyd's "Gender and Ritual: Giving Birth the American Way" challenges the legitimacy of contemporary U.S. medical practices in which childbirth is deeply technologized and women's bodies are figured as "defective" and in need of assistance. In "Fatherhood and the Mediating Role of Women," Nicholas W. Townsend examines the ways in which cultural notions of "mother" and "father" are deeply tied to and limited by traditional gender roles. He considers how new reproductive options for women allow them into motherhood without marriage, although these options do not give men the same flexibility. In "Sexual Dissent and the Family: The Sharon Kowalski Case," Nan D. Hunter addresses the question "who counts as family?" and highlights how gay and lesbian relationships complicate and challenge traditional answers to this question. Luci Tapahonso's poem "Blue Horses Rush In" offers the reader a provocative counterpoint to a "technocratic" model of childbirth and challenges mainstream U.S. notions of women as "the weaker sex."

Witnessing the Death of Love: She Hears Him Tell the Woman That He Will Kill Her . . .

bell hooks

They have never heard their mama and daddy fussing or fighting. They have heard him be harsh, complain that the house should be cleaner, that he should not have to come home from work to a house that is not cleaned just right. They know he gets mad. When he gets mad about the house he begins to clean it himself to show that he can do better. Although he never cooks he knows how. He would not be able to judge her cooking if he did not cook himself. They are afraid of him when he is mad. They go upstairs to get out of his way. He does not come upstairs. Taking care of children is not a man's work. It does not concern him. He is not even interested—that is, unless something goes wrong. Then he can show her that she is not very good at parenting. They know they have a good mama, the best. Even though they fear him they are not moved by his opinions. She tries to remember a time when she felt loved by him. She remembers it as being the time when she was a baby girl, a small girl. She remembers him taking her places, taking her to the world inhabited by black men, the barbershop, the pool hall. He took his affections away from her abruptly. She never understood why, only that they went and did not come back. She remembered trying to do whatever she could to bring them back, only they never came. Growing up she stopped trying. He mainly ignored her. She mainly tried to stay out of his way. In her own way she grew to hate wanting his love and not being able to get it. She hated that part of herself that kept wanting his love or even just his approval long after she could see that he was never, never going to give it.

Out of nowhere he comes home from work angry. He reaches the porch yelling and screaming at the woman inside—yelling that she is his wife, he can do with her what he wants. They do not understand what is happening. He is pushing, hitting, telling her to shut up. She is pleading—crying. He does not want to hear, to listen. They catch his angry words in their hands like lightning bugs—store them in a jar to sort them out later. Words about other men, about phone calls, about how he had told her. They do not know what he has told her. They have never heard them talk in an angry way.

She thinks of all the nights she lies awake in her bed hearing the woman's voice, her mother's voice, hearing his voice. She wonders if it is then that he is telling her everything—warning her. Yelling, screaming, hitting: they stare at the red blood that trickles through the crying mouth. They cannot believe this pleading, crying woman, this woman who does not fight back, is the same person they know. The person they know is strong, gets things done, is a woman of ways and means, a woman of action. They do not know her still, paralyzed, waiting for the next blow, pleading. They do not know their mama afraid. Even if she does not hit back they want her to run, to run and to not stop running. She wants her to hit him with the table light, the ashtray, the one near her hand. She does not want to see her like this, not fighting back. He notices them, long enough to tell them to get out, go upstairs. She refuses to move. She cannot move. She cannot leave her mama alone. When he says What are you staring at, do you want some, too? she is afraid enough to move. She will not take her orders from him. She asks the woman if it is right to leave her alone. The woman—her mother—nods her head yes. She still stands still. It is his movement in her direction that sends her up the stairs. She cannot believe all her sisters and her brother are not taking a stand, that they go to sleep. She cannot bear their betrayal. When the father is not looking she creeps down the steps. She wants the woman to know that she is not alone. She wants to bear witness.

All that she does not understand about marriage, about men and women, is explained to her one night. In her dark place on the stairs she is seeing over and over again the still body of the woman pleading, crying, the moving body of the man angry, yelling. She sees that the man has a gun. She hears him tell the woman that he will kill her. She sits in her place on the stair and demands to know of herself is she able to come to the rescue, is she willing to fight, is she ready to die. Her body shakes with the answers. She is fighting back the tears. When he leaves the room she comes to ask the woman if she is all right, if there is anything she can do. The woman's voice is full of tenderness and hurt. She is in her role as mother. She tells her daughter to go upstairs and go to sleep, that everything will be all right. The daughter does not believe her. Her eyes are pleading. She does not want to be told to go. She hovers in the shadows. When he returns he tells her that he has told her to get her ass upstairs. She does not look at him. He turns to the woman, tells her to leave, tells her to take the daughter with her.

5   The woman does not protest. She moves like a robot, hurriedly throwing things into suitcases, boxes. She says nothing to the man. He is still screaming, muttering. When she tries to say to him he is wrong, so wrong, he is more angry, threatening. All the neat drawers are emptied out on the bed, all the precious belongings that can be carried, stuffed, are to be taken. There is sorrow in every gesture, sorrow and pain—like a dust collecting on every-

thing, so thick she can gather it in her hands. She is seeing that the man owns everything, that the woman has only her clothes, her shoes, and other personal belongings. She is seeing that the woman can be told to go, can be sent away in the silent, long hours of the night. She is hearing in her head the man's threats to kill. She can feel the cool metal as if it is resting against her cheek. She can hear the click, the blast. She can see the woman's body falling. No, it is not her body, it is the body of love. She witnesses the death of love. If love were alive she believes it would stop everything. It would steady the man's voice, calm his rage. Love would take the woman's hand, caress her cheek and with a clean handkerchief wipe her eyes. The gun is pointed at love. He lays it on the table. He wants his wife to finish her packing, to go.

She is again in her role as mother. She tells the daughter that she does not have to flee in the middle of the night, that it is not her fight. The daughter is silent, staring into the woman's eyes. She is looking for the bright lights, the care and adoration she has shown the man. The eyes are dark with grief, swollen. She feels that a fire inside the woman is dying out, that she is cold. She is sure the woman will freeze to death if she goes out into the night alone. She takes her hand, ready to go with her. Yet she hopes there will be no going. She hopes when the mother's brother comes he will be strong enough to take love's body and give it, mouth-to-mouth, the life it has lost. She hopes he will talk to the man, guide him. When he finally comes, her mother's favorite brother, she cannot believe the calm way he lifts suitcase, box, sack, carries them to the car without question. She cannot bear his silent agreement that the man is right, that he has done what men are able to do. She cannot take the bits and pieces of her mother's heart and put them together again.

I am always fighting with mama. Everything has come between us. She no longer stands between me and all that would hurt me. She is hurting me. This is my dream of her—that she will stand between me and all that hurts me, that she will protect me at all cost. It is only a dream. In some way I understand that it has to do with marriage, that to be the wife to the husband she must be willing to sacrifice even her daughters for his good. For the mother it is not simple. She is always torn. She works hard to fulfill his needs, our needs. When they are not the same she must maneuver, manipulate, choose. She has chosen. She has decided in his favor. She is a religious woman. She has been told that a man should obey god, that a woman should obey man, that children should obey their fathers and mothers, particularly their mothers. I will not obey.

She says that she punishes me for my own good. I do not know what it is I have done this time. I know that she is ready with her switches, that I am to stand still while she lashes out again and again. In my mind there is the memory of a woman sitting still while she is being hit, punished. In my mind I am remembering how much I want that woman to fight back. Before I can think clearly my hands reach out, grab the switches, are raised as if to hit her back. For a moment she is stunned, unbelieving. She is shocked. She tells me that I must never *ever* as long as I live raise my hand against my mother. I tell her I do not have a mother. She is even more shocked. Enraged, she lashes out again. This time I am still. This time I cry. I see the hurt in her eyes when I say I do not have a mother. I am ready to be punished. My desire was to stop the pain, not to hurt. I am ashamed and torn. I do not want to stand still and be punished but I never want to hurt mama. It is better to hurt than to cause her pain. She warns me that she will tell daddy when he comes home, that I will be punished again. I cannot understand her acts of betrayal. I cannot understand that she must be against me to be for him. He and I are strangers. Deep in the night we parted from one another, knowing that nothing would ever be the same. He did not say good-bye. I did not look him in the face. Now we avoid one another. He speaks to me through her.

Although they act as if everything between them is the same, that life is as it was. It is only a game. They pretend. There is no pain in the pretense. Everything is hidden. Secrets find a way out in sleep. My sisters say to mama She cries in her sleep, calls out. In her sleep is the place of remembering. It is the place where there is no pretense. She is dreaming always the same dream. A movie is showing. It is a tragic story of jealousy and lost love. It is called *Crime of Passion.* In the movie a man has killed his wife and daughter. He has killed his wife because he believes she has lovers. He has killed the daughter because she witnesses the death of the wife. When they go to trial all the remaining family come to speak on behalf of the man. At his job he is calm and quiet, a hardworking man, a family man. Neighbors come to testify that the dead woman was young and restless, that the daughter was wild and rebellious. Everyone sympathizes with the man. His story is so sad that they begin to weep. All their handkerchiefs are clean and white. Like flags waving, they are a signal of peace, of surrender. They are a gesture to the man that he can go on with life.

Questions for Thought and Writing

1. In paragraph 4, hooks writes, "All that she does not understand about marriage, about men and women, is explained to her one night." Write about what you think is explained to the narrator about these things the night she witnesses the fight between her parents.

2. As her mother packs up to leave her own house, the narrator watches her uncle standing by and "cannot bear his silent agreement that the man is right, that he has done what men are able to do." What does the narrator believe men are "able to do"? Identify and discuss other examples from contemporary culture of conspiracies or partnerships among men that seem to exclude, harm, or negate women.

3. In the heat of a passionate argument, the narrator says "I do not have a mother." In what way does she believe her mother has failed her? Are our expectations for mothers realistic? If not, how might they be adjusted to make them more realistic?

Gender and Ritual: Giving Birth the American Way

Robbie E. Davis-Floyd

Although the array of new technologies that radically alter the nature of human reproduction is exponentially increasing, childbirth is still an entirely gendered phenomenon. Because only women have babies, the way a society treats pregnancy and childbirth reveals a great deal about the way that society treats women. The experience of childbirth is unique for every woman, and yet in the United States childbirth is treated in a highly standardized way. No matter how long or short, how easy or hard their labors, the vast majority of American women are hooked up to an electronic fetal monitor and an IV (intravenously administered fluids and/or medication), are encouraged to use pain-relieving drugs, receive an episiotomy (a surgical incision in the vagina to widen the birth outlet in order to prevent tearing) at the moment of birth, and are separated from their babies shortly after birth. Most women also receive doses of the synthetic hormone pitocin to speed their labors, and they give birth flat on their backs. Nearly one-quarter of babies are delivered by Cesarean section.

Many Americans, including most of the doctors and nurses who attend birth, view these procedures as medical necessities. Yet anthropologists regularly describe other, less technological ways to give birth. For example, the Mayan Indians of Highland Chiapas hold onto a rope while squatting for birth, a position that is far more beneficial than the flat-on-your-back-with-your-feet-in-stirrups (lithotomy) position. Mothers in many low-technology cultures give birth sitting, squatting, semi-reclining in their hammocks, or on their hands and knees, and are nurtured through the pain of labor by experienced midwives and supportive female relatives. What then might explain the standardization and technical elaboration of the American birthing process?

One answer emerges from the field of symbolic anthropology. Early in this century, Arnold van Gennep noticed that in many societies around the world, major life transitions are ritualized. These cultural *rites of passage* make it appear that society itself effects the transformation of the individual. Could this explain the standardization of American birth? I believe the answer is yes.

I came to this conclusion as a result of a study I conducted of American birth between 1983 and 1991. I interviewed over 100 mothers, as well as many of the obstetricians, nurses, childbirth educators, and midwives who attended them.[1] While poring over my interviews, I began to understand that the forces shaping American hospital birth are invisible to us because they stem from the conceptual foundations of our society. I realized that American society's deepest beliefs center on science, technology, patriarchy, and the institutions that control and disseminate them, and that there could be no better transmitter of these core values and beliefs than the hospital procedures so salient in American birth. Through these procedures, American women are repeatedly told, in dozens of visible and invisible ways, that their bodies are defective machines incapable of giving birth without the assistance of these other, male-created, more perfect machines. . . .

PRESERVATION OF THE STATUS QUO

A major function of ritual is cultural preservation. Through explicit enactment of a culture's belief system, ritual works both to preserve and to transmit the culture. Preserving the culture includes perpetuating its power structure, so it is usually the case that those in positions of power will have unique control over ritual performance. They will utilize the effectiveness of ritual to reinforce both their own importance and the importance of the belief and value system that legitimizes their positions.

In spite of tremendous advances in equality for women, the United States is still a patriarchy. It is no cultural accident that 99 percent of American women give birth in hospitals, where only physicians, most of whom are male, have final authority over the performance of birth rituals—an authority that reinforces the cultural privileging of patriarchy for both mothers and their medical attendants.

Nowhere is this reality more visible than in the lithotomy position. Despite years of effort on the part of childbirth activists, including many obstetricians, the majority of American women still give birth lying flat on their backs. This position is physiologically dysfunctional. It compresses major blood vessels, lowering the mother's circulation and thus the baby's oxygen supply. It increases the need for forceps because it both narrows the pelvic outlet and ensures that the baby, who must follow the curve of the birth canal, quite literally will be born heading upward, against gravity. This lithotomy position completes the process of symbolic inversion that has been in motion ever since the woman was put into that "upside-down" hospital gown. Her normal bodily patterns are turned, quite literally, upside-down—her legs are in the air, her vagina totally exposed. As the ultimate symbolic inversion, it is ritually appropriate that this position be reserved for the peak tranformational moments of the initiation experience— the birth itself. The doctor—society's official representative— stands in control not at the mother's head nor at her side, but at her bottom, where the baby's head is beginning to emerge.

Structurally speaking, this puts the woman's vagina where her head should be. Such total inversion is perfectly appropriate from a social perspective, as the technocratic model promises us that eventually we will be able to grow babies in machines—that is, have them with our cultural heads instead of our natural bottoms.

In our culture, "up" is good and "down" is bad, so the babies born of science and technology must be delivered "up" toward the positively valued cultural world, instead of down toward the negatively valued natural world. Interactionally, the obstetrician is "up" and the birthing woman is "down," an inversion that speaks eloquently to her of her powerlessness and of the power of society at the supreme moment of her own individual transformation.

The episiotomy performed by the obstetrician just before birth also powerfully enacts the status quo in American society. This procedure, performed on over 90 percent of first-time mothers as they give birth, expresses the value and importance of one of our technocratic society's most fundamental markers—the straight line. Through episiotomies, physicians can deconstruct the vagina (stretchy, flexible, part-circular and part-formless, feminine, creative, sexual, non-linear), then reconstruct it in accordance with our cultural belief and value system. Doctors are taught (incorrectly) that straight cuts heal faster than the small jagged tears that sometimes occur during birth. They learn that straight cuts will prevent such tears, but in fact, episiotomies often cause severe tearing that would not otherwise occur (Klein 1992; Shiono et al. 1990; Thorp and Bowes 1989; Wilcox et al. 1989[2]). These teachings dramatize our Western belief in the superiority of culture over nature. Because it virtually does not exist in nature, the line is most useful in aiding us in our constant conceptual efforts to separate ourselves from nature.

10   Moreover, since surgery constitutes the ultimate form of manipulation of the human body-machine, it is the most highly valued form of medicine. Routinizing the episiotomy, and increasingly, the Cesarean section, has served both to legitimize and to raise the status of obstetrics as a profession, by ensuring that childbirth will be not a natural but a surgical procedure.

EFFECTING SOCIAL CHANGE

Paradoxically, ritual, with all of its insistence on continuity and order, can be an important factor not only in individual transformation but also in social change. New belief and value systems are most effectively spread through new rituals designed to enact and transmit them; entrenched belief and value systems are most effectively altered through alterations in the rituals that enact them.

Nine percent of my interviewees entered the hospital determined to avoid technocratic rituals in order to have "completely natural childbirth," yet ended up with highly technocratic births. These nine women experienced extreme cognitive dissonance between their previously held self-images and those internalized in the hospital. Most of them suffered severe emotional wounding and short-term post-partum depression as a result. But 15 percent did achieve their goal of natural childbirth, thereby avoiding conceptual fusion with the technocratic model. These women were personally empowered by their birth experiences. They tended to view technology as a resource that they could choose to utilize or ignore, and often consciously subverted their socialization process by replacing technocratic symbols with self-empowering alternatives. For example, they wore their own clothes and ate their own food, rejecting the hospital gown and the IV. They walked the halls instead of going to bed. They chose perineal massage instead of episiotomy, and gave birth like "primitives," sitting up, squatting, or on their hands and knees. One of them, confronted with the wheelchair, said "I don't need this," and used it as a luggage cart. This rejection of customary ritual elements is an exceptionally powerful way to induce change, as it takes advantage of an already charged and dramatic situation.

During the 1970s and early 1980s, the conceptual hegemony of the technocratic model in the hospital was severely challenged by the natural childbirth movement which these 24 women represent. Birth activists succeeded in getting hospitals to allow fathers into labor and delivery rooms, mothers to birth consciously (without being put to sleep), and mothers and babies to room together after birth. They fought for women to have the right to birth without drugs or interventions, to walk around or even be in water during labor (in some hospitals, Jacuzzis were installed). Prospects for change away from the technocratic model of birth by the 1990s seemed bright.

Changing a society's belief and value system by changing the rituals that enact it is possible, but not easy. To counter attempts at change, individuals in positions of authority often intensify the rituals that support the status quo. Thus a response to the threat posed by the natural childbirth movement was to intensify the use of high technology in hospital birth. During the 1980s, periodic electronic monitoring of nearly all women became standard procedure, the epidural rate shot up to 80 percent, and the Cesarean rate rose to nearly 25 percent. Part of the impetus for this technocratic intensification is the increase in malpractice suits against physicians. The threat of lawsuit forces doctors to practice conservatively—that is, in strict accordance with technocratic standards. As one of them explained:

> Certainly I've changed the way I practice since malpractice became an issue. I do more C-sections . . . and more and more tests to cover myself. More expensive stuff. We don't do risky things that women ask for—we're very conservative in our approach to everything. . . . In 1970 before all this came up, my C-section rate was around 4 percent. It has gradually climbed every year since then. In 1985 it was 16 percent, then in 1986 it was 23 percent.

The money goes where the values lie. From this macrocultural perspective, the increase in malpractice suits emerges as society's effort to make sure that its representatives, the obstetricians, perpetuate our technocratic core value system by continuing through birth rituals to transmit that system. Its perpetuation seems imperative, for in our technology we see the promise of our eventual transcendence of bodily and earthly limitations—already we replace body parts with computerized devices, grow babies in test tubes, build space stations, and continue to pollute the environment in the expectation that someone will develop the technologies to clean it up!

We are all complicitors in our technocratic system, as we have so very much invested in it. Just as that system has given us increasing control over the natural environment, so it has also given not only doctors but also women increasing control over biology and birth. Contemporary middle-class women *do* have much greater say over what will be done to them during birth than their mothers, most of whom gave birth during the 1950s and 1960s under general anesthesia. When what they demand is in accord with technocratic values, they have a much greater chance of getting it than their sisters have of achieving natural childbirth. Even as hospital birth still perpetuates partriarchy by treating women's bodies as defective machines, it now also reflects women's greater autonomy by allowing them conceptual separation from those defective machines.

Epidural anesthesia is administered in about 80 percent of American hospital births. So common is its use that many childbirth educators are calling the 1990s the age of the "epidural epidemic." As the epidural numbs the birthing woman, eliminating the pain of childbirth, it also graphically demonstrates to her through lived experience the truth of the Cartesian maxim that mind and body are separate, that the biological realm can be completely cut off from the realm of the intellect and the emotions. The epidural is thus the perfect technocratic tool, serving the interests of the technocratic model by transmitting it, and of women choosing to give birth under that model, by enabling them to use it to divorce themselves from their biology:

> Ultimately the decision to have the epidural and the Cesarean while I was in labor was mine. I told my doctor I'd had enough of this labor business and I'd like to . . . get it over with. So he whisked me off to the delivery room and we did it. (Elaine)

For many women, the epidural provides a means by which they can actively witness birth while avoiding "dropping into biology." Explained Joanne, "I'm not real fond of things that remind me I'm a biological creature—I prefer to think and be an intellectual emotional person." Such women tended to define their bodies as tools, vehicles for their minds. They did not enjoy "giving in to biology" to be pregnant, and were happy to be liberated from biology during birth. And they welcomed advances in birth technologies as extensions of their own ability to control nature.

In dramatic contrast, six of my interviewees (6 percent), insisting that "I am my body," rejected the technocratic model altogether. They chose to give birth at home under an alternative paradigm, the *holistic model*. This model stresses the organicity and trustworthiness of the female body, the natural rhythmicity of labor, the integrity of the family, and self-responsibility. These homebirthers see the safety of the baby and the emotional needs of the mother as one. The safest birth for the baby will be the one that provides the most nurturing environment for the mother.[3] Said Ryla,

> I got criticized for choosing a home birth, for not considering the safety of the baby. But that's exactly what I was considering! How could it possibly serve my baby for me to give birth in a place that causes my whole body to tense up in anxiety as soon as I walk in the door?

Although homebirthers constitute only about 2 percent of the American birthing population, their conceptual importance is tremendous, as through the alternative rituals of giving birth at home, they enact—and thus guarantee the existence of—a paradigm of pregnancy and birth based on the value of connection, just as the technocratic model is based on the principle of separation.

The technocratic and holistic models represent opposite ends of a spectrum of beliefs about birth and about cultural life. Their differences are mirrored on a wider scale by the ideological conflicts between biomedicine and holistic healing, and between industrialists and ecological activists. These groups are engaged in a core value struggle over the future—a struggle clearly visible in the profound differences in the rituals they daily enact.

Endnotes

1. The full results of this study appear in Davis-Floyd 1992.
2. See Goer 1995: 274–284 for summaries and interpretations of these studies and others concerning electronic fetal monitoring.
3. For summaries of studies that demonstrate the safety of planned, midwife-attended home birth relative to hospital birth, see Davis-Floyd 1992, Chapter 4, and Goer 1995.

References

Davis-Floyd, Robbie E. 1992. *Birth as an American Rite of Passage*. Berkeley: University of California Press.

Goer, Henci. 1995. *Obstetric Myths Versus Research Realities: A Guide to the Medical Literature*. Westport, CT: Bergin and Garvey.

Jordan, Brigitte. 1993. *Birth in Four Cultures: A Cross-Cultural Investigation of Birth in Yucatan, Holland, Sweden and the United States* (4th edition revised). Prospect Heights: Waveland Press.

Klein, Michael, et al. 1992. "Does Episiotomy Prevent Perineal Trauma and Pelvic Floor Relaxation?" *Online Journal of Current Clinical Trials* 1 (Document 10).

Shiono, P., M. A. Klebanoff, and J. C. Carey. 1990. "Midline Episiotomies: More Harm Than Good?" *American Journal of Obstetrics and Gynecology* 75 (5): 765–770.

Thorp, J. M., and W. A. Bowes. 1989. "Episiotomy: Can Its Routine Use Be Defended?" *American Journal of Obstetrics and Gynecology* 160 (5Pt1): 1027–1030.

Wilcox, L. S., et al. 1989. "Episiotomy and Its Role in the Incidence of Perineal Lacerations in a Maternity Center and a Tertiary Hospital Obstetric Service." *American Journal of Obstetrics and Gynecology* 160 (5Pt1): 1047–1052.

Questions for Thought and Writing

1. This essay discusses binary categories through which men and women are traditionally conceptualized in the Western world, beginning with normative/other (in which everything male and

male-identified is considered "the norm," and everything female or female-identified is compared against that male norm and labeled "other"). What are some of the other binaries through which we typically view the differences between men and women? What are the costs and challenges for the women in the study who attempt to challenge these divisions?

2. The wheelchair requirement and the lithotomy position for childbirth are two of the visual symbols created by a patriarchal medical system to reinforce cultural beliefs in women's bodies as defective and/or needing medical help in order to properly function. What other visual images circulating in our culture suggest that women's bodies are inadequate in their natural state?

3. The author argues that the core values of American society are "technocratic." How does this compare to traditional ideas of "baseball, motherhood, and apple pie" as core American values? Do both sets of values reinforce the principles of patriarchy?

Fatherhood and the Mediating Role of Women

NICHOLAS W. TOWNSEND

In this chapter I confront an apparent paradox in men's accounts of fatherhood. Men say they want to be involved fathers but they do not seem to be acting that way.

Nearly all the men I talked to in my research said they wanted to be more involved as fathers than their own fathers had been, and this stated desire is very common for men in the United States. But men in the United States do not put much time into domestic work or child care (Coltrane, 1996), and after divorce many men in the United States pay very little or nothing in child support and frequently maintain no contact with their children (Furstenberg and Cherlin, 1991; Arendell, 1995). I argue that we can understand some of this paradox if we consider what men do as fathers as well as what they do not do, and if we listen to what they have to say about being fathers.

Parenting is deeply gendered. And by this I do not mean only that fathers and mothers do different things, though that is clearly the case, but also that being a parent means different things to mothers and fathers, and that being a father means different things to men and women. Parenting is also gendered in other ways, such as men's stated preference for sons and the ways they treat daughters and sons differently. I have discussed these aspects of fatherhood elsewhere (Townsend, n.d.). In this chapter, I am focusing on the gendered relationship between fathers and mothers. Seeing men and their accounts as gendered in this way helps us to understand how men think about being fathers and about relationships in general. . . .

My discussion in this chapter is based on talking to men who graduated from the same high school in 1972 and were in their late thirties when I interviewed them.[1] Because they all graduated from the same high school, I was able to learn a lot about the community in California in which they grew up, the events of their youth, and the opportunities they faced as adults. I can speak with confidence about the attitudes these men shared, and about the differences between them, and I would argue that these men are in many ways typical of men in the United States, but these men's experiences and meanings cannot be used to support universal or essential ideas about "male" experience or fathering as a universal pattern of behavior.[2]

5   What emerged from my conversations is that, for the men I talked to, the father–child relationship could not be described or thought about independent of the relationship between husband and wife. When I ask men about their parents, they talk mostly about their fathers, but when I ask them about becoming fathers they talk about their wives. Some of the paradoxes of men's relations to their children may be resolved by understanding the relative positions of men, women, and children, and specifically the crucial linking or mediating role of women.

Appreciating the linking role of women is not the same as saying that men do not care about children, or that they think that children are entirely women's business. Certainly becoming a parent is more separated from biological reproduction for men than for women. One can scarcely imagine a woman saying, as one of my male informants did: "Actually I have had a child before, although through very strange circumstances. I didn't know I had a child before he was a year old and someone sent me a Christmas card saying: 'This is your baby.' " Equally certainly, men consider childbearing and child rearing to be predominantly women's responsibility. This is not to say that men are indifferent to having children. They have strong feelings about the number, timing, and kind of children they want, but at crucial points in their lives they find that their paternity depends on the cooperation of women. The men are not passively dependent on women's motivations—they actively select and try to persuade, pressure, and coerce women, but the mediating link provided by women remains crucial.

It is not just that men need, and realize that they need, a woman's physical cooperation in order to become fathers. There is also an asymmetry in the ways that men and women *think* about becoming parents. For instance, many women are prepared to think about single parenthood as a possible, though usually less desirable, route to motherhood; the men I talked to, on the other hand, do not even register it as a possibility. Many single, childless women are able to think and talk directly about whether they want to have children. In doing so, and in reading the advice and examples they are offered in books and magazines, it is clear that they see having a child on one's own as an option. It is an option with definite emotional, social, and financial drawbacks as well as opportunities, and it is an option that they may well reject, but it remains a possibility. That having a child on her own is a possibility to be considered means that women are able to weigh and articulate their specific desire for children outside the matrix of family and relationship with a man. The relationship between mother and child, the activity of mothering, and the transformation of self into a mother, are things women can think about directly and in isolation. The men I talked to could not talk about having children without talking about "having a family" or "being a family man." For these men, "having children" is part of "being married and having a family." They can only conceptualize the relationship between father and children within the matrix of family relationships.

Of course, the relationships between men and their wives are very important in their own right, but my interest here is in the way that marital relationships are structurally important for men's relationships with their children. Women, as wives and mothers, mediate and facilitate fatherhood. The word "mediate" describes women's role in the relationship between men and children because it captures, in its various meanings, some of the complexity of that role. Women are in the middle of this relationship, they frequently do mediate in the most literal sense of operating as go-betweens or negotiators between their husbands and their children, and their presence and activity makes possible the reproduction, both biological and social, that is at the heart of fatherhood.

For men, having children is a reproduction of fatherhood—a patrilineal process of the movement of males through the statuses of son, father, and grandfather and of child, adult, and old man (Townsend, 1998). There are five moments, phases, or aspects of reproduction at which women's mediating role is most apparent: at marriage, when decisions are made about the timing and number of children, in the structural division of labor after children are born, in gendered parenting, and after divorce.

MARRIAGE AND CHILDREN: WIFE AND MOTHER

"We always knew we wanted to get married and have a family" was a frequent comment of men who married women they had known in high school. For my informants, marriage is almost always considered to be a relationship that will involve having children. In most first marriages, husbands say they either "knew" or "assumed" that their wives would want children. For the men, marriage meant getting a "wife and family" as a sort of package deal.

As is often the case, it is when obstacles to meeting a norm arise that its existence is made most clear. Several men told me that they did not marry women with whom they had "good relationships" because those women did not want or could not have children. Conversely, men who had actually wanted to have children told me that they had ended relationships with women they did not want to marry by telling them that they did not want to have children. That this was an excuse is made clear by the rapidity with which they subsequently met, married, and had children with other women. Regardless of whether the particular men or women in any relationship or marriage really wanted children or not, the point is that the cultural idea that marriage and children go together was so clear to all that it could be used as a reason to end a relationship without rejecting the other person by saying: "I don't want to marry you." Men are making a simultaneous decision about "a wife and a mother to my children." . . .

"THE DRIVING FORCE": WOMEN, TIMING, AND BIRTH CONTROL

In general, the men I talked to assumed that, in their own lives, conception and birth were events that could be controlled. They assumed that sexual intercourse without pregnancy was a reasonable expectation, so that premarital sex, a space of time between marriage and their first birth, a controlled space between their children's births, and a cessation of childbearing were all things to be reasonably expected and planned for. Their confidence in their ability to plan was, to a certain extent, justified by the technological innovations of the birth control pill, the IUD, and safe and easy techniques for male and female sterilization.

Previous fertility declines and control, at the level of populations and of couples, have depended on a mix of methods, including heavy reliance on abstinence and withdrawal (Schneider and Schneider, 1996). These are methods that involve at least the participation, if not the active initiation, of men. The Pill and the IUD, by contrast, are methods that are used by women and that do not require contraceptive action by men or women at the time of intercourse. They are, particularly for men, much less psychically costly than withdrawal or abstinence. For men in the United States, these methods have had the double effect of enabling a conceptual and physical separation between sexual activity and reproduction and of moving control over reproduction to women. Control over reproduction was seen as not only technically, but also morally, women's responsibility.

Barry, for example, does not say the decision about when to have children was his wife's alone, but he does put the primary responsibility on her.

> She was probably the driving force. Again, I wanted children too. So it wasn't like: "OK, I'll just give in. If you want children, we'll have children." But she was probably more the driver of that issue than myself. I could have been content to wait a couple years. But again, we both wanted children. It wasn't just because she wanted children. If she would have been very insistent against it, it would have been something we probably would have had to talk about. It's really hard to say, but I think I wanted to have children also, but not to the same degree as she did. It would have been nice to have them, but if I didn't, I could have lived without them. It wouldn't have been a decision I may have regretted.

Notice that while she is the "driving force" behind the timing, he also makes it clear that he too wanted children. But he then questions his own desire when he says "I *think* I wanted to have children" and "I could have lived without them." In the face of this uncertainty, he placed the initiative with his wife. . . .

MEN AT WORK, WOMEN AT HOME:
THE STRUCTURAL DIVISION OF LABOR

The archetypical picture of family life in the United States has been of a nuclear household, composed of a married heterosexual couple and their children, in which the man is the breadwinner and the woman is the homemaker. This has not, of course, been an accurate picture of the family lives of many people, but it has been a cultural archetype, or hegemonic image, that shapes people's perceptions even when it does not represent their reality.[3] Even when they become very common, however, behaviors that do not conform to hegemonic cultural norms continue to be perceived as "exceptions." When people's lives diverge from cultural norms they have to do cultural work to deny, explain, or reinterpret, this divergence. Some husbands of employed women who wanted to emphasize that they were the primary providers for their families explained that their wives' incomes were used for "extras" or "luxuries." Others described their wives' work as something they did mainly for variety, social contacts, or to "get away from the kids." But in either case they were doing cultural work to interpret their arrangements as conforming to a hegemonic picture of the structural division of labor in marriage. In support of this division of labor, the men I talked to made three interlocking arguments: that they liked or chose the arrangement, that it was best for the children, and that it was natural.

Gordon, the engineer with three sons who felt "more married" once he had children, expressed very clearly the structural division of labor between parents: one parent should stay home to raise the children, and it should be the mother.

> I think it's wrong to have kids and then lock them in daycare centers while you're working. That's why I'm really grateful that my wife can stay home. And although at times we were real tight for money, and I told her she might have to start looking for a job if we were going to make ends meet, I was grateful when things worked out and she didn't have to. Because this is really the place the kids need a full-time mother, to watch them.

This arrangement works, Gordon says, because "She's not the working type." This gendered division of labor between husband and wife is a reproduction of his parents' pattern. His father had been a skilled machinist, his mother, with a college degree, had stayed home and not worked outside the home until her children were in high school. Gordon explains the arrangement he has with his wife as the result of their "choice" and in accord with his wife's personality. Although Gordon described both the division of labor and the fact that he followed his father into working on machines as "natural," this couple is an instance of a social fact: in the overwhelming number of cases where one of a couple works full time, it is the husband. . . .

DISCIPLINE, CARING, AND PROVIDING: GENDERED PARENTING

In parenting and child rearing men once again place women between themselves and their children. Their interactions with their children are controlled, arranged, or supervised by their wives. Women have most of the responsibility for arranging and enforcing children's activities, with men exerting their influence through their wives. Some men do put a lot of energy into their children's activities, especially into their athletic activities, and even more express the desire to do so, especially to do more with their children than their fathers did with them. But studies of time use continue to find differences between working husbands and wives in the total number of hours worked when paid labor, childcare, and housework are combined.[4]

Not only is there a difference in the number of hours men and women spend in child rearing, but fathers and mothers approach parenting very differently. The men I talked to express the belief that mothers are the "default parent." They act on this belief and by their actions make it true. Being the default parent means being on terms of greater intimacy, being the one to whom a child turns first, and being the one with the responsibility for knowing what the child's needs and schedules are. The default parent, ultimately, is the one who has to be there, to whom parenting is in no sense optional (Walzer, 1998). For example, fathers may go to meetings at their children's schools or take their children to sports practice, but it is usually mothers who keep track of when the meetings and practices are, and who are, therefore, the default parents. Lareau (2000a, 2000b) reports that fathers are very vague and general in their accounts of their children's daily routine, in contrast to the detailed and specific responses of mothers. In general, my informants indicated that it was their wives who kept the mental and physical calendar, and I would simply add that the person who keeps track of scheduling has a good deal of control over what is scheduled.

Even in the area of discipline and punishment, where it would seem that the father's position as ultimate authority was secure, mothers are the gatekeepers or mediators. Consider the proverbial threat of mothers to their children: "Just you wait until your father gets home!" This expression was used as an example by a number of men to express that they were deeply involved in their children's lives. It was meant to indicate that they were the source of discipline even if they were not in a position of direct supervision most of the time. On closer examination, however, the expression indicates a very different relationship, for it is the mother who decides when and what the father is told, and thus when he can act. Rather than being in an immediate disciplinary relationship with his children, he is a resource to be mobilized by his wife in her dealings with the children, and thus in a relationship mediated by his wife.

20   The disciplinary dynamic in families can take several forms, but two are common. While they may seem very different, in both of them the wife and mother is ultimately responsible for discipline. In the first, the husband is an authority figure and disciplinarian who sees himself as supporting or backing up his wife. In the second, the husband is allowed to be fun because his wife is the disciplinarian. . . .

The gendered division of labor in parenting not only distributes work and fun differentially between fathers and mothers, it also distributes who gets taken for granted, and who gets the credit for what they do. Hochschild shows how couples negotiate not only a material division of labor, but also an economy of gratitude (1989): people do not just want to be appreciated, they want to be appreciated for the contributions *they* think are important. Psychologists Carolyn and Philip Cowan (1999) observed that, for men, paid employment "counts" as childcare—when men work they are seen as doing something for their children. In addition, wives see their husbands' attention to their children as contributions to the marriage relationship. Women's employment, on the other hand, is seen as detracting from their mothering, and their husbands do not see the care mothers give their children as couple time or as building the marriage. For the men I talked to, their fathers' employment was remembered and appreciated, while their mothers' employment was minimized or forgotten. In addition, their mothers' parenting was taken for granted, while their fathers' more occasional attention was treasured. . . .

These examples illustrate that the structural division of labor, in which men are seen as providers and women as homemakers, is connected to a gendered division of parenting. Mothers not only do more child care and domestic work, they also know more about what their children are doing and feeling, they talk to them more, and they control the flow of information between fathers and children. They also schedule their children's lives and the interactions they have with their fathers. As part of this gendered system, the relationship that mothers have with their children even influences the quality of the interactions men have with their children. Mothers may invoke their husbands as disciplinarians and enforcers, so that the fathers are stricter or sterner than they might otherwise be. Or mothers may maintain the structure of family life, giving men the space to be spontaneous and fun.

Within this gendered system of parenting, men and women act out and reinforce gender stereotypes. Men are expected to play more actively with children than women do, and as a general rule they do so. Mothers, so I was told, control male exuberance, calming people down and discouraging dangerous or over-exuberant play. It is mothers, I am told, who set limits on the activity of men and children. By doing so, they constrain themselves or, rather, are constrained by an entire system of expectations from being "fun" in quite the same way that men are. Men's playfulness and men's anger, their distance and their sense of inadequacy, are reproduced in the daily interactions of family life. A crucial element of these interactions is the mediating position of women, as wives and mothers. . . .

Endnotes

1. The interviews involved an interaction between my personal situation, the perceptions of the men I talked to, and my conclusions (Townsend, 1999). I refer to all the men by pseudonyms. The quotations are taken from the transcripts of tape-recorded interviews. I have not changed or added to what men said, but because I do not want to distract attention from the content of what they told me, I have not presented all the "ers," "ums," and "you knows" with which real speech is studded. In the quotations, a dash (–) indicates an incomplete sentence or change of topic, ellipsis (. . .) indicates that I have omitted words or sentences from a quotation.

2. I do not mean to imply that all men, or all women, think and feel alike. Certainly, fatherhood means something different to men in the contemporary United States than it does to men in India, in the Congo basin, or in New Guinea. Fatherhood also has different meanings to men in the United States now than it did to men in the nineteenth century or in the colonial period. Fatherhood also means different things to different groups of men in the contemporary United States. Fathers in the upper classes, for instance, have concerns about inheritance and family status that are very different from those of fathers in the middle class who are worried about their children's college education and the dangers of downward mobility, or from working class fathers whose positions in families are being transformed by declining real wages and an increasing family dependence on two incomes.

3. The "father breadwinner, mother homemaker" family has been both historically recent and short-lived as a dominant pattern. From 1850 until the Second World War, the decline of farm families was matched by an increase in the percentage of children in "father breadwinner, mother homemaker, nonfarm families" which reached almost 60 percent by 1930 and then fluctuated around that level until 1960, when it began a rapid drop to 27 percent by 1989. From 1950 onward, the declines in farm and father breadwinner families has been matched by a rise in the percentage of children in dual-earner and one-parent families, which was approaching 70 percent by 1990. Since 1970, less than half of the children in the United States have been in families of the father breadwinner, mother homemaker type (Hernandez, 1993: 103).

4. Hochschild (1989: 3–4 and 271–273) summarized studies that concluded that there was a difference of ten to twenty hours of total work between working husbands and wives. Other studies have found that men and women spend approximately equal amounts of time on the combination of housework and paid work (Ferree, 1991; Pleck, 1985; Schor, 1991), but certain domestic tasks continue to be overwhelmingly women's work (Coltrane, 1996; Shelton, 1992), and men's contribution to housework still tends to be thought of, by both husbands and wives, as helping (Coltrane, 1989; Walzer, 1998). When married couples have children, the division of domestic labor tends to become more traditionally gendered (Cowan and Cowan, 1999) and women spend less time in the paid labor force while men spend more (Shelton, 1992).

References

Arendell, Terry. 1995. *Men and Divorce.* Thousand Oaks, CA: Sage.
———. 1996. *Family Man: Fatherhood, Housework, and Gender Equity.* New York: Oxford University Press.
Coltrane, Scott. 1989. "Household Labor and the Routine Production of Gender." *Social Problems* 36: 473–490.
———. 1996. *Family Man: Fatherhood, Housework, and Gender Pay Equity.* New York: Oxford University Press.

Cowan, Carolyn, and Philip A. Cowan. 1999. *When Partners Become Parents: The Big Life Change for Couples.* Mahwah, NJ: Lawrence Erlbaum.

Ferree, Myra Marx. 1991. "The Gender Division of Labor in Two-Earner Marriages: Dimensions of Variability and Change." *Journal of Family Issues* 12:158–80.

Furstenberg, Frank F. and Andrew Cherlin. 1991. *Divided Families: What Happens to Children When Parents Part.* Cambridge: Harvard University Press.

Hernandez, Donald J. 1993. *America's Children: Resources from Family, Government, and the Economy.* New York: Russell Sage Foundation.

Hochschild, Arlie. 1989. *The Second Shift: Working Parents and the Revolution at Home.* New York: Viking.

Lareau, Annette. 2000a. "Vague Answers: Reflections on Studying Fathers' Contributions to Children's Care." Paper presented at "Work and Family, Expanding the Horizons," University of California, Berkeley.

———. 2000b. "Social Class and the Daily Lives of Children: A Study from the United States," Childhood 7 (2): 155–171.

Pleck, Joseph. 1985. *Working Wives/Working Husbands.* Beverly Hills, CA: Sage.

Schneider, Jane C. and Peter Schneider. 1996. *Festival of the Poor: Fertility Decline and the Ideology of Class in Sicily, 1860–1980.* Tucson: University of Arizona Press.

Schor, Juliet B. 1991. *The Overworked American: The Unexpected Decline of Leisure.* New York: Basic Books.

Shelton, B. A. 1992. *Women, Men, Time.* New York: Greenwood.

Townsend, Nicholas W. 1998. "Fathers and Sons: Men's Experience and the Reproduction of Fatherhood," pp. 363–76 in *Families in the U.S.: Kinship and Domestic Politics,* edited by Karen V. Hansen and Anita Ilta Garey. Philadelphia: Temple University Press.

———. 1999. "Fatherhoods and Fieldwork: Intersections Between Personal and Theoretical Positions." *Men and Masculinities* 2(1):89–99.

———. n.d. *The Package Deal: Marriage, Work, and Fatherhood in Men's Lives.*

Walzer, Susan. 1998. *Thinking About the Baby: Gender and Transitions into Parenthood.* Philadelphia: Temple University Press.

Questions for Thought and Writing

1. The author says that "parenting is deeply gendered." What does it seem to mean for something to "be gendered" or "deeply" gendered? How does this language highlight the socially constructed nature of gender (the understanding of gender as a phenomenon defined by the society in which one lives, rather than an inherent quality or characteristic)?

2. According to the author, men need the marital relationship to conceive of themselves as parents, whereas many women are comfortable with the idea of motherhood outside of mar-

riage. Do new birth control technologies and habits contribute to this distance between men and children? How?

3. What does it mean to be the "default parent"? How does the "economy of gratitude" that often operates in families reflect a cultural devaluing of mothers' work and contributions to childraising? How do the parental dynamics described by the author accord with your own family experience?

Sexual Dissent and the Family: The Sharon Kowalski Case
Nan D. Hunter

No connection between family, marriage, or procreation on the one hand and homosexual activity on the other has been demonstrated.
SUPREME COURT, BOWERS V. HARDWICK, 1986

Sharon Kowalski is the child of a divorce between her consanguineous family and her family of affinity, the petitioner Karen Thompson. . . . That Sharon's family of affinity has not enjoyed societal recognition in the past is unfortunate.
MINNESOTA STATE DISTRICT COURT, IN RE:
GUARDIANSHIP OF SHARON KOWALSKI, WARD, 1991

In the effort to end second-class citizenship for lesbian and gay Americans, no obstacle has proved tougher to surmount than the cluster of issues surrounding "the family." The concept of family functions as a giant cultural screen. Projected onto it, contests over race, gender, sexuality and a range of other "domestic" issues from crime to taxes constantly create and recreate a newly identified zone of social combat, the politics of the family. Activists of all persuasions eagerly seek to enter the discursive field, ever ready to debate and discuss: Who counts as a family? Which "family values" are the authentic ones? Is there a place in the family for queers? As battles are won and lost in this cultural war, progressives and conservatives agree on at least one thing—the family is highly politicized terrain.

For lesbians and gays, these debates have dramatic real-life consequences, probably more so than with any other legal issue. Relationship questions touch almost every person's life at some point, in a way that military issues, for example, do not. Further, the unequal treatment is blatant, *de jure* and universal, as compared with the employment arena, where discrimination may be more subtle and variable. No state allows a lesbian or gay couple to marry. No state recognizes (although a number of counties and cities do) domestic partnership systems under which unmarried couples (gay or straight) can become eligible for certain benefits usually available only to spouses. The fundamental inequity is that, barring mental incompetence or consanguinity, virtually any straight couple has the option to marry and thus establish a next-of-kin relationship that the state will enforce. No lesbian or gay couple can. Under the law, two women or two men are forever strangers, regardless of their relationship.

One result is that every lesbian or gay man's nightmare is to be cut off from one's primary other, physically incapacitated, stranded, unable to make contact, without legal recourse. It is a nightmare that could not happen to a married couple. But it did happen to two Minnesota women, Sharon Kowalski and Karen Thompson, in a remarkable case that threaded its way through the courts for seven years.

Sharon Kowalski, notwithstanding the Minnesota State District Court's characterization of her as a "child of divorce," is an adult with both a committed life partner and parents who bitterly refuse to acknowledge either her lesbianism or her lover. Kowalski is a former physical education teacher and amateur athlete, whose Minnesota women's high school shot-put record still stands. In 1983, she was living with her lover, Thompson, in the home they had jointly purchased in St. Cloud. Both women were deeply closeted; they exchanged rings with each other but told virtually no one of their relationship. That November, Kowalski suffered devastating injuries in a car accident, which left her unable to speak or walk, with arms deformed and with major brain damage, including seriously impaired short-term memory.

After the accident, both Thompson and Kowalski's father petitioned to be appointed Sharon's guardian; initially, an agreement was entered that the father would become guardian on the condition that Thompson retain equal rights to visit and consult with doctors. By the summer of 1985, after growing hostilities, the father refused to continue the arrangement, and persuaded a local court that Thompson's visits caused Kowalski to feel depressed. One doctor hired by the father wrote a letter stating that

Kowalski was in danger of sexual abuse. Within twenty-four hours after being named sole guardian, the father cut off all contact between Thompson and Kowalski, including mail. By this time, Kowalski had been moved to a nursing home near the small town where she grew up in the Iron Range, a rural mining area in northern Minnesota.

Surely one reason the Kowalski case is so compelling is that, for millions of parents, learning that one's son is gay or daughter is lesbian would be *their* worst nightmare. That is all the more true in small-town America, among people who are religiously observant and whose expectations for a daughter are primarily marriage and motherhood. "The good Lord put us here for reproduction, not that kind of way," Donald Kowalski told the *Los Angeles Times* in 1988. "It's just not a normal life style. The Bible will tell you that." Karen Thompson, he told other reporters, was "an animal" and was lying about his daughter's life. "I've never seen anything that would make me believe" that his daughter is lesbian, he said to the *New York Times* in 1989. How much less painful it must be to explain a lesbian daughter's life as seduction, rather than to experience it as betrayal.

In 1988, Thompson's stubborn struggle to "bring Sharon home" entered a new stage. A different judge, sitting in Duluth, ordered Kowalski moved to a new facility for medical evaluation. Soon thereafter, based on staff recommendations from the second nursing facility, the court ordered that Thompson be allowed to visit. The two women saw each other again in the spring of 1989, after three and a half years of forced separation. Kowalski, who can communicate by typing on a special keyboard, said that she wanted to live in "St. Cloud with Karen."

In May 1990, citing a heart condition for which he had been hospitalized, Donald Kowalski resigned as his daughter's guardian. This resignation set the stage for Thompson to file a renewed petition for appointment as guardian, which she did. But in an April 1991 ruling, Minnesota State District Court Judge Robert Campbell selected as guardian Karen Tomberlin—a friend of both Kowalski and her parents, who supported Tomberlin's request. On the surface, the court sought balance. The judge characterized the Kowalski parents and Karen Thompson as the "two wings" of Sharon Kowalski's family. He repeatedly asserted that both must have ample access to visitation with Kowalski. He described Tomberlin as a neutral third party who would not exclude either side. But the biggest single reason behind the decision, the one that he characterized as "instrumental," seemed to be the judge's anger at Thompson for ever telling Kowalski's parents (in a private letter), and then the world at large, that she and Kowalski were lovers.

The court condemned Thompson's revelation of her own relationship as the "outing" of Sharon Kowalski. Thompson did write the letter to Kowalski's parents without telling Kowalski (who was at the time just emerging from a three-month coma after the accident) and did build on her own an active political organization around the case, composed chiefly of disability and lesbian and gay rights groups. Of course, for most of that period, she could not have consulted Kowalski because the two were cut off from each other.

In truth, though, the judge's concern seemed to be more for the outing of Kowalski's parents. He describes the Kowalskis as "outraged and hurt by the public invasion of Sharon's privacy and their privacy," and he blames this outing for the bitterness between Thompson and the parents. Had Thompson simply kept this to herself, the court implies, none of these nasty facts would ever have had to be discussed. The cost, of course, would have been the forfeiture of Thompson's relationship with her lover.

An openly stated preference for ignorance over knowledge is remarkable in a judicial opinion. One imagines the judge silently cursing Thompson for her arrogance in claiming the role of spouse, and for her insistence on shattering the polite fiction of two gym teachers living and buying a house together as just good friends. Women, especially, aren't supposed to be so stubborn or uppity. One can sense the court's empathetic response of shared embarrassment with the parents, of the desire not to be told and thus not to be forced to speak on this subject.

The final chapter in the Kowalski case vindicated Karen Thompson's long struggle. The Minnesota Court of Appeals granted Thompson's guardianship petition in December, 1991, reversing the trial judge on every point.

The conflict in the Kowalski case illustrates one of the prime contradictions underlying all the cases seeking legal protection for lesbian and gay couples. This culture is deeply invested with a notion of the ideal family as not only a zone of privacy and a structure of authority (preferably male in the conservative view) but also as a barrier against sexuality unlicensed by the state.

Even many leftists and progressives, who actively contest male authority and at least some of the assumptions behind privacy are queasy about constructing a family politics with queerness on the inside rather than the outside.

When such sexuality is culturally recognized *within* family bounds, "the family" ceases to function as an enforcer of sexual norms. That is why the moms and dads in groups like P-FLAG, an organization primarily of parents supportive of their lesbian and gay children, make such emotionally powerful spokespersons for the cause of civil rights. Parents who welcome sexual dissenters within the family undermine the notion that such dissent is intrinsically antithetical to deep human connection.

15   The theme of cultural anxiety about forms of sexuality not bounded and controlled by the family runs through a series of recent judicial decisions. In each case, the threat to norms did not come from an assault on the prerogatives of family by libertarian outsiders, a prospect often cited by the right wing to trigger social anxieties. Instead, each court faced the dilemma of how to repress, at least in the law, the anomaly of unsanctioned sexuality within the family.

In a stunning decision in 1989, the Supreme Court ruled in *Michael H. v. Gerald D.* that a biological father had no constitutionally protected right to a relationship with his daughter, despite both paternity (which was not disputed) and a psychological bond that the two had formed. Instead, the Court upheld the rule that because the child's mother—who had had an affair with the child's biological father—was married to another man, the girl would be presumed to be the husband's child. It was more important, the Court declared, to protect the "unitary family," that is, the marriage, than to subject anyone to "embarrassment" by letting the child and her father continue to see each other. The Court ruled that a state could properly force the termination of that bond rather than "disrupt an otherwise harmonious and apparently exclusive marital relationship." We are not bound, the Court said, to protect what it repeatedly described as "adulterous fathers."

In *Hodgson v. Minnesota,* the Supreme Court upheld a Minnesota requirement that a pregnant teenager had to notify both of her parents—even if they were divorced or if there was a threat of violence from her family—prior to obtaining an abortion, so long as she had the alternative option to petition a court. The decision was read primarily as an abortion decision and a ruling on the extent of privacy protection that will be accorded a minor who decides to have an abortion. But the case was also, at its core, about sex in the family and specifically about whether parents could rely on the state for assistance in learning whether a daughter is sexually active.

In two very similar cases in 1991, appellate courts in New York and California ruled that a lesbian partner who had coparented a child with the biological mother for some years had no standing to seek visitation after the couple split up. Both courts acknowledged that the best interests of the child would be served by allowing a parental relationship to continue, but both also ruled that the law would not recognize what the New York court called "a biological stranger." Such a person could be a parent only if there had been a marriage or an adoption.

Indeed, perhaps the most important point in either decision was the footnote in the California ruling that invited lesbian and gay couples to adopt children jointly: "We see nothing in these [statutory] provisions that would preclude a child from being jointly adopted by someone of the same sex as the natural parent." This opens the door for many more such adoptions, at least in California, which is one of six states where lesbian- or gay-couple adoption has occurred, although rarely. The New York court made no such overture.

The effort to legalize gay marriage will almost certainly   20
emerge as a major issue in the next decade. Lawsuits seeking a right to marry have been filed in the District of Columbia and Hawaii, and activists in other states are contemplating litigation. In 1989, the Conference of Delegates of the State Bar of California endorsed an amendment of that state's law to permit lesbian and gay couples to marry.

The law's changes to protect sexual dissent within the family will occur at different speeds in different places, which might not be so bad. Family law has always been a province primarily of state rather than federal regulation, and often has varied from state to state; grounds for divorce, for example, used to differ dramatically depending on geography. What seems likely to occur in the next wave of family cases is the same kind of variability in the legal definition of the family itself. Those very discrepancies may help to denaturalize concepts like "marriage" and "parent," and to expose the utter contingency of the sexual conventions that, in part, construct the family.

Questions for Thought and Writing

1. At the beginning of the essay, the author asks the question: "Who counts as a family?" How do her examples offer an answer? How do examples from popular culture answer this question?
2. Does the Kowalski case provide convincing evidence that gay and lesbian relationships/marriages should be legalized? If not, why?
3. The traditional family has consistently functioned as an enforcer of patriarchal sexual norms. How would the legalization of gay/lesbian marriages affect this function? Are we better off having our sexual norms enforced by law or by family?
4. Sharon Kowalski's parents refused to believe that their daughter would willingly have been involved in a lesbian relationship. What does this say about how our culture treats nontraditional sexualities? Do you believe the attitude demonstrated by the Kowalski family is still a prevalent one? If not, why?

Blue Horses Rush In
Luci Tapahonso (Navajo)

For Chamisa Bah Edmo, Shisói 'aláájí naaghígíí

Before the birth, she moved and pushed inside her mother.
Her heart pounded quickly and we recognized
the sound of horses running:
      the thundering of hooves on the desert floor.

Her mother clenches her fists and gasps.   5
She moans ageless pain and pushes: This is it!

Chamisa slips out, glistening wet, and takes her first breath.
      The wind outside swirls small leaves
      and branches in the dark.
Her father's eyes are wet with gratitude.   10
He prays and watches both mother and baby—stunned.

This baby arrived amid a herd of horses,
    horses of different colors.

White horses ride in on the breath of the wind.
White horses from the east   15
where plants of golden chamisa shimmer in the moonlight.

She arrived amid a herd of horses.

Blue horses enter from the south
bringing the scent of prairie grasses
from the small hills outside.   20

She arrived amid a herd of horses.

Yellow horses rush in, snorting from the desert in the south.
It is possible to see across the entire valley to Niist'áá from Tó.
Bah, from here your grandmothers went to war long ago.

She arrived amid a herd of horses.   25

Black horses came from the north.
They are the lush summers of Montana and still white
    winters of Idaho.

Chamisa, Chamisa Bah. It is all this that you are.
You will grow: laughing, crying,
and we will celebrate each change you live.   30

You will grow strong like the horses of your past.
You will grow strong like the horses of your birth.

Questions for Thought and Writing

1. How does the birth described in the poem's first stanza contrast with the "technocratic" model of childbirth? In what
   ways are women and their bodies linked with strength and
   competency—rather than with weakness and incompetence—in this poem?
2. In a patriarchal society, one of the binaries by which men and
   women are categorized is culture/nature, with culture as the
   more positive term and nature as the negative term. In this
   poem, how is nature understood? What qualities are attributed to women when nature is linked with femininity?

Exploring Connections

1. In the hooks essay, the narrator claims that "for the mother it is not simple. She is always torn." How does this statement relate to the idea from "Fatherhood and the Mediating Role of Women" that mothers traditionally become their children's "default" parents, while parenting can often remain "optional" for men? Identify examples from popular culture in which the traditional roles for parents are reversed. What are the effects?

2. In "Sexual Dissent and the Family: The Sharon Kowalski Case," the author offers the Kowalski case as a way to highlight the potential conflicts between traditional and legal ways of defining who "counts" as a family. How does the Kowalski case reflect the idea of "nostalgia" described in "Family" from *Morality USA?* Identify and discuss other examples from contemporary culture, such as the debate over gay adoptions, that call into question traditional ideas of family.

3. In "The Transformation of Family Life," male resistance to female demands for increased support centered around the issue of "legitimacy" and what women have the right to expect. How does the male-dominated medical system discussed in "Gender and Ritual: Giving Birth the American Way" undercut women's legitimacy? Which other readings from this chapter address the issue of women's legitimacy? In which areas do women seem to be achieving greater legitimacy? In which areas does the patriarchy still prevail?

CHAPTER 2

Gender and Popular Culture

OVERVIEW

The Overview articles "Image-Based Culture: Advertising and Popular Culture" and "How Does a Supermodel Do Feminism? An Interview with Veronica Webb" provide readers with two very different perspectives on the ways advertising culture affects women. While Sut Jhally charges advertisers with the responsiblity for creating unrealistic needs and expectations in U.S. consumers (particularly women), Veronica Webb argues that the "beauty culture" and modeling industry operate in response to desires that already exist. In tandem, the articles will provide readers with an opportunity to reflect on the roots of their own consumerist impulses and to re-examine pervasive associations in popular culture between women and sexuality.

Image-Based Culture: Advertising and Popular Culture
Sut Jhally

Because we live inside the consumer culture, and most of us have done so for most of our lives, it is sometimes difficult to locate the origins of our most cherished values and assumptions. They simply appear to be part of our natural world. It is a useful exercise, therefore, to examine how our culture has come to be defined and shaped in specific ways—to excavate the origins of our most celebrated rituals. For example, everyone in this culture knows a "diamond is for-ever." It is a meaning that is almost as "natural" as the link between roses and romantic love. However, diamonds (just like roses) did not always have this meaning. Before 1938 their value derived primarily from their worth as scarce stones (with the DeBeers cartel carefully controlling the market supply). In 1938 the New York advertising agency of N. W. Ayers was hired to change public attitudes toward diamonds—to transform them from a financial investment into a *symbol* of committed and everlasting love. In 1947 an Ayers advertis-ing copywriter came up with the slogan "a diamond is forever" and the rest, as they say, is history. As an N. W. Ayers memorandum put it in 1959: "Since 1939 an entirely new generation of young people has grown to marriageable age. To the new generation, a diamond ring is considered a necessity for engagement to virtually everyone."[1]

This is a fairly dramatic example of how the institutional structure of the consumer society orients the culture (and its atti-tudes, values, and rituals) more and more toward the world of commodities. The marketplace (and its major ideological tool, advertising) is the major structuring institution of contemporary consumer society. . . .

In the contemporary world, messages about goods are all per-vasive—advertising has increasingly filled up the spaces of our daily existence. Our media are dominated by advertising images, public space has been taken over by "information" about prod-ucts, and most of our sporting and cultural events are accompa-nied by the name of a corporate sponsor. There is even an attempt to get television commercials into the nations' high schools under the pretense of "free" news programming. As we head toward the twenty-first century, advertising is ubiquitous—it is the air that we breathe as we live our daily lives.

ADVERTISING AND THE GOOD LIFE: IMAGE AND "REALITY"

I have referred to advertising as being part of "a discourse through and about objects" because it does not merely tell us about things but of how things are connected to important domains of our lives. Fundamentally, advertising talks to us as individuals and ad-dresses us about how we can become *happy*. The answers it pro-vides are all oriented to the marketplace, through the purchase of goods or services. To understand the system of images that consti-tutes advertising we need to inquire into the definition of happi-ness and satisfaction in contemporary social life.

Quality of life surveys that ask people what they are seeking   5
in life—what it is that makes them happy—report quite consistent results. The conditions that people are searching for—what
they perceive will make them happy—are things such as having
personal autonomy and control of one's life, self-esteem, a happy
family life, loving relations, a relaxed, tension-free leisure time,
and good friendships. The unifying theme of this list is that these
things are not fundamentally connected to goods. It is primarily
"social" life and not "material" life that seems to be the locus of
perceived happiness. Commodities are only *weakly related* to
these sources of satisfaction.[2]

A market society, however, is guided by the principle that satisfaction should be achieved via the marketplace, and through its
institutions and structures it orients behavior in that direction.
The data from the quality of life studies are not lost on advertisers. If goods themselves are not the locus of perceived happiness,
then they need to be connected in some way with those things
that are. Thus advertising promotes images of what the audience
conceives of as "the good life": Beer can be connected with anything from eroticism to male fraternity to the purity of the old
West; food can be tied up with family relations or health; investment advice offers early retirements in tropical settings. The marketplace cannot directly offer the real thing, but it can offer vi-
sions of it connected with the purchase of products.

Advertising thus does not work by creating values and attitudes out of nothing but by drawing upon and rechanneling concerns that the target audience (and the culture) already shares. As
one advertising executive put it: "Advertising doesn't always mirror how people are acting but how they're *dreaming*. In a sense
what we're doing is wrapping up your emotions and selling them
back to you." Advertising absorbs and fuses a variety of symbolic
practices and discourses, it appropriates and distills from an un-
bounded range of cultural references. In so doing, goods are knit-
ted into the fabric of social life and cultural significance. As such,
advertising is not simple manipulation, but what ad-maker Tony
Schwartz calls "partipulation," with the audience participating in
its own manipulation.

What are the consequences of such a system of images and
goods? Given that the "real" sources of satisfaction cannot be provided by the purchase of commodities (merely the "image" of that
source), it should not be surprising that happiness and content-
ment appear illusory in contemporary society. Recent social

thinkers describe the contemporary scene as a "joyless economy,"[3] or as reflecting the "paradox of affluence."[4] It is not simply a matter of being "tricked" by the false blandishments of advertising. The problem is with the institutional structure of a market society that propels definition of satisfaction *through* the commodity / image system. The modern context, then, provides a curious satisfaction experience—one that William Leiss describes as "an ensemble of satisfactions and dissatisfactions" in which the consumption of commodities mediated by the image-system of advertising lead to consumer uncertainty and confusion.[5] The image-system of the marketplace reflects our desire and dreams, yet we have only the pleasure of the images to sustain us in our actual experience with goods.

The commodity image-system thus provides a particular vision of the world—a particular mode of self-validation that is integrally connected with what one *has* rather than what one *is*—a distinction often referred to as one between "having" and "being," with the latter now being defined through the former. As such, it constitutes a way of life that is defined and structured in quite specific political ways. Some commentators have even described advertising as part of a new *religious* system in which people construct their identities through the commodity form, and in which commodities are part of a supernatural magical world where anything is possible with the purchase of a product. The commodity as displayed in advertising plays a mixture of psychological, social, and physical roles in its relations with people. The object world interacts with the human world at the most basic and fundamental of levels, performing seemingly magical feats of enchantment and transformation, bringing instant happiness and gratification, capturing the forces of nature, and acting as a passport to hitherto untraveled domains and group relationships.[6]

10   In short, the advertising image-system constantly propels us toward things as means to satisfaction. In the sense that every ad says it is better to buy than not to buy, we can best regard advertising as a propaganda system for commodities. In the image-system as a whole, happiness lies at the end of a purchase. Moreover, this is not a minor propaganda system—it is all pervasive. It should not surprise us then to discover that the problem that it poses—how to get more things for everyone (as that is the root to happiness)—guides our political debates. The goal of *economic growth* (on which the commodity vision is based) is an unquestioned and sacred proposition of the political culture. As the envi-

ronmental costs of the strategy of unbridled economic growth become more obvious, it is clear we must, as a society, engage in debate concerning the nature of future economic growth. However, as long as the commodity image-system maintains its ubiquitous presence and influence, the possibilities of opening such a debate are remote. At the very moment we most desperately need to pose new questions within the political culture, the commodity image-system propels us with even greater certainty and persuasion along a path that, unless checked, is destined to end in disaster.

Moreover, this problem will be exponentially compounded in the twenty-first century, as more and more nations (both Third World and "presently existing socialist") reach for the magic of the marketplace to provide the panacea for happiness. One of the most revealing images following the collapse of the Berlin Wall was the sight of thousands of East German citizens streaming into West Berlin on a Sunday (when the shops were closed) to simply stare in rapture and envy at the commodities in the windows. Transnational corporations are licking their lips at the new markets that Eastern Europe and China will provide for their products. Accompanying the products (indeed preceding them, preparing the way) will be the sophisticated messages of global advertising emerging from Madison Avenue. From a global perspective, again at the very moment that there needs to be informed debate about the direction and scope of industrial production, the commodity propaganda system is colonizing new areas and new media, and channeling debate into narrower confines.

THE SPREAD OF IMAGE-BASED INFLUENCE

While the commodity image-system is primarily about satisfaction, its influence and effect are not limited to that alone. I want to briefly consider four other areas in the contemporary world where the commodity system has its greatest impact. The first is in the area of gender identity. Many commercial messages use images and representations of men and women as central components of their strategy to both get attention and persuade. Of course, they do not use any gender images but images drawn from a narrow and quite concentrated pool. As Erving Goffman has shown, ads draw heavily upon the domain of gender display—not the way that men and women actually behave but the ways in which we think men and women behave.[7] It is because these conventions of gender display are so easily recognized by the audience that they figure so prominently in the image-system. Also, images having to do with gender strike at the core of individual identity; our understanding of ourselves as either male or female (socially defined within this society at this time) is central to our understanding of who we are. What better place to choose than an area of social life that can be communicated at a glance and that reaches into the core of individual identity.

However, we should not confuse these portrayals as true reflections of gender. In advertising, gender (especially for women) is defined almost exclusively along the lines of sexuality. The image-system thus distorts our perceptions and offers little that balances out the stress on sexuality. Advertisers, working within a "cluttered" environment in which there are more and more messages must have a way to break through the attendant noise. Sexuality provides a resource that can be used to get attention and communicate instantly. Within this sexuality is also a powerful component of gender that again lends itself even easier to imagistic representation.

If only one or two advertisers used this strategy, then the image-system would not have the present distorted features. The problem is that the vast majority do so. The iconography of the culture, perhaps more than any previous society, seems to be obsessed with sexuality. The end result is that the commodity is part of an increasingly eroticized world—that we live in a culture that is more and more defined erotically through commodities.

15 Second, the image-system has spread its influence to the realm of electoral politics. Much has been written (mostly negatively) about the role that television advertising now plays within national electoral politics. The presidency seems most susceptible to "image-politics," as it is the office most reliant on television advertising. The social commentary on politics from this perspective has mostly concerned the manner in which the focus has shifted from discussion of real "issues" to a focus on symbolism and emotionally based imagery.

These debates are too important and complex to be discussed in any depth here, but there is a fundamental point to be made. The evidence suggests that George Bush won the 1988 presidential race because he ran a better ad and public relations campaign. Given the incredible swings in the polls over a relatively short period of time, when media information was the only thing that voters had to go on, it seems to be a conclusion with some substance.

The implications of such a conclusion, though, have not really been explored the way they should. The fact that large numbers of people are changing their minds on who to vote for after seeing a thirty-second television commercial says a great deal about the nature of the political culture. It means that politics (for a significant portion of the electorate) is largely conducted on a symbolic realm, and that a notion of politics that is based upon people having a coherent and deep vision of their relationship to the social world is no longer relevant. Politics is not about issues; it is about "feeling good" or "feeling bad" about a candidate—and all it takes to change this is a thirty-second commercial.

The grammar of these images, then, clearly is different to the grammar of verbal or written language. The intrusion of the image-system into the world of electoral politics has meant that the majority of committed voters are held ransom by those who are uncommitted (the undecided or swing votes), and that these groups are influenced differently—and have a different relationship to politics—than those who have an old style view of politics. These huge swings of opinion, based upon information provided by the image-system, suggest that the political culture is incredibly superficial and does not correspond to what we normally think of as "politics."

Third, the commodity image-system is now implicated, due to changes in the way that toys are marketed, in the very structure and experience of children's play. With both children's television programming and commercials oriented around the sale of toys, writers such as Stephen Kline argue that the context within which kids play is now structured around marketing considerations. In consequence, "Children's imaginative play has become the target of marketing strategy, allowing marketers to define the limits of children's imaginations. . . . Play in fact has become highly ritualized—less an exploration and solidification of personal experiences and developing conceptual schema than a rearticulation of the fantasy world provided by market designers. Imaginative play has shifted one degree closer to mere imitation and assimilation." Further, the segmentation of the child audience in terms of both age and gender has led to a situation where parents find it difficult to play with their children because they do not share the marketing fantasy world that toy advertisers have created and where there is a growing divide between boys and girls at play. "Since the marketing targets and features different emotional and narrative elements (action/conflict vs. emotional attachment and maintenance) boys and girls also experience difficulty in playing together with these toys."[8]

Fourth, the visual image-system has colonized areas of life that were previously largely defined (although not solely) by auditory perception and experience. The 1980s has seen a change in the way that popular music commodities (records, tapes, compact discs) are marketed, with a music video becoming an indispensable component of an overall strategy. These videos are produced as commercials for musical commodities by the advertising industry, using techniques learned from the marketing of products. Viewing these videos, there often seems to be little link between the song and the visuals. In the sense that they are commercials for records, there of course does not have to be. Video makers are in the same position as ad makers in terms of trying to get attention for their message and making it visually pleasurable. It is little wonder then that representations involving sexuality figure so prominently (as in the case of regular product advertising). The visuals are chosen for their ability to sell.

20   Many people report that listening to a song after watching the video strongly effects the interpretation they give to it—the visual images are replayed in the imagination. In that sense, the surrounding commodity image-system works to fix—or at least to limit—the scope of imaginative interpretation. The realm of listening becomes subordinated to the realm of seeing, to the influence of commercial images. There is also evidence suggesting that the composition of popular music is effected by the new video context. People write songs or lines with the vital marketing tool in mind. . . .

POLITICAL IMPLICATIONS: EDUCATION IN AN IMAGE-SATURATED SOCIETY

There really is not much to dispute in the analysis I have offered of the history, character, and consequences the commodity image-system may have. The real question concerning these issue has to do with the political implications that one may draw from this kind of approach. Put simply: Is there a problem with this situation, and if so what precisely is it? Further, what solutions may be offered? . . .

I would focus a cultural politics on two related strategies. First, the struggle to reconstruct the existence and meaning of the world of substance has to take place on the terrain of the image-system. In some progressive cultural politics the very techniques associated with the image-system are part of the problem—that is, images themselves are seen as the problem. A struggle over definitions of reality (what else is cultural politics?) needs to use other mediums of communication. I believe such a strategy surrenders the very terrain on which the most effective battles can be fought—the language of the contemporary world.[9]

The second aspect of the strategy centers less on revealing matters of substance (the underlying reality) than on opening up further the analysis of the contemporary image-system, in particular, *democratizing* the image-system. At present the "discourse through and about objects" is profoundly authoritarian—it reflects only a few narrow (mostly corporate) interests. The institutions of the world of substance must be engaged to open up the public discourse to new and varied (and dissenting) voices.

The other set of concerns are connected to issues of *literacy* in an image-saturated society. As Raymond Williams has pointed out, in the early development of capitalism workers were taught to read but not to write. The skills of reading were all that were required to follow orders and to understand the Bible. Contemporary society is in a similar position. While we can read the images quite adequately (for the purposes of their creators) we do not know how to *produce* them. Such skills, or knowledge of the process, must be a prerequisite for functional literacy in the contemporary world. Basic course work in photography and video production should be required in all high schools. Moreover, while messages can be read adequately, most people do not understand *how* the language of images works. Just as knowledge of grammar is considered vital in learning foreign languages, so the grammar of images (how they work) needs to be integrated into the high school curriculum. "Visual literacy" courses should be taken right after the production courses.

Finally, information about the institutional context of the production and consumption of the image-system should be a prerequisite for literacy in the modern world. Advertisements, for example, are the only message forms that are not accompanied by credits in terms of who has produced them. In this sense, movies and television programs have a different status within the image-system in that at least *some* of their process of production is revealed. At minimum, we know that they are made by lots of people!

Ads, on the other hand, simply appear and disappear without any credits. A third set of courses could focus on the political economy of the media and advertising industries. Stripping away the veil of anonymity and mystery would by itself be of great value in demystifying the images that parade before our lives and through which we conceptualize the world and our role within it. As Noam Chomsky puts it (talking about the media in general) in his book *Necessary Illusions:* "Citizens of the democratic societies should undertake a course of intellectual self-defense to protect themselves from manipulation and control, and to lay the basis for meaningful democracy."[10] Such a course of action will not be easy, for the institutional structure of the image-system will work against it. However, the invigoration of democracy depends upon the struggle being engaged.

Endnotes

1. See Epstein (1982).
2. See Hirsch (1976).
3. Scitovsky (1976).
4. Hirsch (1976).
5. Leiss (1976).
6. See Jhally (1987) and Kavanaugh (1981).
7. Goffman (1979).
8. Kline (1989, pp. 299, 315).
9. For more on progressive cultural politics, see Angus and Jhally (1989, Introduction).
10. Chomsky (1989).

References

Angus, I., & Jhally, S. (1989). *Cultural politics in contemporary America.* New York: Routledge.

Chomsky, N. (1989). *Necessary illusions: Thought control in democratic societies.* Boston: South End Press.

Epstein, E. (1982). *The rise and fall of diamonds.* New York: Simon & Schuster.

Goffman, E. (1979). *Gender advertisements.* New York: Harper & Row.

Hirsch, F. (1976). *Social limits to growth.* Cambridge, MA: Harvard University Press.

Jhally, S. (1987). *The codes of advertising.* New York: St. Martin's.

Kavanaugh, J. (1981). *Following Christ in a consumer society.* New York: Orbis.

Kline, S. (1989). Limits to the imagination: Marketing and children's culture. In I. Angus & S. Jhally (Eds.), *Cultural politics in contemporary America.* New York: Routledge.

Leiss, W. (1976). *The limits to satisfaction.* Toronto: Toronto University Press.

Scitovsky, T. (1976). *The joyless economy.* New York: Oxford University Press.

Questions for Thought and Writing

1. Jhally describes the dilemma faced by the advertising industry by saying that "If goods themselves are not the locus of perceived happiness, then they need to be connected in some way to those things that are." Using specific advertisements, identify the concepts, such as freedom, romance, and so on, that are most frequently connected to products marketed to women. How do they differ from those connected to products marketed to men? How do these concepts reinforce or challenge traditional notions of femininity and masculinity?

2. If ads typically "draw heavily upon the domain of gender display—not the way that men and women actually behave but the ways in which we think men and women behave," what do you think are the greatest differences between the "display" and the reality? What variations of masculinity and femininity are not featured in the "display" version? Why not?

3. Jhally argues that "our understanding of ourselves as either male or female (socially defined within this society at this time) is central to our understanding of who we are." In an attempt to examine the truth of this statement, consider and write about how you think your life would change if your gender changed.

4. According to Jhally, advertisers use sexual images to sell almost everything because such images are instantly recognizable in a crowded marketplace. The effect of this strategy is that "gender (especially for women) is defined almost exclusively along the lines of sexuality." Imagine that you work in an advertising agency and have been charged with designing a series of ads that define gender without using sexuality to get attention. What could you do instead?

How Does a Supermodel Do Feminism?
An Interview with Veronica Webb

Rebecca Walker

REBECCA WALKER: Do you consider yourself a feminist?

VERONICA WEBB: Yes, I consider myself a feminist, but not in the fist-in-the-air kind of way. It's kind of hard to define, because so much is taken for granted by our generation. We just assume women are supposed to be paid equally and all the rest. I mean, I march for reproductive freedom, and I raise money for breast cancer research, and I am definitely concerned about women getting what they need in order to be in control of their lives.

You know, I was sitting on the couch crossed legged on a cold night a few weeks ago, and it was just one of those nights where nothing was going on, and I was flipping through the channels on TV and Vanessa Redgrave was on PBS doing this dramatic reading of Virginia Woolf's *A Room of One's Own*. There she was, in this dark oak corridor of some university somewhere and she starts reading Virginia's essay about going to this university and being shut out of the library and shut out of knowledge because she is a woman. You know, the beetles chase her off the grass, and she tries to go into the library and they tell her she can't because she is not a male student. Woolf is really talking about women's lack of access and where access comes from: knowledge and money. And not just money, but money that comes with no strings attached. And I found myself really moved, because what she was talking about is something I so relate to, a need for access and privacy, a need for sovereignty. And I think all women need that, sovereignty. And by sovereignty I mean having the freedom to be self-governed. And by self-governed I mean that there's nobody up in your house standing over you telling you what to do because they control the purse strings.

RW: Do you feel there's any conflict between being a "feminist" and working in a profession that many feminists say objectifies women?

VW: Well, first let me say that I think that all people are judged by their looks, especially women, and that we cannot escape it. I'm not saying it's right or wrong, it's just what it is: a part of human nature, the same way we have certain associations, both positive and negative, about people because of what race they are. I personally don't feel objectified, because I control the way my looks are used, not the other way around. There is a lot more self-expression involved than people realize. I mean, people always ask models, do they make you cut your hair? Do they make you pose nude? And it's like, no, models *choose* what they want to do. Everyone at the top of their profession has looked at themselves and said this is who I am naturally, or this is the persona that I want to create, this is how I want to use my looks to create an enterprise. That's why Cindy Crawford chose to do *Playboy,* because that's what she is naturally, she is very very very very sexy, and that was her springboard to a professional empire.

And that's on a grand scale, but on an everyday scale, the way I look gives me power in different situations, and this is nothing new. There's something about being pulled together and in control that makes people want to emulate you, which makes people begin to have certain associations about how you run your business and how you run your life, it's a very persuasive thing. When you are in a meeting you can be well spoken, but when you are well spoken *and* pulled together you have a whole other kind of power.

RW: What do you think about the whole debate about the standard of beauty—that models create a standard of beauty that most women can't attain and which ends up making women dissatisfied with themselves?

VW: Well, I did a lecture at Vanderbilt University and there was a girl there who was very upset because she said I set an impossible standard and was participating in an industry that makes impossible standards. And that made me think of this Kurt Vonnegut story about a society where everyone has to be equal. So there's a musician who has to wear lead earmuffs all the time, and there is an artist who has to wear these gloves that make him clumsy, so that anything special about people is muted so that everyone can be equal.

Anyway, at one point she just blew up at me and she screamed, "You're just a piece of meat, you have absolutely no power!"

RW: And what did you say?

VW: I said, "Well, first of all, for you to get that upset at me already tells me that I have emotional power over you." And then I began to tell her about different work I'd done to raise public awareness about different issues, not to pat myself on the back, but just to say this is an influential and powerful business and it could be used to our advantage. She walked out, but a lot of women started to raise their hands, and they were saying, "Well, my boyfriend loves you and he has your picture on the wall and I feel that I could never ever look like you." And I said, "No one can ever look like anybody else, sorry I can't look like you either, but if it makes you feel really bad, if it makes you feel inferior, either ask him to take it down, or put your own icon up and tell him to live up to it."

Listen, no woman can be an air-brushed photograph. Just like most men cannot be a Arnold Schwarzenegger, they just can't yet men are not held back by the fact they don't have movie-star looks, and women are. There is obviously something else going on there that I am not so sure you can blame on modeling.

I mean, I'm sure the fashion industry is culpable on some level for causing women to have feelings of desperation or inadequacy, but you know, I have friends who have a daughter who is physically deformed. She has a very big head and is very odd looking. She is not unconscious and can process almost everything that goes on around her. Her mother and father and brothers gave her almost perfect love and worked very hard on accepting her, and she actually has more self-confidence than I do. She has really made me see that how much self-confidence and self-esteem you have comes from how you were raised and how much attention and value people placed on you as a child. It has to do with other things you are exposed to, but a lot of it has to do with how much you were loved for being you.

RW: What was your mother like?

VW: Well, my mother was born in 1922 and in her time you had to do what you were told to do, and being black there were two things you could do professionally: you could be a school-teacher or a nurse. So my mother's parents made sure she became a nurse even though she wanted to go to an ivy league school and become a concert pianist.

My mother worked really really really really hard to make sure I was educated in a way that would teach me to think and which would allow me to compete on a lot of different levels and to have entrée into a lot of different places. She would tell me, I don't care what you do with you life, I can't tell you what to do or how to spend it, just make sure you do what you want.

You know, all through my upbringing if I did something right or discovered something new my mother would clap her hands over her head and shake them in the air to cheer me on, and you know, any lesson I wanted to take she would make sure I had it, and she was always there with information but never there with too much direction because she wanted me to find my own way. And I'm really lucky that I got put on that track because there were no other examples for me really, and it wasn't until much later in life that intellectually it clicked, and it was because of *A Room of One's Own*. I realized that without any rhetoric or expectation of payback, my mother had basically set up a room of my own for me. Pushing me to find my own way was what my mother gave me.

RW: Have you ever felt guilty about what you are doing? Do you ever feel like you are playing into stereotypes of women, or creating them?

VW: I felt a lot of the guilt in the beginning of my career, and certainly it comes back every once in a while, from what people from Naomi Wolf to Gloria Steinem have said about models presenting negative images to young girls, images which hold all women back, and all that. But you know, being black and growing up, I went through school in the sixties and the seventies, and there were not a lot of images out in popular culture for me to relate to. I felt almost invisible. I mean, the world was going on. There was Angela Davis, Barbara Jordan, and all those people, but they were far from my age range, and they were doing things that, as a child, I couldn't really understand. That's not to knock or diminish them, but in terms of there being some kind of intermediary professional image of a black woman that I could relate to, there just wasn't one. So, on some level I feel that the fact that I'm there visually and I'm represented is helpful to young black women looking out into the culture and trying to see themselves.

RW: I was at a Third Wave board meeting last week and we were naming people for our advisory board, and I suggested you and one of the other board members said, "Oh—I just hate models, they're just like little dolls, not in control, and I don't think that's the right image." Another member then said, "I wouldn't want to participate in an industry that makes women spend billions of dollars trying to improve the way they look." What do you think about these responses?

VW: I think sometimes people think that if women use and manipulate their sexuality in any way it makes them a prostitute, which leads to that whole question of being in control. As for the second question, the industry doesn't *make* women spend billions of dollars, people *want* to. We're a nation of consumers, people want to go out and have something new, a new dress, a new shade of lipstick or nail polish, or a new cream because it makes you feel renewed, it brings something new into your life. I do think the industry is at fault when it makes false promises. Like when women read ads and magazines and things are presented in a very real way, promising that if you do this you will get "x" results, rather than saying this is an idea, this is a suggestion. You can't let yourself believe that there is a plastic surgeon or a genie in the bottle, cosmetics are just a little pick-me-up.

RW: What kind of role model would you say you are?

VW: I put emphasis on thinking, on being outspoken. I mean I'm certainly not an ivy league scholar or anything like that, but I just think it's really important to be self-educated and self-determined. I also think that if you are a woman, any way that you can amass power and money you have to do it as long as it's ethical, because it's just something that we don't have. And you know, it's funny, because you go back to when people say well, women trading off their looks strips them of their power, but it has empowered a lot of women. If you look at me, Cindy Crawford, Claudia Schiffer, Naomi Campbell, Elle McPherson, and many others, we've become phenomenally empowered by trading off our looks, the same with Hollywood actresses. The bottom line is how you do or don't use your power.

I am not saying that you have to create some kind of colony or alternative life-style, that's not what I'm suggesting at all. I mean, I feel that I can use my power to really do something to educate young black people, I can set up a foundation or a school. And hopefully I can amass enough capital at some point to give my life over to a charitable enterprise.

You know, some people say that what models get paid devalues other women in the workplace, and I don't think that is true. What making money does allow me to do is hire other black people and other women, because I'm an enterprise and I can create jobs, and certainly if there are women in my employ we can have a better working environment and get farther in general than if someone has to go into a huge corporate system, or be at the mercy of a Newt Gingrich.

RW: Speaking of Newtie, what do you think about the welfare debate?

VW: Well, first of all, I think welfare is the code word for black.

RW: Black women.

VW: No, welfare means nigger, that's what welfare means. I think that during elections, when it's time for us to make important decisions, that is when the racial debate gets thrown up. Do you remember when the welfare debate started there was a cover story in the *New York Times* with a photograph of an overweight dark-skinned black woman getting ready to put these two chickens in the oven, did you read that story?

RW: Umm, I might have missed it.

VW: Well anyway, the story was this: she has three kids, she gets off welfare and she finds a job where she can make $7 an hour and at the end of the week she makes something like $300. But she has to wake up every morning at three, get her two infants dressed, and take them to her grandmother's house, drive her son to school by six, and get herself to work. She can't receive phone calls at her job, and if her mother has a heart attack they won't put the phone call through for her to know, and if one of her kids gets sick or her car breaks down, then she is totally back in the hole again, in debt, and her life goes back into a tailspin. It was very manipulative because here she is being used as the poster child for welfare—see, if she can do it, then anybody can do it—and anybody who isn't willing to live a life that is so totally distorted is lazy and someone who is working this hard shouldn't be, quote, humiliated, by any help.

RW: Yeah, no one seems to be talking about the cost of child care, the unavailability of birth control and information, instead they're talking about the woman who's getting over on the system. And what about the sixteen-year-olds in my neighborhood pushing baby carriages who know about birth control, but who live in a culture that says you don't become a real woman until you have a baby?

VW: Maybe I'll write about the welfare debate in my next column for *PAPER*.

RW: Where do you find strength?

VW: First of all, from my mother, from knowing how much she loved me, knowing that she would lay down her life for me. I also get a lot of strength from knowing that I am the object of love from a Divine Being.

RW: How do you know that?

VW: I know that from growing up in the Church, from reading the Bible, and from looking around myself and seeing how many blessings I have. I consider myself very lucky that God does not test me very often.

RW: Did you always believe in God as defined by the Bible?

VW: Not at all. I grew up having different relationships with God my whole life. Like, I have always thought that Jesus was really cool and really sexy, and that God is like the Prince symbol: both sexes at once. But that's really obvious.

RW: Do you feel connected to other models? Is there any kind of sisterhood?

VW: Well, certainly Karen Alexander, Cindy Crawford, Tyra Banks, and Elle McPherson are friends of mine, they're all people I turn to for comradeship and advice in the business. And Cindy especially, she will always help you. She is a very firm believer that we have to be really open about what kind of commission structures we have and how much money we make, so that we don't get ripped off. I think most of us work hard to eliminate any feelings that we're fighting against each other.

RW: Are there any principles you live by?

VW: Don't do anything you can't own up to. And always be grateful.

Questions for Thought and Writing

1. What do you think Webb means when she says she is a feminist "but not in the fist-in-the-air kind of way"? What do you believe are the most important criteria by which to define a feminist or feminism?

2. Webb explains that she does not feel objectified by the modeling industry because she "control[s] the way [her] looks are used and not the other way around." In an essay that explains what you think it means to be objectified, decide whether or not you find her answer convincing.

3. Webb defends her work as a model with the conviction that "if you are a woman, any way that you can amass power and money you have to do it as long as it's ethical, because it's just something we don't have." Critics of "the beauty culture," however, argue that the modeling industry *is* unethical because it sets unrealistic standards for women and makes them feel badly for not being able to meet them. To what extent do you believe modeling and feminism are contradictory? Can a supermodel truly "do feminism"?

ISSUES

Issues begins with "'Where Do the Mermaids Stand?': Voice and Body in *The Little Mermaid*," in which author Laura Sells considers how Disney's *The Little Mermaid* "sanitizes" the original Hans Christian Andersen story in an effort to hide the costs paid by many women seeking access to the benefits of patriarchal culture. Yet, she also sees how the representation of Ursula the sea witch presents the the potentially liberatory effects of gender as performance. In "Sexism and the Art of Feminist Hip-Hop Maintenance," Eisa Davis discusses double standards for women in hip-hop and other media. She also highlights the particular dangers for women in looking to popular culture figures as a way to develop a stable identity. Mary Douglas Vavrus introduces the term "postfeminism" in "Putting Ally on Trial: Contesting Postfeminism in Popular Culture" to reflect a pervasive message in contemporary U.S. media that feminism is dead. She argues that feminism has been turned by television shows like "Ally McBeal" into an explanation for working women feeling conflicted and anxious. The imperative to be perfect in the home and in the workplace in order to achieve a "balanced life" leads to impossible standards most women have trouble meeting. In their effort to succeed, working women find their options shrinking rather than expanding.

"Where Do the Mermaids Stand?": Voice and Body in *The Little Mermaid*

Laura Sells

Where to stand? Who to be?

—Cixous (1975) [1986], 75)

A young pastor, finding himself in charge of some very energetic children, hit upon a game called "Giants, Wizards and Dwarfs." "You have to decide now," the pastor instructed the children, "Which you are . . . a giant, a wizard or a dwarf?" At that, a small girl tugging on his pants leg asked, "But where do the mermaids stand?" The pastor told her there are no *mermaids. "Oh yes there are," she said. "I am a mermaid."*

—Barbara Bush (1990)

In spring 1990 Barbara Bush addressed the graduating class of Wellesley College, facing a hostile crowd of young feminist women who challenged her ability to represent the woman they all hoped to become as they entered the "real world." Arguing that Bush was selected as the wife of an important figure rather than as someone with accomplishments of her own, students first circulated a petition that one-fourth of the class signed, and later wore to the graduation ceremony purple armbands, which signified their protest, their graduating class color, and their first-ranked choice of commencement speaker, Alice Walker. The controversy received national media coverage, which, incidentally, characterized the protesting students as hysterics.[1]

In response to her audience's rejection, Bush gracefully defended her lifestyle, spoke about the need for women to have multiple choices, and implicitly criticized the limits placed on women by American feminism. After indirectly exalting women's role as wife and mother in the heterosexual family, she invoked the image of a mermaid as the master trope of her speech: "For over 50 years, it was said that the winner of Wellesley's annual hoop race would be the first to get married. Now they say the winner will be the first to become C.E.O. Both of those stereotypes show too little tolerance for those who want to know where the mermaids stand." The mermaid thus became Bush's attempt to broaden the spectrum of representations of women while simultaneously invoking a cartoon-like, stay-at-home Mom as a viable option. Framed by this oxymoron, the mermaid is an ironic figure that critiques the narrowness of identity politics in contemporary feminism; yet it simultaneously valorizes an equally narrow and conservative image of acceptable positions for women in American culture. This speech marks an interesting moment in the struggle to invent appropriate and liberatory images for American women, a moment in which "woman" slides between the complicated terms of mother, citizen, and subject.

Earlier that school year, in November, the Walt Disney Corporation conjured another cartoon image of woman as mermaid in their animated feature *The Little Mermaid* (1989).[2] A hallmark Disney film, *The Little Mermaid* is their first commercially successful animated feature since Walt's death in 1966, and the first in a spate of new animated features that reaffirm Disney's position as one of the largest producers of "acceptable" role models for young girls. The film portrays the story of the teenage mermaid, Ariel, who first desires independence and entry into the human world, and who eventually desires the handsome Prince Eric. She trades her voice to the Sea Witch Ursula for a human body and for access to the Prince and his world. The narrative recounts the ritual slaughtering of the archetypal evil feminine character and the marital union of the girl and her prince. Embedded within this classic narrative about an adolescent girl's coming of age is a very contemporary story about the costs, pleasures, and dangers of women's access to the "human world." . . .

Clearly, both Bush's and Disney's versions of the mermaid can be read as conservative images. Yet both versions of the mermaid critique the narrow range of options that constrain women's lives, and both emphasize issues of choice and agency. This essay situates *The Little Mermaid* within the context of contemporary American feminism and the struggle over the cultural definitions of "woman." By reading against the backdrop of Bush's speech, and the media's representation of the Wellesley students, I find that *The Little Mermaid* reflects some of the tensions in American feminism between reformist demands for access, which leave in place the fixed and complementary definitions of masculine and feminine gender identities, and radical refigurings of gender that assert symbolic change as preliminary to social change. In this context, then, the mermaid figure becomes both an icon of bourgeois feminism and a sign of the stakes in reinventing the category of "woman," or reimagining women as speaking subjects.

UPWARD MOBILITY

"Bright young women, sick of swimmin', ready to stand. . . ."

—ARIEL'S SONG

5   In 1837, Hans Christian Andersen wrote the original literary fairy tale of "The Little Mermaid." Like most of Andersen's work, the tale is considered autobiographical, an expression of his lack of social acceptance in the aristocratic circles that offered him patronage, a personal narrative of the pleasures and dangers of "passing." Ever the outsider, Andersen "projects his nagging sense of deprivation" in his writings (Spink n.d.; Bredsdorff 1975; Zipes 1983).[3] If a fairy tale is chameleon-like, as Joseph Campbell suggests, putting on "the colors of its background," living and shaping itself to "the requirements of the moment" (1972, 850), then Disney's contemporary version has shifted colors from class to gender privilege. Given the autobiographical theme of "passing" in Andersen's literary version, the Disney version, along with its ritual affirmation of women's coming of age, invites a reading of this film as a parable of bourgeois feminism. Ariel's ascent to the

"real world" easily becomes metonymic of women's access to the white male system.

The Little Mermaid establishes the world on land and the world under the sea as two contrasting spaces, one factual and one fictive, one real and the other imaginary. In this dualistic and hierarchical construction, the human world can be aligned with the white male system and the water world situated outside that system. In *Women's Reality* (1981), Ann Wilson Schaef uses the term "white male system" to characterize the dominant culture of American patriarchy. According to Schaef, the white male system operates on several contradictory myths, at least two of which are relevant to the complementary worlds of this film. First, nothing exists outside the white male system; and second, the white male system knows and understands everything (8–9). Those who are privileged by the white male system are oblivious to anything outside the system, while those outside the system know about the dominant culture as well as their own marginalized culture. These two contradictory myths speak to the relationship between the land and sea worlds: the sea world is rendered either invisible or mythic while the land world is endowed with cultural validity. As contradictory and complementary, the two-world motif creates permeable yet dangerous borders, furthers the plot, and establishes a hierarchy of desires. . . .

In these contrasting worlds of dominant and muted cultures, Ariel's song "Part of Your World" becomes more than an adolescent yearning for adulthood. As Ariel sings of access, autonomy and mobility, she yearns for subjecthood and for the ability to participate in public (human) life. She is figuratively and literally an upwardly mobile mermaid.[4] As the film opens, her adolescent curiosity and rebelliousness are both immediately apparent. She is late for her singing debut, a coming-of-age ritual ordained by her father, because she is out and about salvaging forbidden human objects from sunken ships.[5] Her curiosity about the human world, and her rebelliousness toward her father and his prohibitions against human contact, are particularly evident in her song. The song intones her desire to run, walk, and dance, all synonyms for mobility. While singing, she caresses a book that she cannot read, expressing her longing for knowledge. Her desire for access is characterized by her hunger and fascination with a different world in which she believes she can have autonomy and independence.

Autonomy and independence, as many feminists have recognized, is never easy; the cost for participating in the white male system can be quite dear. About to enter the real world, Ariel faces the pain of conforming to impossible ideals as she physically mutilates her own body by exchanging her fins for the mobility of human legs. Even more disheartening, she purchases this physical transformation with her voice. Like so many women who enter "the workforce" or any other "male sphere," Ariel wrestles with the double-binding cultural expectations of choosing between either voice or access, but never both. Our culture's continued difficulty with sexual difference is evident in the public persona of figures such as Geraldine Ferraro and Hillary Clinton. Ferraro failed in her 1984 vice-presidential bid in part because voters considered her too aggressive after hearing her forceful "masculine" speaking style (Jamieson 1988). Similarly, Hillary Clinton has been called the "Lady Macbeth of Little Rock," the "Evita Peron of America," and Bill's co-president. The Bush presidential campaign sought to discredit Hillary Clinton by suggesting she was "not a real woman" (qtd. in Wood 1994, 299–300). Women so often find themselves in a position much like Andersen's, a position in which access is really just a form of passing that compromises personal integrity and immolates voice.

Disney, however, obscures these costs through several related sanitizing maneuvers that contrive to create a bizarre erasure of "the feminine." Irigaray writes that Western patriarchy is constructed on a history of matricide, and on the expropriation of women from the mother's genealogy to the father's. As the film concludes with Ursula being impaled on a phallic mast from a ship and with Ariel being passed from her father to her prince, *The Little Mermaid* enacts this expropriation and makes Ariel's choices appear to be cost-free.

10   First, Ariel's fascination with the human world becomes transformed into love for Prince Eric. Through this sanitizing maneuver Disney obscures Ariel's interest in the human world as metonym for access to power. Once she meets the prince, her curiosity is minimized and her drive becomes externally motivated rather than self-directed. As Ariel passes from her father's hands to her husband's hands, the autonomy and willfulness that she enacted early in the film becomes subsumed by her father's "permission" to marry Eric. In other words, the marriage plot (Radner 1993) prevails as her interest in the role of citizen becomes supplanted by her interest in the role of wife.

Many feminists found objectionable this transformation from the Andersen version. In Andersen's tale the mermaid dies because she fails to earn the prince's love. Upon her death, the daughters of the air grant her the ability to earn an immortal soul through three hundred years of service. Trites argues that the Disney version subverts the mermaid's self-actualization process, and that Andersen wanted the mermaid to earn a soul on her own, not as an attachment of someone else: "Andersen offers women several paths toward self-realization, so the message to children is much more farsighted than Disney's limited message that only through marriage can a woman be complete" (1990/91, 150). Andersen's version, however, is not quite that liberatory. As Zipes suggests, Andersen's reward was never power over one's own life, but security in adherence to power—in the little mermaid's case, the power of servitude to god (1983, 84).

Second, Disney erases the pain of access by sanitizing the physical, bodily pain of Ariel's self-mutilation when she trades her fins for feet. Within the context of the first sanitization, and of Ursula's song about beauty and looks ("poor unfortunate souls . . . this one longing to be thinner . . ."), the legs indicate Ariel's compliance with the beauty culture, rather than her desire for access, mobility, and independence. Ariel becomes "woman as man wants her to be" rather than "woman for herself." In Andersen's version, the mermaid feels incredible pain, as if a sword goes through her body and knives pierce her feet with each step; the pain is so deep that her feet bleed. For Andersen, the pain reflected his discomfort and the price of his own integrity as a peasant whose literary talents earned him entry into aristocratic circles (Zipes 1983). His story expressed his own discomfort and loss of voice as he attempted to "pass" in high society. Disney masks the pain of self-mutilation that often accompanies this access by excising the pain from Andersen's story. By eliminating this pain, however, Disney only enhances Andersen's original version. As Zipes puts it, "Ideologically speaking, Andersen furthered bourgeois notions of the self-made man or the Horatio Alger myth, which was becoming so popular in America and elsewhere, while reinforcing a belief in the existing power structure that meant domination and exploitation of the lower classes" (1983, 81). The Disney version thus becomes a bourgeois feminist success story in which access is achieved with minimal cost.[6]

Third, Ariel sacrifices her connection to the feminine in the matricide of Ursula, the only other strong female character in the film. Eventually, Ariel achieves access by participating with Eric in the slaughtering of Ursula, relegating her and that which she signifies to silence and absence. Ursula is reassigned to the position of the repressed that keeps the system functioning. Embedded in gynophobic imagery, Ursula is a revolting, grotesque image of the smothering maternal figure (Trites 1990/91). Of course, within Disney's patriarchal ideology, any woman with power has to be represented as a castrating bitch. Ariel's entry into the white male system is at the expense of her connection with the mother. The gynophobic imagery sanitizes this cost, making it more palatable. By vilifying feminine power in the figure of Ursula, Disney simplifies Ariel's choice: in the white male system it is much easier to be silent than to be seen as monstrous.

Admittedly, the film is a problematic text for a feminist resistant reading, because it teaches us that we can achieve access and mobility in the white male system if we remain silent, and if we sacrifice our connection to "the feminine." We all know the storyline about Ariel sacrificing her voice. Indeed, Ursula tells an ancient story when she convinces Ariel that her voice will be useless in the human world. Although Ariel severs her connection with the one strong female character of the film, Ursula, she ultimately retrieves her voice. This final sanitization is clearly the product of Disney's compulsion for rainbows, violins, and happy endings. If voice is a symbol of identity, then Ariel retains a measure of autonomy and subjecthood. Philosopher Margaret Whitford argues that women cannot be social subjects until they are subjects of language (1991, 43). In this final sanitization lies the film's undoing.

IN THE HOUSE OF DIVINE

"This little girl knew what she was and she was not about to give up on either her identity or the game."

—Barbara Bush (1990)

If the Little Mermaid is, indeed, a budding young woman severing her connection to the feminine symbolic, what possible sites of resistance and pleasure are available? Where do I find hope for Ariel as she enters the white male system, passed from the hands of her father to the hands of her husband? How can Ariel's compliance with the laws of the Father be recuperated? Much like Ariel, I find myself turning to Ursula for answers to these questions. Trites tells us that the wealth of gynophobic imagery precludes us from reading Ursula's wry comments ironically: "Although some viewers might perceive those of Ursula's statements that capitalize on Ariel's inexperience as ironic and as an intended tribute to feminism, these comments are voiced in the midst of too much gynophobic imagery to honestly promote feminism" (1990/91, 152, n. 7). But beyond the gynophobic imagery, the character of Ursula, who is unlike any other Disney villain, teaches a different lesson about access, mobility, and voice. Ursula can retrieve Ariel from her destined alliance with patriarchy. Not only does she give Ariel legs, she schools her in disruptive reconstructions of gender and harbors her voice in the feminine home of *jouissance*. Ursula teaches Ariel that performance and voice are manifestations and liberations of gender.

The lessons that Ursula gives Ariel about womanhood offer   15 an important position from which to resist narrowly drawn patriarchal images of women, a position absent in Disney's previous fairy tales. During her song about body language, Ursula stages a camp drag show about being a woman in the white male system, beginning "backstage" with hair mousse and lipstick. She shimmies and wiggles in an exaggerated style while her eels swirl around her, forming a feather boa. This performance is a masquerade, a drag show starring Ursula as an ironic figure. According to the directing animator, Ruben Acquine, Ursula was modeled on the drag queen Divine, while the voice and ethos behind Ursula belong to Pat Carroll. Both of these character actors are known for their cross-dressing roles. Ursula's theatricality is undeniable; to prepare her voice for her role, Carroll envisioned Ursula as an aging Shakespearean actress because, as she says in *People* (11 December 1989), "only someone who has done the classics has that kind of arrogance." A composite of so many drag queens and camp icons—Joan Collins, Tallulah Bankhead, Norma Desmond, Divine—Ursula is a multiple cross-dresser; she destabilizes gender. . . .

In Ursula's drag scene, Ariel learns that gender is performance; Ursula doesn't simply symbolize woman, she *performs* woman. Ursula uses a camp drag queen performance to teach Ariel to use makeup, to "never underestimate the importance of body language," to use the artifices and trappings of gendered behavior. Ariel learns gender, not as a natural category, but as a performed construct. As Ariel stumbles away from the shore into Eric's arms, she winks to her undersea companions, indicating that she is *playing:* "The game is dangerous, and has a compulsive quality, but it *is* play. We may hope that when this game isn't fun any more Ariel may use her stubbornness, if not her beauty, to play another, more interesting one" (White 1993, 191).

Drag performances such as Ursula's and Ariel's are spectacles that can teach us something important about gender. Gender is composed of repeated, publicly performed, regulated acts that are "dramatic" and therefore "contingent" embodiments of meaning. Drag denaturalizes gender by showing us its imitative structure; it operates on the contradiction between anatomical sex and gender identity, a contradiction that is interrupted by the performance itself. Defining gender as a performative production dismantles the illusion of a natural category (Butler 1990; Butler 1991; Capo and Hantzis 1991; Garber 1992). Mary Russo puts it more simply: "To put on femininity with a vengeance suggests the power of taking it off" (1986, 224). Butler, however, refutes this equation of gender with style, as something to be put on or taken off as a conscious choice: "Performativity has to do with repetition, very often with the repetition of oppressive and painful gender norms to force them to resignify. This is not freedom, but a question of how to work the trap that one is inevitably in" (1992, 84).

Andersen, who inhabited a position that was radically other than himself, struggled with working this trap. "Throughout his life Andersen was obliged to act as a dominated subject within the dominant culture despite his fame and recognition as a writer," as Zipes reminds us (1983, 77). Indeed a recurrent theme in many of Andersen's fairy tales is to dismantle what Butler calls "zones of legitimacy": *pace* "The Emperor's New Clothes." Andersen's writing is often simply about passing, but passing in itself is not subversive. For drag to be subversive, it must go beyond exposing an ideal as uninhabitable. Drag becomes subversive when it "dissolves and rearticulates" ideals (Butler 1992, 89). The ideal woman represented by the mermaid image is immobile, her only power in her sexuality. As one journalist describes Bush's mermaid: "Those free-floating mermaids she mentioned are sheathed in glittering, confining, fantasy fins that really get the sailor going but leave the woman foundering if she tries to walk" (Johnson 1990). Ariel is a dissolution and rearticulation of this gender ideal: she is a mermaid passing as a human with both legs and voice, or mobility and subjecthood.

Just as Ursula's drag performance destabilizes and deconstructs gender, her excessive figure provides the site upon which we can reconstruct the image of the mermaid. It is no accident that Ursula is an octopus, an inverted Medusa figure. Very early in the film we learn that she is exiled by King Triton from the world of the merpeople. She represents that which is outside even the patriarchally domesticated outside, and hence, outside patriarchal language. Ariel's outside, the undersea world, is a colonized outside ruled by the patriarchal father, King Triton, who has the power to name his daughters. Ursula, who is banished from Triton's realm, is outside the outside. Ursula is a double-voiced, multiple character. The sprawling seascapes of Ursula's home are what Cixous calls "the dark continent" of the feminine body. To visit Ursula, Ariel must enter through the toothy jaws of a gigantic mouth, and swim through womb-like caves. Ursula is the female symbolic encoded in patriarchal language as grotesque and monstrous; she represents the monstrosity of feminine power. This is why Ariel trades her voice to the Sea Witch in the first place.

Feminist theories of women's *jouissance* help us to understand the metaphors of voice, body, and language as they create a force that displaces the dualistic order of the white male system. The multiplicity of women's *jouissance*, or women's bodily, sexual pleasure, cannot be represented dualistically. Although it means woman's pleasure, *jouissance* cannot simply be translated into bodily pleasure. It connotes sensual enjoyment, the enjoyment of rights, and the enjoyment of language. *Jouissance* implies "total access, total participation, as well as total ecstasy." The multiplicity of woman's sexuality indicates "she has the potential to attain something more than total, something extra—abundance and waste, Real and unrepresentable" (Wing 1986, 165–66). The language of women's bodies jams the machinery of phallocentric discourse that generates a dualistic world view, disrupting the symbolic system that demands the complementarity of gender and the dual world construction of land and sea. A voice that has spent time with Ursula, that has spoken in the language of *jouissance*, could never return to innocence.

The configuration of voice, bodily excess, rupture and the feminine is established by the visual alignment of images in the climax of the film. In the first wedding scene, Ursula wears Ariel's voice in a shell around her neck in her disguise as Vanessa, Ariel's evil double. The bird Scuttle swoops down and shatters the shell, freeing Ariel's voice. The metaphor of flying/stealing (*voler*) is central to Cixous's notion of *l'écriture feminine*, because "to fly/steal is a woman's gesture, to steal into language to make it fly . . . for all the centuries we have only had access to having by flying/stealing" (1986, 96). Ariel's voice literally becomes "the spoken word, exploded, blown to bits by suffering and anger, demolishing discourse. Broken from her body where it was shut up and forbidden" (94). The freeing of Ariel's voice literally interrupts the wedding, or the ritual enactment of patriarchal symbolic order.

This release of Ariel's voice also releases Ursula, who then seizes King Triton's crown and the phallic scepter. Just as Disney transforms Ariel's desire for autonomy and access into desire for a husband. Disney also warps Ursula's desire into a form of penis envy, or in this case, scepter envy. With the scepter in hand, Ursula swells into an enormous monster, exploding, diffusing, overflowing. Her growth is more rupturing than an erection. Eventually, Ursula dies as Eric pierces her with the phallic mast of a ship. This undeniable event makes a recuperation of *The Little Mermaid* rather questionable. As the film concludes with Ariel in Prince Eric's arms, the dangerous message about appropriation and the sanitized cost of access cannot be ignored. Yet, even though Ariel has been complicit in the death of Ursula, and the destined alliance with patriarchy is fulfilled, I remain hopeful. After all, Ariel enters the white male system with her voice—a stolen, flying voice that erupted amidst patriarchal language, a voice no longer innocent because it resided for a time in the dark continent that is the Medusa's home.

Endnotes

The author would like the thank the women of the Pagoda at St. Augustine, Florida, for providing the space to draft this essay.

1. See, for instance, Mike Barnicle's *Boston Globe* column in which he describes Wellesley students as "a pack of whining, unshaved feminists" who cause the Boston College students to "appreciate the virtue of celibacy" (*Boston Globe*, 26 April 1990). The controversy provoked the production of T-shirts sporting the slogan: "Just a bunch of whiny unshaven radical spinster tartlets" ("The Wellesley Protest, Beyond Barbara Bush," *The Washington Post*, 29 May 1990).
2. *The Little Mermaid* is the first animated fairy tale released by Disney in thirty years. It broke national box office and video store records for "first release" animations, making it Disney's most successful feature-length animation (surpassed by *Beauty and the Beast* in 1991) (Thomas 1991). As Susan White points out in "Split Skins," mermaids have become a pervasive cinematic symbol of the girl's difficult rite of passage to womanhood (1993, 186): *Splash* (1984), a Disney/Touchstone film directed by Ron Howard; Richard Benjamin's *Mermaids* (1990); and of course, Madonna's music video "Cherish"

(1991). Likewise, Tori Amos's song, "Silent All These Years" (1991), evokes the configuration of the mermaid and voice.

3. See Zipes for a brief discussion of the literary and folk origins of the tale, and for an insightful class analysis of Andersen's version (Zipes 1983, chapter 4).

4. Ann Wilson Schaef's (1981) terminology is particularly useful to discuss Ariel's desire to participate in the human world. Like many people who theorize about dominant and marginal cultures, Schaef agrees that marginalized people often experience a double consciousness, or an awareness both of dominant culture and of their own marginalized cultural systems (see also, for instance, Sandra Harding 1991). Unlike cultural critics who see this double consciousness as a product of political struggle, Schaef recognizes this double vision as simply the (frequently inchoate) recognition of being disenfranchized and disconfirmed as a member of a muted group. While Ariel certainly doesn't have a politicized consciousness, she is indeed aware of her own relative lack of power.

5. Ariel's desire to acquire human objects is interesting within the context of Hilary Radner's (1993) discussion of consumption as a way for women to negotiate the constraints placed on a sexual identity within the public sphere. *The Little Mermaid* can be seen as a variation on that theme. Indeed, a frenzy of consumption has sprung up around the mermaid motif as young girls buy everything from Mermaid toothbrushes to Mermaid video games (White 1993). In addition, the obvious analogy between Ariel and Barbie suggests that Ariel teaches girls that adult female sexuality is inextricably linked to consumption (see Motz 1983).

6. By shifting the focus from class to gender, Disney creates what one reviewer calls "the fall of a fishy, feminist Horatio Alger" (Roberts 1992).

7. To be fair to Eleanor Clift, Ann McDaniel, and Clara Bingham, the authors of this article, they conclude with a more favorable (although questionable) assessment of Bush's character: "It is unlikely that Barbara Bush will change her style. It is equally unlikely that she will ever submerge her identity to that of her husband, even if he is the president."

References

Andersen, Hans Christian. (1837) 1974. "The Little Mermaid." *The Complete Fairy Tales and Stories*. Trans. Erik Christian Haugaard. Garden City, NY: Doubleday.

Braidotti, Rosi. 1987. "Envy: Or, With My Brains and Your Looks." In *Men in Feminism*, ed. Alice Jardine and Paul Smith. New York: Methuen.

Bush, Barbara. 1990. Remarks of Mrs. Bush at Wellesley College Commencement. Wellesley, MA: Wellesley College Office of Public Affairs.

Butler, Judith. 1990. *Gender Trouble*. New York: Routledge.

———. 1991. "Gender Trouble, Feminist Theory, and Psychoanalytic Discourse." In *Feminism/Postmodernism*, ed. Linda J. Nicholson. New York: Routledge.

Campbell, Joseph. 1972. "Folkloristic Commentary." In *The Complete Grimm's Fairy Tales*. New York: Pantheon, Random House.

Capo, Kay Ellen, and Darlene M. Hantzis. 1991. "(En)Gendered (and Endangered) Subjects: Writing, Reading, Performing and Theorizing Feminist Criticism." *Text and Performance Quarterly* II: 249–66.

Garber, Marjorie. 1992. *Vested Interests: Cross-Dressing and Cultural Anxiety*. New York: Harper Perennial, Harper Collins.

Harding, Sandra. 1991. *Whose Science, Whose Knowledge?* Ithaca: Cornell University Press.

Jamieson, Kathleen Hall. 1988. *Eloquence in an Electronic Age: The Transformation of Political Speechmaking*. New York: Oxford University Press.

Johnson, Rheta Grimsley. 1990. "What Mrs. Bush Didn't Say." *Dallas Morning News*, 10 June.

Motz, Marilyn Ferris. 1983. "I Want to Be a Barbie Doll When I Grow Up: The Cultural Significance of the Barbie Doll." In *The Popular Culture Reader*, ed. Christopher D. Geist and Jack Nachbar. Bowling Green: Bowling Green University Popular Press.

Radner, Hilary. 1993. "Pretty Is as Pretty Does." In *Film Theory Goes to the Movies*, ed. Jim Collins, Hilary Radner, and Ava Preacher Collins. New York: Routledge.

Roberts, Susan C. 1992. "Fractured Fairy Tales." *Common Boundary*, September/October: 17–21.

Russo, Mary. 1986. "Female Grotesques: Carnival and Theory." In *Feminist Studies/Critical Studies*, ed. Teresa de Lauretis. Bloomington: Indiana University Press.

Schaef, Anne Wilson. 1981. *Women's Reality*. San Francisco: Harper and Row.

Spink, Reginald. n.d. "Hans Christian Andersen: Fairy Tales in a Hundred Languages." *Fact Sheet/Denmark*. Copenhagen: Press and Cultural Relations Department of the Ministry of Foreign Affairs of Denmark.

Thomas, Bob. 1991. *Disney's Art of Animation: From Mickey Mouse to Beauty and the Beast*. New York: Hyperion.

Trites, Roberts. 1990/1991. "Disney's Sub/Version of *The Little Mermaid*." *Journal of Popular Television and Film* 18: 145–59.

Whitford, Margaret. 1991. *Philosophy in the Feminine*. New York: Routledge.

Wing, Betsy. 1986. "Translator's Glossary." In *The Newly Born Woman*, by Hélène Cixous and Catherine Clément. Trans. Betsy Wing. Minneapolis: University of Minnesota Press.

Wood, Julia T. 1994. *Gendered Lives*. Belmont, CA: Wadsworth.

Zipes, Jack. 1983. *Fairy Tales and the Art of Subversion: The Classical Genre for Children and the Process of Civilization*. New York: Wildman Press.

Questions for Thought and Writing

1. Author Laura Sells argues that both the Barbara Bush and the Disney figures of the mermaid "critique the narrow range of options that constrain women's lives, and both emphasize

issues of choice and agency." What aspects of the Disney version are more hopeful, in the author's view, than the Barbara Bush version?

2. Sells argues that the Disney version of *The Little Mermaid* differs from the Andersen original in many ways, including the fact that it "sanitizes" the costs that Ariel pays in order to gain access to the "white male system." What are some of the costs? To what extent do contemporary women still face them?

3. What is the value of the idea of "gender as performance" that Ariel learns from Ursula? In what way(s) can "drag" be "subversive?" What must it be able to do? Consider your own gender identity as a "performance." Which aspects of it are the easiest, the most enjoyable to "perform"? Which ones would you prefer not to perform? Why not?

4. Describe the approach author Sells takes in examining *The Little Mermaid*. How does she challenge its authority as a positive cultural representation? How might you pose a similar challenge to a different Disney film or story?

Sexism and the Art of Feminist Hip-Hop Maintenance
Eisa Davis

I belong to the church of hip hop. Just as people my parents' age remember precisely where they were when JFK was shot, my fellow believers and I can recall every detail about the first time we heard "Rapper's Delight." Hip-hop beats are always thumping somewhere in my chest every time I feel at home with myself, under lyrics that stir politics, music, and theatrical performance into a hearty gumbo that tastes different each time I try it. Hip hop gave me a language that made my black womanhood coherent to myself and the world; hip hop revived me when my soul was blanched from neglect. So I knew something was up when I found myself at the record store, a vein in my temple near to bursting, trying to decide whether to buy Snoop Doggy Dogg's *Doggystyle* or Queen Latifah's *Black Reign* with my last $15.

This didn't make any sense. Latifah had virtually saved my life in college: her music and public image were intimately, almost inextricably, connected to my awakening personal and political identity. How could I walk out on her at this critical moment, this election of the marketplace, by casting a cash vote for sexism, violence, Snoop and Dre? What could have precipitated this Cardinal Sin?

Back in my sophomore year in college, Latifah was the woman I had been waiting for, the woman who could be me. Black, female, nineteen-year-old royalty. With her hair and sexuality tucked underneath crowns, knee-high boots, and military garb trimmed with kente, she tore up every single track on *All Hail the Queen*, her debut album, her deep voice commanding complete respect. She not only inspired idolatry in young women like me and in our parents, but she got props from the hard rocks: the B-boys with Ph.D.s in vinyl archaeology, and the exclusively male jury of rappers, producers, and magazine editors in whose ears the hip-hop canon is constructed.

The first time I saw Latifah in person, I left my feminism and classical political theory class early so that I could hear her speak over the electric fence between a (white) feminism that many Harvard students and faculty wanted to hear her advocate, and a (black) womanism that the nebulous B-boy council and many black students needed her to defend so that she could retain her ghetto pass. White women wanted her to prioritize sexism and "transcend" racism; black men wanted her to address racism and spirit away her knowledge and experience of sexism. She navigated the thicket of competing loyalties and emerged completely intact, being everything to everybody, occasionally clipping or silently blotting out her answers altogether so as not to put anyone out.

5   I bumrushed the stage after her talk, to meet her, hoping that some of her energy, strength, boldness, and creativity would osmose into me. On that day, Latifah seemed so perfect to me because she evoked a recognizable ideal: the quintessentially strong, virtuous woman my grandmother always exhorted me to become. The woman everyone loves—from a distance. Never loose, never trivial, never bitchy or butchy. The talented, disciplined, powerful woman who is too generous and down-to-earth to constitute a threat. The woman who keeps her panties up and practices the art of no, who polices any moral injustice or infraction of etiquette and never misses an opportunity to speak up for herself or any oppressed groups in words that are clear, just, and listened to.

Latifah was like a young Rosa Parks getting open on the mike, a symbol with whom everyone could identify. Her Afrocentric imaging, full-bodied voice, and collaboration with some of hip hop's pioneers (such as KRS-One, De La Soul, and Daddy-O of Stet-sasonic) set her apart from female rappers like Lyte and Shante who'd come before her. She meant safety and strength to me, a way for me to come out as a black woman. Not that I was planning on rhyming any time soon. But she was my age, and that made her the first mainstream black female role model with whom I could identify in a practical way. Latifah was a step toward an entirely new epistemology for me. My political awareness and self-esteem began to put on some weight as I started to connect more mean-ingfully with my mother and my aunt, took a trip to West Africa with my family, moved into an artsier, blacker dormitory, took classes in African-American history and culture, sat twelve hours for microbraids, and fell in love with a black man.

When I got Latifah's next album, *Nature of a Sista'*, I laid on my couch and cried because she was talking about men! I could-n't believe that she was singing about love, loneliness, and rela-tionships and occasionally even sounding like Madonna to top it all off. R&B was moving toward her; she (and hip hop) were mov-ing toward R&B. All the iconography was changing, tending to-ward a heightened corporeality in an expanding discourse on sex. And just like Lyte and her lipstick, Janet and her belly button, Lat-ifah was only a woman after all. She had gone "soft," the ultimate insult in the hip-hop phallo-universe, experiencing the same wounds and joys I was petrified of revealing to myself, let alone to the world. I felt betrayed. How could she do this to me? A little makeup now and again was fine, but did she have to display the holes in her heart, and the reality that she needed a man from the bully pulpit of hip hop?

And yet I had identified so powerfully with Latifah that after I listened to the album a few more times, the shock eased and I started to absorb, unconsciously at first, a wider concept of my own femininity through Latifah's own expanding notions of self. By accepting Latifah's growth, by allowing her to be someone I didn't want her or myself to be while still admiring her, I made a subtle but distinct break with my inherited tradition of who I, Black Woman, was supposed to be.

Then came Latifah's movie roles, her business acumen, and *Living Single*. As her identities began to compound instanta-neously in the Hollywood dream bank, I lost that initial sense of connectedness. She still managed to balance the needs of her hard-core and lay feminist contingencies while making an empire of herself, keeping Nielsen ratings high and the mall rats in stitches every Thursday night. But who was she? I no longer recognized myself in her work or in her persona.

10   Which brings me back to my dilemma: *Doggystyle* or *Black Reign?* Was I in the mood for bluesy misogyny over the fattest, most addictive beats known to humankind, or did I want to hear "positive" messages I already knew nestled into Latifah's latest product? The devil or Daniel Webster? Toxic chocolate sundae or nine-grain granola?

I ended up buying *Doggystyle;* seven hours later, I was singing "g'z up hoes down." But I did acquire a free copy of *Doggystyle* later that week and traded it in for *Black Reign* so that I could have both, which is what I wanted in the first place. In my post-Latifah phase, I don't fit into a puritanical, dualistic feminism that recognizes only indignant innocence (buying *Black Reign*) or unenlightened guilt (buying into *Doggystyle*). I don't have to choose.

My dilemma, then, was not one of rational consumerism, or how to voice my own opinion best, given the products and their attendant philosophies. While that remains an important issue, the actual dilemma I was experiencing was how to explain that I don't feel oppressed by Snoop or defined by his conception of women—without denying that in Snoop's world, he is defining me and all women, even if he separates the queens from the hoes in his life off wax. How can I love me some Dre beats with sexist Snoop lyrics while responding to him in language that criticizes the misogynist reality he's been born into and continues to build for himself?

When I was introduced to Latifah in 1990, Afrocentric racial consciousness and progressive gender politics joined hands in hip hop, and the version of female empowerment I had borrowed from my elders wouldn't even allow me to say or hear bitch. Even in jest. Even as a verb. But now, like many women I know, I have acquired an immunity to sexist lyrics. While some may call this immunity a weariness, or a numb defeat, could it be the first inexplicable taste of inner power? I can't stuff my ears with cotton and refuse to hear those who have different politics than I do. I don't want to censor or dismiss my culture, my language, my sense of community regardless of the form in which it comes. Hip hop, after all, is the chosen whipping boy for a misogyny that is fundamental to Western culture. Why should I deny myself hip hop but get a good grounding in Aristotle? I'd rather listen and listen well, and have a conversation with the artist-philosophers who are repeating the sexist ways they have been taught, and then have chosen, to see the world.

As part of my work as a journalist, I've had some illuminating discussions with Ice Cube, Scarface, Apache, Snoop, the members of Brand Nubian and many other rappers regarding their use of sexist lyrics. These conversations have underscored the need to be sensitive to the rapper's or listener's specific context when deciphering lyrical meaning. The terms "bitch" or "ho" (or "nigga") can be used playfully, lovingly, even fictively at times. "Bitch" can even be used as an anodyne for lost love (for instance, on "Bitches Ain't Shit").

The second point I've heard from male rappers is that there really are bitches and hoes. And they need to be told about themselves. Even rappers who are socially conscious qualify these lyrics by saying things like, "This song isn't for an African queen like you or like my lady or like my mama," but this, as Jeru the Damaja says, "is for the 'bichez.'" In other words, if you're not a bitch or a ho, why do you have a problem? (Just insert the word "nigga" flying out of a white mouth and watch the script flip.) Why do you come when you weren't being called in the first place? I only disrespect those who disrespect themselves. I'm a correct black man, a god, only a nigga on weekends. I learned my history. Now why can't these bitches get themselves together?

This response has little validity for me, because while I am immune to a sexist reality on record, I'm not yet free, to steal from The Coup. When used jokingly between equals, these terms are fine, and when I'm getting my groove to "Bitches Ain't Shit (But Hoes and Tricks)" in a club, I'm cool. But don't let a black man call me "bitch" other than in jest. The word can become a sledgehammer, sometimes even a bullet that grazes my heart. It's as if, for one unbearably painful moment, I believe him more than I believe myself.

I also don't buy the claim that there are "real" bitches and hoes. I think it is a trap that punishes women for playing their expected roles in figuring the rapper's persona. Onstage, hip-hop artists invite women's desire and pursuit, bragging about their conquests far in advance of the reality. But when the women go back to the hotel after the show and get what they came for, the artists reject the women who have legitimated their player persona, channeling their own morning-after disgust into a litany of bitches and hoes.

There are no excuses for lyrical sexism. I can't fantasize that it's dead, embalmed, and on exhibit at the Smithsonian, or convince myself that it's an historical, cultural condition that black women have to accept in order to understand and stand by "our" men. Yet I still feel virtually untouched by this verbal and visual violence toward women, and I believe this feeling springs from an increased sense of freedom rather than from apathetic resignation.

As sexist as these lyrics and attitudes can be, my immunity is fortified by a growing number of male rappers who consciously and humorously espouse a chauvinism they know to be antiquated because they are beginning to understand that their position is as fragile and as powerful as a woman's. Male hip-hop artists recognize that they are the hunted; they flesh out all of white America's fears by carrying out, lyrically, unthinkable acts of sociopathic destruction. The fantastical crime setting of gangsta and horrorcore rap, starring protagonists who drip with testosterone, features a masculinity that defines itself by an ability to annihilate any challenger, female or male. When this protagonist commits sexual and violent crimes, he satisfies a specifically black male yet generic desire for total power. This protagonist also embodies the newly formulated national enemy: in the absence of the Red Threat, the specter of the criminalized black male steps into its place. Thus the criminalized enemy is contained and made fictive, consumed, pitied, or condemned by the haves, and disowned or celebrated by the have-nots. Misogyny here becomes a reactionary act with a subversive gloss.

20   When I peer into this hip-hop shadow box where the stock characters of seventies' blaxploitation are revisited—how poignant this swan song, how funny this compulsive reenactment of a sexist past—I consume the performance of sexism, thereby assuring myself that the reality of sexism depicted in the lyrics is happening to an imaginary woman, not a real one. Unlike white hip-hop fans who confirm and celebrate their own perceived distance from racism by identifying with the purveyor of explicit antiracist, even antiwhite lyrics, I think there's a new woman on the dance floor who can chant "Bitch Betta Have My Money" and identify with neither the lyricist nor the sexual object, discovering instead a humor in sexist lyrics whose possible truth removes rather than implicates her. She realizes that AMG can't really be talking to her or anyone else, and if he is, he's got to be kidding.

There are also women out on the dance floor who accept these lyrics as truths about themselves—sometimes playing the bitch or ho role in the same spiteful way that the men explode the stereotype of criminalization. Or sometimes there's a recognition that a woman who dares to step out of her place, a woman who is willful or sexually uninhibited, may be called a bitch or ho, respectively. These women not only have a sense of humor about being called bitches and hoes, they have a sense of pride that they are finally being spoken to. The hip-hop ode to women has evolved from L.L. Cool J's "Around the Way Girl" to Sir Mix-A-Lot's "Baby Got Back" to Apache's "Gangsta Bitch," giving the ideal woman a rare multiplicity. These songs reveal how male hip-hop artists actually have provided public acceptance, not just degradation, for women who would never receive it elsewhere in popular culture.

Whether women respond with pride, a sense of humor, or righteous anger upon hearing sexist lyrics—or if they don't pay attention to the lyrics at all—there is and always has been a strong public dialogue between male and female rappers, between black men and women. That's another reason why I can croon along with Nate Dogg on "Ain't No Fun (If The Homies Can't Have None)" because I know that I and every other woman are always talking back. Call this dialogue the racist legacy of Moynihan's matriarchal pathology or the retention of an African mother goddess; it doesn't matter. We all know that if we'd ever been blessed with a blaxploitation sequel entitled *Coffy v. Dolemite*, Pam Grier and Rudy Ray Moore would kill each other before letting the other win. More likely, they'd call it a draw and join forces against evil. In the same way, female and male rappers battle each other within or between songs, with neither sex ever having the final word. Hip-hop dialogue has a male advantage by sheer number and by male privilege in the language, genre, and social custom, but just one female who gets the crowd hype can rebut all the men if her style is identical to none. With dis artists like Shante and Bytches With Problems, with spirits like Mecca of Digable Planets, Nefertiti, Medusa and Koko of Sin, T-Love, Lauryn from the Fugees, 99, and Rage, and with mainstream presences like Latifah, Lyte, Yo Yo, and Salt-N-Pepa, the burden of representation is spread wide on strong shoulders. And the mainstream media's strategy of coopting this dialogue for racist purposes, restaging black women and men's struggle against racialized sexism as a bloody cockfight, can be reappropriated as an opportunity to truly resolve the conflicts we have with one another and with the larger hegemony.

Recognizing that there is an uncut umbilical cord between hip hop's art and life as well as an infinite amount of exaggeration and fantasy only leads me to want to change the reality of sexism off of wax. Who would these rappers be, I wonder, if no ladies wanted to get with them? If all women, like the Athenian and Spartan coalition of Aristophanes' *Lysistrata*, agreed to abstain from sex with all rappers, could we end sexism in hip hop? Why is there so little space for public, artistic declaration of meaningful relationships? (Method Man's "All I Need" is a wonderful exception to the rule.) And aren't the women who do have recreational sex with hip-hop artists or who put on a thong bikini to play a "video ho" just searching for that place where we women can celebrate our bodies, where we can express our eroticism freely, where we can have sexual agency?

I had a dream in which TLC members Left Eye and Chilli were sitting on a couch on the beach (embarrassingly, this is a real dream, hardly invented for the purposes of this piece). I sat on the couch and told Left Eye that the (real) *ViBe* cover with the trio in fireman's slickers might have been in bad taste since she'd just burned down her abusive boyfriend's mansion, and that the new (dreamworld) cover *ViBe* had replaced it with after recalling the original was even worse because it featured T-Boz by herself draped in white and discussed only her in the cover story. I wanted to share how incensed I was by *ViBe*'s mistreatment of them. Looking at T-Boz dipping her toes in the water, Left Eye and Chilli said, "No, you're wrong." Left Eye explained in dreamy, lush language how T-Boz had enlightened her and Chilli about feminist practice. How T-Boz had this amazing mind and was using her corporeality as a tool to free women, not to entice men. Elegy complete, Left Eye had tears in her eyes as she gazed toward her latter-day saint. I woke up and wondered if she could be right.

25   When sexist lyrics are not self-conscious but instead are full of vitriol and anger, they do still hurt, they still feel real. This pain only helps me diagnose the problem; it does nothing to solve it. And I don't have to throw away all the old words and the people who say them in order to have a new conversation. I can't have a vision of political practice anymore that makes no space for pleasure, conflict, personal and collective responsibility to cohabitate simultaneously. I have to genuflect to Dr. Dre for his genius as a producer and an artist while I lacerate him for his physical violence toward women. I commend and criticize. I speak not

from the vengeful state I was in when I heard he'd beaten "Pump It Up" host Dee Barnes, but from the place where I want to be when sexism is all over.

I often think about these issues through the lens of humor because it often provides freedom, creativity, and a language that dispenses with blame and guilt, precisely what we need in our work toward transcending sexism. When I hear self-conscious sexism in rap and laugh at it, I am releasing a painful past and garnering power to shape a new future. For example, I love the two-syllable variation of "bitch" pronounced "beeotch," because the word is distorted explicitly for humor, making light of the namer as well as the named, ridiculing the term itself. "We don't love them hoes," goes the misogynistic, faintly homoerotic Dogg Pound refrain, and damnit, the shit is funny. Admittedly, it's a humor that still operates on an uneven playground, where hoes and bitches get bullied much more than the niggaz. "Sexist hoes, they wanna get with this," flows Snoop, but since I've had Latifah's "U.N.I.T.Y." in my back pocket since long before she recorded it, I don't even have to let him know that I ain't a "bitch" or a "ho," because I know for myself.

An organic act of laughter upon hearing a lyric reminds me that the present manifestations of sexism in hip hop have a value for me: they are simply a tradition, like a woman wearing white when she marries, that I recognize and enjoy as such precisely because I know I am not bound to it. Although Snoop is talking to me, he isn't defining me, and this position spawns a new politics that protects our identities as women without sentencing us to life in a prison of identity we didn't choose. I want to infuse some of the necessary energy we spend fighting men's rules into working on a new extinction agenda, to sample Organized Konfusion, that will render sexism, racism, homophobia, and classism old sitcoms that we watch in syndication only to see how much we've changed.

When women no longer feel bound by sexist representations, when we initiate a dialogue that doesn't turn on the axis of anger, blame, or victimology, then artists who should attend Ism Anonymous meetings (treating compulsive sexism, nihilism, and marijuana use in lyrics) are finally recognized as valuable people who can become even stronger by assuming self-worth through constructing themselves rather than destroying others. I would love to see hip-hop battles, conference panels, and articles and essays like this one that talk about issues of sexism in hip hop supplemented by other formats for dialogue. While I have some drafty ideas for in-store listening stations with hardware for immediate on-line responses, the most effective formats are informal: relationships between artists and critics (in the loosest sense of that term) which probe these issues honestly, over time, are probably the best and most difficult way to get anything done. I am encouraged by relationships such as the one fostered between Harvard professor and novelist Carolivia Herron and Public Enemy, coinciding with Chuck D.'s lyrics moving from the misogyny of "She Watch Channel Zero" to the womanism of "Revolutionary Generation."

Even considering growth like Chuck D.'s, I don't look to hip-hop artists with the same religious zeal for The Answers that I once did, because I know those answers only pose more questions; I'm a big ho now and I don't depend on hip hop to tell me that I'm not or that I am or that I'm just joking. Since I no longer need hip hop to provide me with a fixed identity, I have no need to control hip hop's representation of women. I just want to continue talking to and hearing from the artists who do control these representations, as I have in the past through interviews, and in the future within these valuable long-term relationships I mentioned above.

30   More important to me than my conversations with artists is the conversation between Ice Cube and a woman who wants to produce a track for his next album, the conversation between a male higher-up and a woman marketing executive at a record label who wants to try something other than bikini and booty art on an album cover, the conversation between a woman and a man in a club who's called her a stanky bitch for not dancing with him. We must make a world outside of hip hop in which we and our daughters are equals in these conversations—and we can't make it with only guns, money, and tears to choose from.

In my personal/political upbringing, I got my theory at home and my praxis from hip hop. And I think I've grown up enough to know where else I need to grow. Latifah in all her avatars—Afrocentric, introspective, and relationship-hungry; plain old Dana; Khadijah on "Living Single"—isn't a model that was once useful for me and then thrown out; instead she has given me a foundation of bedrock to build upon. She and all women artists, mainstream and underground, get props for relentlessly transforming the taboo into the cool because we all privilege from the truth. My grandmother's version of black womanhood isn't a tradition that restricts me, either; rather it has allowed me to break those patterns that confine my growth, yet remains a home for me to return to and feed my spirit. Grandma continues to inform my choices, values, and dreams. Her lifelong work as an educator makes me want to make time for the children who are being raised by hip hop and Sega to sit down and actively analyze and filter what they learn. And I would love to see a public hip-hop library and studio to give access to anybody who wants to learn about and make music, because is there anything more joyful, more weary, more expressive of our humanity than hip hop, ever transforming, encompassing the universe of all music?

Fighting sexism isn't only about being offended by the forty-five bitches and twenty-three hoes on someone's record. I hope that the strength we gain from realizing that we women—and men—are not bound to hip hop's representations can help to dismantle the sexism we've internalized, and empowers us to combat the sexism outside of us.

Questions for Thought and Writing

1. Why does the author credit Latifah with having "saved [her] life" in college? Why was Davis so disappointed by Latifah's later songs "about men" and by the realization that "Latifah was only a woman after all"? How does this change help the author rethink her own ideas of femininity?
2. Davis argues that while "There are no excuses for lyrical sexism. . . . I still feel virtually untouched by this verbal and visual violence toward women." How does she explain her ability to not feel oppressed by such music? Do you find her rationale convincing? Why or why not?
3. In attempting to explain why so many male rappers continue "consciously and humorously" perpetuating sexist ideas and images in their music, Davis suggests that they do so, in part, because they, as black males, are also "hunted." By whom, in her view, are they hunted and for what reasons?
4. Davis suggests that the way male rappers treat women who are willing to have sex with them reflects a cultural double-standard about female sexuality. Explain how the double-standard operates in the world of hip hop and in other contemporary media.
5. Davis explains that she no longer needs "to let [Snoop] know that I ain't a 'bitch' or a 'ho,' because I know it for myself" and also that she "no longer need[s] hip hop to provide [her] with

a fixed identity." Why not? From what sources does the author derive her identity now? Trace some of the key sources
from which you derive your identity, including positive and
negative influences.

Putting Ally on Trial: Contesting Postfeminism in Popular Culture

MARY DOUGLAS VAVRUS

In the last two years, a number of media texts have addressed
women and so-called women's issues by exploring, and often
implicating, the way feminism has played out in their private and
public lives. In this essay, I examine some of these texts in order
to illuminate the ideological patterns they share. I argue that,
taken together, these texts convey a culturally significant message
to their audiences: that feminism is a problematic social movement that should be superseded instead by a set of beliefs and
assumptions I call "postfeminism." Postfeminism is privileged in
discursive patterns that constitute a solipsistic perspective on
women: generalizing about women using particular women's
voices and concerns to the exclusion of others. The worldview
that emerges represents a minority of elite women's interests and
negates the needs of other women. Postfeminist solipsism parallels a concept popularized by Adrienne Rich (1979), "white solipsism:" thinking, imagining, and speaking "as if whiteness
described the world" (p. 299). Postfeminist solipsism functions
similarly, but is based on the positionality of elite, white, straight
women. Postfeminist solipsism is constructed from problematic
assumptions and claims exemplified in mainstream media texts
that I examine here.

WOMEN AND EVERYDAY LIFE

The everyday lives of women have become the subject of a great
deal of media examination: the *USA Weekend* newspaper supplement is one recent example of such an examination. According to
USA Weekend, women are approaching the next century being "fo-

cused more on their families and homes, and less on meeting career goals or society's expectations, than at any other time in the past two decades." In other words, for today's women, "now the word is balance" ("Now the word," 1998, p. 4). This article reports the findings of the *Update: Women* survey, conducted by two marketing researchers, which found that its women respondents were scaling back their expectations and aspirations in workplaces and replacing them with filial and domestic concerns; an archetypal respondent was one who was working for pay part-time, while attending to children and home for the remainder of her time.

This particular article, short and "factoid-y," is indicative of a trend in much popular culture (and here I include non-fictional as well as fictional media) that purports to report on women's lives: that of implicitly or explicitly blaming feminist politics and feminists for the dissatisfactions and problems faced by women today, while eschewing or negating an expansive notion of politics and community. Alongside this feminist-blaming, a similar tendency exists: that of pointing out a few high-profile examples of women in powerful positions—or simply public women—as representative of feminism's successes. This rests on a meritocracy argument: a few women have made it in a corporate or professional setting, therefore those who haven't must be to blame for not succeeding.

The word "balance" is key here, I believe, for its perceived value in personal life, public life, and journalism. That is, balance connotes a space between extremes where one (presumably) finds harmony between competing forces, demands, and circumstances. Balance is not a bad goal for which to strive; we don't often hear of people credibly promoting imbalance as a worthwhile goal. However, it is worthwhile to consider what we mean when we talk about balance. For example, which elements are we trying to balance? To what end are we striving for balance, or is this an end in itself? And finally, is it the case that the elements we are attempting to balance are as extreme and oppositional as might be suggested in some public discourse?

In a recent essay, Justin Lewis argues that certain patterns in   5
political reporting result in persistently reproducing what he calls the "hegemony of corporate center-right interests" (1999, p. 251). These patterns, he argues, are at least indirectly responsible for the way in which the majority of respondents to a poll he and his colleagues conducted implicitly consented to aspects of a political

ideology that work against them. One of the patterns of reporting Lewis identifies as being both prevalent and insidious he refers to as the "Left versus Right framework of political reporting." This framework divides politicos and commentators into one of two dichotomous realms: those who represent Left-wing politics and those who represent the Right. One of the (many) problems with this framework is that, rather than representing liberal to actual leftist values, spokespersons identified with the Left are usually centrist in their beliefs—if not to the right of centrist. When combined with a tendency to emphasize conflict, this frame, Lewis (1999) asserts, stresses political differences "while areas of agreement are *assumed to take place somewhere in the political center*" (p. 256, emphasis in original).

Lewis's analysis could be applied as well to reporting on so-called women's issues and feminism. In fact, the framework he describes undergirds some recent—and high-profile—mainstream media accounts of women's lives and/or feminism's role in them. But just as Lewis argues the Left is misrepresented in political reporting, so too is feminism in its construction in mainstream media. That is, feminism is vilified and depicted as an extreme politics that has benefited few and harmed many. What is constructed as middle ground, between the feminist and prefeminist extremes, is postfeminism: an essentialist ideology which privileges individualism and the interests of elite, white, straight women at the expense of a collective politics of diverse women's needs.

BLAMING FEMINISM

News about women is often saturated with commentary about harried mothers who have discovered that parenting and working for pay are realms whose demands are mutually exclusive (though similarly draining)—an opposition that has provoked various anti-feminist tracts suggesting feminists are to blame. By suggesting that women could work for pay *and* be good parents, feminists have created unrealistic and unrealizable expectations for women, they say. In such discourse, "balance" is to be found only when women capitulate to their essential natures: procreating and then caring for their progeny as their first and most gratifying priority.

In much public discourse, feminism has become a scapegoat social movement—a straw figure easy to attack because it has been constructed as so extreme and counterproductive to women's lives as to be laughable. . . .

This version of feminism has become a social movement made accountable for any issue, problem, or concern even remotely related to women. As Melissa Deem (1999) has argued recently, feminism and women are typically conflated in media discourse, a tactic that makes feminists spokespersons for all women. Throughout the publicity and impeachment events of President Clinton's affair with Monica Lewinsky, Deem notes that feminists were called on the carpet in various mainstream media venues to explain Clinton's behavior. Because women were involved, and the power disparity between Clinton and Lewinsky suggested the possibility of sexual harassment, feminists were called upon to make sense of it. When they responded, media commentators didn't like what they heard, blaming feminism for what they said was a weak response. This is a typical public response to feminism, Deem argues, when feminists are held accountable for the actions of all women—and feminist-sympathetic men.

The (now-defunct) candidacy of Elizabeth Dole evoked similar responses from news workers; that is, commentators used Dole as a symbol of women's equality with men, and if feminists didn't support her, then they were betraying their loyalties to their sex. Dole equivocated on the specifics of her political agenda, but politically. Dole's record suggests that she is anything but a feminist. She aligned herself with religious right activists and organizations such as Pat Robertson and the Christian Coalition, stated that she would support "'the idea of'" a constitutional amendment prohibiting abortion, and fought hard against the Family and Medical Leave Act (Nichols, 1999, pp. 31–32). Yet, Patricia Ireland, president of the National Organization for Women, reported that she had spoken with NOW members who were torn on the issue of whether to support Dole or Al Gore—simply because Dole is female and they supported the presence of women in high political offices (Nichols, 1999, p. 31). But is such support of Dole a move that supports feminism? If women and feminism are conflated, then the answer is "yes": supporting any woman under these circumstances could be construed as feminist. But if we stop to consider the past record of Dole as a predictor of her future policies, then the answer is likely to be "no." And although newsworkers have seemed to enjoy covering Dole—and gave her much flattering

10

coverage—the mere fact of her persistent presence in news narratives does not translate into the concrete realities of support for policies that could help large numbers of women (see, for example, Bayer, 1999; Cocco, 1999; & Sobieraj, 1999).

Marjorie Ferguson (1990) points out that women who rise to positions of power are often held up in public discourse as evidence of the success of feminism. And surely feminism, with its push to make powerful positions open to women, is in large part responsible for Dole's ascendance. But Dole's place in power is only a part of the story. How she acts in the service of women's issues is quite another. And in Dole's case, it is clear that she is far from feminist—and wants it that way. Like Margaret Thatcher, Dole demonstrates what Ferguson detected in Thatcher: that rather than being altruistic and encouraging women to follow her up the ladder of success, Dole instead saws "the ladder away from beneath the feet of those on the lower rungs, fearful that" if she doesn't do so, she will risk losing her status and power in the process of sharing it (1990, pp. 223–24).

Ferguson refers to this expectation as the "feminist fallacy": the idea that the presence of women in media texts—including some women in positions of power—translates into "cultural visibility and institutional empowerment" (1990, p. 215). This fallacy was illustrated recently in *TV Guide* magazine from the week of October 9, 1999. The cover featured Katie Couric (of *The Today Show*) posing in a pink sweater, set off by a bold headline: "How Women Took Over the News." The story that followed the headline (and its suggestion of an invasion by foreign forces in the nation's newsrooms) celebrated the increased numbers of women in TV journalism and strongly suggested that women had achieved gender parity with their male counterparts. Along with that good news came Diane Sawyer's observations: that this women's coup was responsible for more "soft news" stories women really cared about (e.g., day care), and a different slant on those about which women were less interested (e.g., "'what's happening in Sri Lanka,'" [Murphy, 1999, p. 22]). Lesley Stahl, of *60 Minutes*, noted that her style of reporting can now be " 'more and more of me. It's a style of naturalness' " (Murphy, 1999, p. 20).

There's no doubt that women in journalism have had to fight against sexism. But is the picture for women as rosy today as *TV Guide* suggests? Maybe not. According to Fairness and Accuracy in Reporting (FAIR), women are still nowhere near majority status in journalism: In 1998, they constituted only 1/3 of all correspondents and they covered just 28% of news stories. None of the top 25 media corporations have women at their helms (FAIR, 1999b). In other words, the fact that a few women have "made it" in TV journalism is no reason to think that the news industry is not still dominated by men. That "style of naturalness" might work to make Lesley Stahl more comfortable in her job, and the soft news focus touted by Diane Sawyer may be interesting to some viewers (although persistently referring to issues of interest to women as "soft news" is problematic). But what does this do for the way feminism is constructed in mainstream news? I would argue that it works to privilege both meritocracy and elitism, thus constructing a postfeminism constituted of a glowing, but unrepresentative, picture of journalism for women; thus, if anti-feminist coverage, or coverage clearly *lacking* feminist interpretation, emerges, it must be legitimate—in other words, it's there because feminists and feminism are in legitimate need of re-tooling. After all, great correspondents like Cookie Roberts and Katie Couric wouldn't permit *unfounded* criticisms of feminism, would they?

Clearly, this sort of cheerleading for women overlooks structural issues in media organizations—such as male dominance in the upper echelons of media management or the intense competition between network news and cable news that drives a bottom-line mentality. These structural issues make it unlikely that much feminist interpretation occurs. What else could explain the vilification of feminism we saw during the reports on the President Clinton-Monica Lewinsky saga? During the time Clinton and Lewinsky's affair was being broadcast, feminists who supported Clinton were compared to Nazis and prostitutes, were called hypocrites, and were made to seem responsible for this consensual affair between two adults. If the feminist sea-change *TV Guide* reported actually existed, it seems doubtful that such an assault on feminism could have transpired.

Similarly, last June's *Larry King Live* expose on Hillary Clinton's physical appearance and fashion sense would likely never had been broadcast if feminists had clout at CNN. This broadcast of *Larry King Live* featured the commentary of fashion and entertainment reporters on the subject of Hillary Rodham Clinton's "look" as she began to test the idea of running for the Democratic New York state Senate seat. These reporters assessed her weight, the length and size of her legs, her new $500 haircut, and her perceived demeanor: "hard and bitchy and intense" (FAIR, 1999a). 15

That such commentary about male politicians is absent from media coverage suggests that this playing field is far from level. The feminist fallacy is alive and well—and even thriving—in the news.

POSTFEMINISM AND POPULAR CULTURE

In a piece from *The New Republic*, Ruth Shalit argues that "postfeminist" describes many prime-time TV programs that have featured women, such as *Dharma & Greg*, *Veronica's Closet*, and *Ally McBeal*. These female protagonists, who are hyper feminine even as they perform demanding jobs (such as attorney), represent "really nothing but a male producer's fantasy of feminism, which manages simultaneously to exploit and to deplore, to arouse and to moralize" (Shalit, 1998, p. 30). Finally, Shalit notes, these programs—particularly *Ally McBeal*—"have made male power and female powerlessness seem harmless, cuddly, sexy, safe, and sellable. They have merely raised conservatism's hem" (p. 32). Bonnie J. Dow (1996) has made similar observations about postfeminism in older TV programs such as *Designing Women* and *Murphy Brown*.

My point here is to foreground some of the means by which texts and trends promoted as feminist, or even pro-woman, don't hold up as such in meaningful ways. If anything, an *absence* of strong feminism is more evident in mainstream media. For example, *Time* magazine's treatise on the state of feminism, 1998, titled "Is Feminism Dead?" is an example of a news story that purports to comment on the state of the feminist movement, but succeeds instead in smearing it—and in predictable ways. As both Susan Faludi (1991) and Susan Douglas (1994) remind us, this process of trying to publicly bury feminism is one that recurs with regularity in mainstream media. Thus, the *Time* editors once again deferred to the time-worn formula of putting feminism to death—while simultaneously blaming feminists for an appalling array of bad books, and dubiously feminist icons and art.

The *Time* essay was the cover story for the June 29, 1998 edition. The cover featured the faces of four women, three of whom were stalwart feminist activists: Susan B. Anthony, Belly Friedan, and Gloria Steinem. But the fourth—the face of Calista Flockhart representing her TV role, Ally McBeal—was the one that garnered the greatest reaction. Under Ally McBeal's face was posed the question, "Is feminism dead?" When that particular face is paired with this question, the question becomes rhetorical. If wacky, self-absorbed, apolitical Ally McBeal is considered a feminist icon, then feminism *must* surely be dead. In response to this issue, one post-*Time* episode of *Ally McBeal* even included an exchange between Ally and a typical media caricature of a feminist that made Ally's (and producer David Kelley's) stance on feminism all too clear.

As Ally exits a courtroom into a busy courthouse hallway, she is accosted by a loud woman who grabs her by the arm and then announces that she has been nominated as a 1999 professional role model by her group, "Women for Progress." The following dialogue ensues:

FEMINIST: "You're a role model."

ALLY: "I . . . I don't want to be a role model."

The feminist, not listening to Ally's objection, tells her that she's going to have to change how she dresses and "fatten up" because her group doesn't want young girls glamorizing "that thin thing."[1]

FEMINIST: "My sources tell me that you feel an emotional void without a man. You're really going to have to lose that if women are going to look up to you."

ALLY: "I don't want them looking at me at all."

FEMINIST: "Don't be pissy. You're a role model. And you'll do what we tell you to do. And you can start by dropping that skinny, whiny, emotional slut thing, and be exactly who we want you to be. Nothing more, nothing less. Can you do *that* pinhead?"

This dialogue, which turns out to be one of many of Ally's fantasy sequences, concludes with Ally turning to the feminist, biting off her nose, and spitting it out against a door. Later, as she petulantly recounts this dream to co-worker, John Cage, she snarls, "I had a dream they put my face on the cover of *Time* magazine as the *face* of feminism!"

After viewing this episode, one need not wonder about Ally's and producer David Kelley's feelings about feminism and feminists. The fascist, abrasive feminist is a stock stereotype in mainstream media, and works to discredit both feminism and its adherents (see, for example, Kamen, 1991). And Ally's pure disdain for feminism—or even for being a role model for "young girls"—is obvious at a glance. A quick assessment of some of her other statements and behaviors on the program would suggest that Ally is hardly feminist at all.[2] For example, on one program Ally tells her roommate, Renee, that yes, she does, "want to change the world. But first I want to get married." But the *Time* author's conclusion is predictable. The article itself is standard tabloid fare; hyperbolic and replete with dubious evidence to substantiate the claim that feminism is a has-been social movement.

Ginia Bellafante, the author of the *Time* story, has written a polemic which, if it had appeared in *The Star* or *The Weekly World News*, would be easy to dismiss. Bellafante's piece, however, appears in a historically respectable news magazine, and therefore benefits from the halo effect of its context. While it seems fairly obvious that she has constructed this polemic as a straw figure destined to generate increased sales by way of controversy, it still bears the imprimatur of the Time Warner corporation—one of the 10 largest media parent companies in the United States' oligopolistic media world ("100 Leading Media Companies," 1999; Bagdikian, 1997, p. xiii). The Time Warner corporation's importance to the media oligopoly might raise questions as to the intention of *Time*'s editorial board vis-à-vis this commentary on feminism. In other words, *Time*'s recycling of this topic is more a demonstration of its commercial appeal than of its legitimacy as political commentary.

But if that isn't enough to raise questions, then the spurious methods Bellafante uses to make her argument should: she makes claims using—at most—the slimmest of evidence; usually her claims are simply unsubstantiated. Her "that-was-then-this-is-now" examples signify a dead future for feminist politics—hijacked by what she refers to as the "flightiness of contemporary feminism" (Bellafante, 1998, p. 57). Her evidence for such flightiness? Popular culture texts such as the novel *Bridget Jones's Diary* and the television program *Ally McBeal* (contrasted with their secondwave feminist counterparts *The Women's Room* and *The Mary Tyler Moore Show*, respectively). She argues that the female protagonists in these contemporary texts are farther evidence of feminism gone awry:

> Much of feminism has devolved into the silly. And it has powerful support for this: a popular culture insistent on offering images of grown single women as frazzled, self-absorbed girls. . . . The problem with Bridget and Ally is that they are presented as archetypes

of single womanhood even though they are little more than composites of frivolous neuroses (Bellafante, 1998, p. 57).

To Bellafante, Camille Paglia represents what feminism should be. She argues that Paglia's very controversial book, *Sexual Personae,* "helped catapult feminism beyond an ideology of victimhood" (1998, p. 58). That Bellafante accepts the notion that feminism ever relied upon an "ideology of victimhood" places her squarely in a camp with writers like Christine Hoff Sommers and Katie Roiphe who make the same, unsubstantiated, claim. Sommers' and Roiphe's works have been roundly criticized by feminists for their decidedly anti-feminist and even, at times, misogynist, sentiments (see Dow, 1996, for an excellent summary). Moreover, Paglia's book did more to catapult her into the national media limelight to act as a vehicle for her own self promotion than it did to raise public interest in feminist politics.

It's a damned if we do/damned if we don't equation. The media stereotype of feminism is that of a social movement confounded by seriousness and populated by grave, ball-busting women (Douglas, 1994; Kamen, 1991). So if feminists decide to have a little fun with a performance art fund-raiser ("The Vagina Monologues") it's evidence of the devolution of feminism. Similarly, the presence of women starring in television programs must mean that feminism is both responsible for getting them there and for the personalities their characters possess. If there is a logic to this argument, it escapes me. Bellafante even notes that *Ally McBeal's* producer, David Kelley, doesn't suggest that either he or Ally McBeal (the character) are feminist, although Kelley does claim that Ally is "all for equal rights" (Bellafante, 1998, p. 58).

Danielle Crittenden's *What Our Mothers Didn't Tell Us* (1999), uses similarly spurious tactics to make a case against feminism. Crittenden is a spokesperson for the Independent Women's Forum (IWF) and the editor of their "Women's Quarterly" newsletter. The IWF is a conservative anti-feminist group that churns out press releases blaming feminism for all manner of society's ills. Like a latter day incarnation of Phyllis Schlafly and the Eagle Forum, Crittenden aligns herself with conservative causes and politicians; unlike Schlafly, however, Crittenden never names her political ideology. *What Our Mothers Didn't Tell Us* is her book-length attempt to push women back to the days of yore by espousing a return to marrying young, having children quickly thereafter, and staying home with the children at least until they're old enough not to be traumatized by their mothers' outside-the-home job obligations (preferably when they leave home for college or other independent living arrangements).

Crittenden bases her argument on a foundation of anti-feminism; for the last three decades feminists sold women a bill of goods by telling them they could—and should—successfully parent and work for pay, all while managing to have egalitarian romantic relationships. Crittenden especially objects to a feminism that she argues has elevated careers over family, betraying both women and children in the process. Clearly, this has failed women, she argues, because evidence of an epidemic of desperately unhappy, feminist-influenced women is all around us. Her evidence for this? Women's magazine headlines about the proliferation of unhappy single women and the multitude of techniques available for remedying their single status—in other words, to catch a man.

> When the magazines are not terrifying women into celibacy with articles on the dangers of "date rape"[3] and sexually transmitted diseases, they are offering desperate "tips" to catch a man's attention. . . . And once you have managed to turn a man's head, it's assumed that you will have no end of trouble keeping it pivoted in your direction. . . . (Crittenden, 1999, p. 15).

Because second-wave feminists had touted the benefits of single life, then surely they're responsible for such widespread dissatisfaction. When Crittenden conducted a tour of a few East Coast colleges and universities, she found that the few women who were proud to call themselves feminists were "on the fringes of student society . . . women with odd personalities and carefully cultivated grievances. . . . It is because women like these call themselves feminists that so many others have decided that feminism has gone 'too far' " (p. 19).

What feminists failed to realize, Crittenden claims, is that women will always be unhappy when they're unfaithful to their essential natures. Their essential natures, of course, tell them to pair off into marriage early, have children when young, and nest with their babies until they're strong and confident enough to weather life's storms. Then and *only* then should women consider working for pay. Oh, and they should not consider divorce as an option—the case with which couples can become legally uncoupled is one of the main weapons in the morality-obliterating arsenal of feminist doctrine. Independent women can kiss the idea of coupling good-bye, anyway: they're hopelessly self-absorbed and all this independence "has the perverse effect of making it even more difficult even to attract, let alone keep" a man (p. 91).

Ultimately, the legacy of Crittenden's straw-figure feminism is that women now "think of themselves as a victimized subset of humanity and not as active participants in a free and democratic society" (p. 189). Part of Crittenden's claim may be correct—that some women (and probably many men, too) feel alienated by politics of any kind, and therefore disenfranchised. But Crittenden's evidence for blaming feminism for this is weak, at best. In blaming feminism, she betrays her mildly obscured roots in conservative politics. But she is also a victim—of her assumptions, if nothing else. That is, she falls prey to the motion that media texts, such as women's magazines, realistically reflect lived experience—in this case, the quotidian lives of women. Using popular culture and popular media to gauge the success or failure of a social movement is at best a weak method; at worst, it is dishonest.

At a glance around the magazine stand at any grocery store one can easily see women's magazines that portray women as unhappily, dangerously single, or exhausted from trying to deal with the pressures of work and family. But such magazines are, first and foremost, commercial endeavors; they are spaces in which advertisers peddle their products to a target audience of women consumers (an important market, to be sure). Editors of these magazines routinely tweak, alter, and eradicate stories that might alienate advertisers. Editors suggest and select stories that have the greatest potential to attract advertisers; this is the commercial imperative of their business. Crittenden overlooks the possibility that such stories may appear in these magazines not because they are accurate reflections of the state of women's lives, circa the *fin de siecle*, but because their harried protagonists' lives could be represented in a very particular, commercially appealing, fashion; as in need of the remedies offered by the consumer products and service industries that conveniently advertise in their pages. *Cosmopolitan* and *Glamour*, to name but two magazines Crittenden cites, regularly offer stories about the difficulties women face in today's world. But the solutions they offer for diminishing or erasing these difficulties are usually consumerist in nature, and almost always sexist (see, for example, Duffy & Gotcher, 1996; Duke & Kreshel, 1998; Garner, Sterk, & Adams, 1998; and Ruggiero & Weston, 1985). If women's magazines are to be used as data for anything, this should be accompanied by an interrogation of commercialism, which is at the heart of their story-selection process. It is not *feminism* that is to blame for women being unhappy (if, indeed, women are), but commercialism and consumerism. It isn't feminism that provides role models for anorexic and bulimic body types. It isn't feminism that suggests women's existential crises can be ameliorated through the use of bath salts or cellulite cream. In other words, it isn't feminism that has promoted a commercial fix for metaphysical ills. But nevertheless, feminism has been a historically easy target for public commentators of all stripes. . . .

Endnotes

1. This comment is in reference to an issue that has dogged Calista Flockhart in the "real world." That is, tabloid and non-tabloid reporters have pointed out how very thin she is, and have asked her, repeatedly, if she suffers from anorexia or bulimia. Flockhart has denied that she suffers from either of these disorders, and has dismissed any suggestion that she has a problem with her weight.
2. For example, one of *Ally McBeal*'s standard narrative techniques is the catfight—usually between Ally and her former boyfriend's current spouse, Georgia. In a number of scenes, Ally and Georgia duke it out either metaphorically—in a fantasy scene with cat heads—or literally—in a kick-boxing ring. Susan Douglas (1994) has noted that the depiction of female relationships is an important indicator of a producer's/director's stance with respect to feminism. Competition between women—and particularly competition for the attention of men—is often used as a subtle suggestion that women exist in opposition to one another more often than existing cooperatively or with mutually agreed upon goals. The "catfight," Douglas argues, is a "staple of American pop culture" (1994, p. 221) and is a particularly effective means of signifying schism between women.
3. That Crittenden uses quotation marks around the term *date rape* is revealing. Elsewhere in the book she relies upon a Katie Roiphe-like argument about feminism and a cult of victimhood she says is cultivated by it. This is much like Roiphe's argument in *The Morning After: Sex, Fear, and Feminism on Campus* that the concept of date rape was concocted by feminists who needed one more issue that would make women feel like victims and prey to men and patriarchal practices.

References

100 leading media companies. (1999, August 16). *Advertising Age*, pp. S1–S10.
Bayer, A. (1999. August 20). Elizabeth Dole tapping women for campaign funds/fuel. Copley News Service.

Bellafante, G. (1998, June 29). Feminism: It's all about me. *Time*, pp. 54–60.

Cocco, M. (1999, August 30). For women, 2000 race is not a sorority run. *The Des Moines Register*, p. 7.

Crittenden, D. (1999). *What our mothers didn't tell us: Why happiness eludes the modern woman*. New York: Simon & Schuster.

Deem, M. (1999). Scandal, heteronormative culture, and the disciplining of feminism. *Critical Studies in Mass Communication. 16*(1), 86–93.

Douglas, S. (1994). *Where the girls are: Growing up female with the mass media*. New York: Times Books.

Dow, B. J. (1996). *Prime-time feminism: Television, media culture, and the women's movement since 1970*. Philadelphia: University of Pennsylvania Press.

Duffy, M. & Gotcher, J. M. (1996). Crucial advice on how to get the guy: The rhetorical vision of power and seduction in the teen magazine *YM. Journal of Communication Inquiry, 20*(1), 32–48.

Duke, L. L. & Kreshel, P. J. (1998). Negotiating femininity: Girls in early adolescence read teen magazines. *Journal of Communication Inquiry. 22*(1), 48–71.

Fairness & Accuracy in Reporting. (1999a, June 14). Why does Larry King think Hillary Clinton's hair, legs, smile and figure are "news"? [WWW document]. URL http://www.fair.org/

Fairness & Accuracy in Reporting. (1999b, October 12). Women have not "taken over the news." [WWW document]. URL http://www.fair.org/

Faludi, S. (1991). *Backlash: The undeclared war against American women*. New York: Crown Publishers, Inc.

Ferguson, M. (1990). Images of power and the feminist fallacy. *Critical Studies in Mass Communication, 7*(3), 215–230.

Flanders, L. (1994, September/October). The "stolen feminism" hoax: Anti-feminist attack based on error-filled anecdotes. *EXTRA* [WWW document]. URL http://www.fair.org/

Garner, A., Sterk, H. M., & Adams, S. (1998). Narrative analysis of sexual etiquette in teenage magazines. *Journal of Communication, 48*(4), 59–78.

Kamen, P. (1991). *Feminist fatale: Voices from the "twentysomething" generation explore the future of the "Women's Movement."* New York: Donald Fine Inc.

Lewis, J. (1999). Reproducing political hegemony in the United States. *Critical Studies in Mass Communication, 16(3)*, 251–267.

Murphy, M. (1999, October 9–15). How women look over the news. *TV Guide*, pp. 16–23.

Nichols, J. (1999, July). Will any woman do? The candidacy of Elizabeth Dole. *The Progressive*, pp. 31–33.

Now the word is balance. (1998, October 23–25). *USA Weekend*, pp. 4–6.

Rich, A. (1979). *On lies, secrets, and silence*. New York: Norton.

Ruggiero, J. A. & Weston, L. C. (1985). Work options for women in women's magazines: The medium *and* the message. *Sex Roles, 12*(5/6), 535–547.

Shalit, R. (1998, April 6). Canny and Lacy: Ally, Dharma, Ronnie, and the betrayal of postfeminism. *The New Republic,* pp. 27–32.

Sobieraj. S. (1999, August 19). Is Bush eyeing Dole and her female support? The Associated Press.

Questions for Thought and Writing

1. What are the author's objections to the "balance" that professional women are supposedly trying to achieve between home and work? How does this version of "balance" seem to restrict rather than expand options open to contemporary women?

2. Explain what Marjorie Ferguson calls the "feminist fallacy." How does it work to create an "unrepresentative picture" of feminism's progress in certain professional fields such as journalism? What kind of information and facts does it overlook or ignore?

3. How has feminism been turned into a "straw figure" by mainstream media, according to the author? In other words, how has it been made an easy target for all that is wrong with contemporary women's lives? What real obstacles in the path of women's progress get ignored as a result of this strategy?

4. Identify the chief tactics used by mainstream media to convey the agenda of "postfeminism," or the message that feminism is over or "dead." Imagine that you are charged with creating a sitcom character who will challenge this message. What will she or he be like?

Exploring Connections

1. In "Sexism and the Art of Feminist Hip-Hop Maintenance," author Eisa Davis remembers how Latifah represented one of the first "recognizable ideals" she could find as a black woman establishing her identity in the late 1980s. How does her confusion over Latifah's changing images of womanhood and femininity connect with the dilemma faced by Wellesley students over the selection of Barbara Bush as commencement speaker in "'Where Do the Mermaids Stand?': Voice and Body in *The Little Mermaid*"?

2. In "How Does a Supermodel Do Feminism," Veronica Webb argues that "the [modeling] industry doesn't *make* women spend billions of dollars, people want to." How does this belief compare to Sut Jhally's contention that advertisers create desires in their consumer audiences by repackaging and "selling our dreams" back to us?

CHAPTER 3

Gender and Sexuality

OVERVIEW

The Overview articles that follow—"Letters to a Young Feminist on Sex and Reproductive Freedom" and "How Men Have (a) Sex"—provide readers with a framework for considering and critiquing how traditional roles of gender, race, and class shape our understandings of sex and sexuality. Focusing primarily on reproductive freedom, Phyllis Chesler presents a set of critical issues that shaped Second Wave feminism and advises the new generation of feminists of their ongoing importance. She suggests that "sex is more complex and simpler than you've been led to believe," and argues that sex and the nature of sexual orientation has little to do with our cultural perceptions of it. John Stoltenberg similarly argues that there is no "male sex" but rather "only the idea of it," or a set of traits and sexual behaviors that men are culturally required to perform. He encourages young men to stop "acting out" manhood and strive to "touch truthfully."

Letters to a Young Feminist on Sex and Reproductive Freedom

PHYLLIS CHESLER

SEX AND HUMANITY

Sexual pleasure is not a sin. Nor is it a sacrament. It is your right as a human being to exercise as you see fit. It's amazing that I feel the need to say this, but, given our times, I do.

Feminists are not—and never have been—against sexual pleasure. Patriarchy is—and has always been—against sexual pleasure *for women*. Confusing one's own sexual orgasms with radical actions is silly, pretentious. Feeling good physically is important, but it is not political in the same way as freeing prisoners from concentration camps or feeding the poor. Romanticizing female lust as Goddess-given is as dangerous as romanticizing male war lust as God-given.

If you're a woman, sex is not something you have to submit to (or aspire to) only with a man, or only with your husband, in marriage. Sexual pleasure is not necessarily tied to reproduction. If you're a man, sex is not something you can buy or take by force.

Sex is not something that you can only share with members of the opposite sex. Nor is it something that always results in genital orgasm.

5   As human beings, we are more than the sum of our sexual parts. However, women are more often reduced to a collection of eroticized body parts: a pretty face, cleavage, breasts, buttocks. Many parts of a woman's body can be eroticized, i.e., can become the focus of orgasm: a foot in a high-heeled shoe, an exposed back, or hip, or thigh, or calf.

In some countries, a woman's exposed (unveiled) face, her eyes, or eyebrows when seen above a half-veil, immediately suggest a forbidden vagina, an orgasm, an orgy, a brothel.

Even in our sex-saturated society, and despite an increase in teenage pregnancies, young girls today, especially of the inner cities, are not having orgasms any more frequently than the young girls of my generation ever did. I didn't believe this either, until I interviewed counselors who are working with precisely this population.

Sex education in the schools and in the media is still being hotly contested and condemned by religious fundamentalists. There is some good information available; it is hard to find. Know that most women cannot have an orgasm without direct clitoral stimulation. Both men and women enjoy oral sex. And, in the era of AIDS and other sexually transmitted diseases, people should not have unprotected sex.

But they do, they do, young people especially.

10   The solution to unwanted pregnancies, epidemics of sexually transmitted diseases, rape, and incest involves educating the coming generations in radically different ways. Young men must be taught to refrain from using coercion of any sort in

matters sexual; young women must be taught how to resist such coercion.

The same experience—having sex—can have different consequences as a function of gender. For example, many young girls still lose their reputations for having sex; boys rarely do. (SOS— Same Old Shit.) Again, contrary to myth, women can and do sexually contract AIDS from men far more often and easily than men do from women, including from prostitutes. Women get pregnant, men don't, and mothers, no matter how young, often bear sole, lifelong responsibility for a child—more so than most fathers ever do. Women also bear the sole, life-long trauma of having given up a child for adoption.

Sexual desire is fluid, ever-changing, especially if it's more than a masturbation fantasy. Sex may mean one thing when you're eighteen, and an entirely different thing when you're sixty-five. No, all people do not lose their desire for orgasm or affection as they age; some do though, but they're often happy about it. However, health and leisure time free of worry are essential.

You may experience desire one way with one person, another way with another person—or differently over time with the same person.

Some men may experience more sexual desire when they're young, some women when they're older; some men may think the beginnings of sexual relationships are hot, some women that it's hotter when you've come to know and trust your partner.

Trust me, sex is more complex and simpler than you've been led to believe.

Even Dr. Freud said we are all bisexual. This doesn't mean that bisexuals swing from trees, first one way, then another. It means that we all have the potential to love, mate, and experience sexual pleasure with someone of our own sex too. No big deal.

Homophobia is the last acceptable prejudice. I have observed people of all classes, races, and political persuasions bond by mocking homosexuals and lesbians, or by boasting, loudly and non-stop, of their own heterosexuality.

Telling you that I'm either heterosexual or lesbian tells you very little about how often I have genital sex, or how I have orgasms, or what sex or love really means to me. Homosexuals are not what homophobes assume. What being a lesbian means probably has little to do with our culture's general perception of a lesbian.

Both physicists and philosophers tell us that things are not what they seem—sturdy tables, for instance, are no more than

15

molecules in motion—and that all things change, nothing remains the same.

20 I know women and men who were once heterosexual, parented children together, and who later became homosexuals. They still love their children, they are still good parents. I know closet homosexuals who legally married each other as cover, had children, continue to keep up the heterosexual pretense, but still prefer liaisons with others of their own sex.

Things are not always what they seem. Know that.

"NOT THE CHURCH, NOT THE STATE, WOMEN MUST DECIDE THEIR FATE"

No woman should be forced to have an abortion against her will. No woman should be prevented from having an abortion against her will.

This is what choice is about.

I believe in a woman's absolute right to *choose* whether and when she will have a child. Free choice means that a woman must have access to high-quality, physician-assisted, economically affordable, legal abortion *and* have the option of keeping the child she chooses to bear without having to pay an inhuman price for doing so.

25 Inhuman prices include: Children having children, having to drop out of school, having a child alone, without family or community, being condemned to poverty because we have no affordable day care, etc. It is also inhuman to have to surrender a child for adoption. This is a trauma from which many birth mothers never recover.

Abortion is not murder. It is the termination of a fetus. This is my view, and the view of the Supreme Court in 1973, in *Roe v. Wade*. However, if women do not have the legal right to decide whether a pregnancy is a future baby or an unacceptable burden, then it is women who are civilly dead.

Anti-abortion crusaders are more concerned with the rights of the unborn than with the rights—including the right to life—of the living. Abortion opponents actually champion the unborn at the expense of the pregnant woman and her other living children. Anti-abortionists do not demand that the state invade a *man's* body against his will for the sake of his living child—who may, for example, die without his father's kidney, lung, or bone marrow.

For at least 10,000 years of recorded history, most women were forced into biological motherhood, and, unlike men, were severely punished and sometimes killed for having sex outside of marriage.

It was therefore obvious to my generation of feminists that women needed to secure the right to safe, legal, and affordable birth control and abortions. Without them, how could a woman pursue life or liberty? She could not—and cannot. I feel as strongly about the importance of birth control and abortion today as I did thirty years ago.

Ideally, a woman's right to choose an abortion should be a civil, not just a privacy right. A woman must have the right to decide if and when to become a mother—not merely the right to choose abortion when her life or health are at stake.   30

Abortions have always existed. They have not always been illegal, but when they were, wealthy women had them anyway. Poor women either didn't, or risked death at the hands of back-alley practitioners.

In the 1950s, white teenagers who couldn't find or afford an illegal abortion, or who couldn't go through with one, had to endure endless recriminations from their parents; they *had* to drop out of high school or college—no one pregnant was allowed to attend. The "lucky" teenager got to marry someone who didn't really want to marry her and who wasn't ready to be a husband and father. Or she was forced to surrender her child for adoption.

The teenage father was rarely blamed—only the mother was.

I remember thinking, ah, if you're female, one slip and you're down for the count forever. One night of experimental lovemaking, one brief affair, one tragic episode of rape—and a young woman and her child could be condemned, permanently, to lesser, harsher lives.

In 1959, I traveled alone, between college exams, for an appointment with the famed underground physician Dr. Robert Spencer, of Pennsylvania. (Rumor had it that his daughter had died of a botched illegal abortion and that this was his way of making sure it didn't happen again to anyone else's daughter.) When I arrived, Dr. Spencer was "out of town." He frequently was. The man lived one step ahead of the law. I remember sitting on a swing in a nearby park, disconsolate, thinking that my life *as I wanted to live it* might be over if I couldn't find another abortionist.   35

Of course, I went to see Dr. Spencer alone, not with my boyfriend. Back then, men were not supposed to see women in curlers or cold cream, much less in childbirth or having an abortion.

Not all abortionists were trained physicians. They didn't always use anesthesia, and the pain was terrible, but you were more afraid of dying, or of having your parents find out. Some of us also had to contend with the sexual innuendos and gropings of the abortionist. The secrecy and the humiliation were profound.

Over a fourteen-year period, I had other abortions. And yes, I used birth control: first an IUD—until it became embedded in the wall of my uterus, then a diaphragm. Guess what? They failed.

Americans obtained the right to legal abortion in this country not because feminists fought and died for it, but because a sexually positive climate had been created in which both lawyers and physicians emerged who supported a woman's right to choose abortion. They had seen too many women die awful deaths from unsafe, illegal abortions. Perhaps, physicians also viewed abortion as a potentially lucrative practice. Perhaps, both men and women wanted *women* to experience sex without worry, not merely as a way to procreate.

40   My generation initially focused more on a woman's right to abortion than on her right to motherhood—or on the rights of racially persecuted women to resist sterilization, or the "ideal" of a small family. We were not wrong, nor were we right; no movement can do everything at once. Women were so universally obligated to become mothers, so universally condemned for pursuing independence that our feminist path was clear.

I have never softened about a woman's right to choose: not while I was pregnant, not after I gave birth to my son. I did not think that *my* right to choose to have a baby meant that *all* women had to make this same choice, nor did I think that if they didn't they were, somehow, not respecting my love for my own baby. I experience no contradiction between my *choosing* to have a child and the next woman's *choosing* not to have a child.

Make no mistake, I experienced giving birth as a sacred rite of passage.

In the late 1960s, before abortion was legal, I initiated some meetings to discuss how we could *physically* defend our then-underground clinics and networks. I should have kept notes. But who could have imagined that, only thirty years later, the right to a legal abortion would be under such deadly attack?

Never could I have imagined that, in 1997, abortion clinics and their employees would have to suffer prolonged off-site personal harassment, aggressive anti-abortion demonstrations and endless bomb threats, or that they'd be forced to install metal detectors and help train feminists to escort frightened women into and out of clinics.

Who could have foreseen that so many clinics across the country would be forced to close, would be bombed—not once, but repeatedly—that physicians and clinic workers would be forced to wear bulletproof vests, harassed, even killed so that women could exercise their rights to have a legal abortion. We could never have imagined that physicians and medical students might decide not to perform any abortions, because they seemed too dangerous, too much trouble.

Yes, freedom for women means trouble. But without such freedom, women would be in even more trouble.

Abortion has been under serious siege for more than twenty years, ever since Henry Hyde pushed through his infamous amendment to a federal funding bill that made it much harder for poor women to have federally subsidized abortions.

What can you do? There is more than one feminist thing to do. For example, a feminist might, honorably, do any of the following:

1. vote for pro-choice politicians, write them checks, and actively campaign for them;
2. escort women into and out of abortion clinics;
3. open abortion clinics—currently, at least 84 percent of U.S. counties do not have any abortion providers;
4. educate young men about their responsibilities as fathers; educate young women about their responsibilities, too;
5. pioneer research on more effective, less harmful methods of female birth control;
6. develop and distribute a male birth control pill;
7. lobby your church or religious congregation to change its stance on birth control and abortion;
8. campaign for a guaranteed above-minimum wage for all workers, so the choices are more affordable for everyone;
9. *personally* shelter, or become family to, a particular pregnant woman who wants to keep her baby, but who has no education, no money, and no family support—this option is reserved for saints;
10. become a physician willing to perform abortions; or a lawyer willing to represent physicians who perform abortions, clinic owners, and staff.

The list is endless. However, in my view, there are at least two feminist bottom lines. Rendering abortion illegal is not a feminist option, nor is forcing birth mothers to surrender their infants to adoption. Studies have persuaded me that birth mothers end up surrendering their peace of mind and mental health when they surrender their newborns for adoption. And even loved, well-cared-for adopted children suffer, psychologically, more than other children do.

50   Do I think the Second Wave of feminism worked as hard on obtaining the right to mother or parent under *feminist* working conditions as they did on keeping abortion legal? No, I don't. But obtaining the right to an abortion is far easier than redefining the family.

As Americans, we shun collective social solutions to what we still view as individual, private matters. We do so at our own peril.

You've inherited the consequence of our failure to redefine the family. The task is yours.

Questions for Thought and Writing

1. Chesler begins her essay with the statement that "Sexual pleasure is not a sin. Nor is it a sacrament. It is your right as a human being to exercise as you see fit." What does this introduction tell you about the "lens" through which she views sexuality? What kind of argument(s) does she consider to be invalid or irrelevant? Why? How does her position compare to the ways you have been taught to understand sexuality?

2. Chesler is part of what is known as second-wave feminism, which is generally understood to have begun in the 1960s and continued until the defeat of the ERA (Equal Rights Amendment) in 1982. What are the key issues she focuses on in this discussion? To what extent are they still important for your generation, whose feminists are called the third wave?

3. What are the many ways, according to Chesler, in which women—and not their male partners—suffer the consequences of unplanned pregnancies? How are these facts represented or neglected in contemporary debates about abortion?

4. Chesler ends her essay by advising a new generation of feminists that "You've inherited the consequence of our failure to redefine the family. The task is yours." Do you agree with Chesler that the family needs redefinition? If so, what changes do you think need to be made, particularly with regard to traditional notions of sexuality? If not, why?

How Men Have (a) Sex

John Stoltenberg

An address to college students

In the human species, how many sexes are there?
Answer A: *There are two sexes.*
Answer B: *There are three sexes.*
Answer C: *There are four sexes.*
Answer D: *There are seven sexes.*
Answer E: *There are as many sexes as there are people.*

I'd like to take you, in an imaginary way, to look at a different world, somewhere else in the universe, a place inhabited by a life form that very much resembles us. But these creatures grow up with a peculiar knowledge. They know that they have been born in an infinite variety. They know, for instance, that in their genetic material they are born with hundreds of different chromosome formations at the point in each cell that we would say determines their "sex." These creatures don't just come in XX or XY; they also come in XXY and XYY and XXX plus a long list of "mosaic" variations in which some cells in a creature's body have one combination and other cells have another. Some of these creatures are born with chromosomes that aren't even quite X or Y because a little bit of one chromosome goes and gets joined to another. There are hundreds of different combinations, and though all are not fertile, quite a number of them are. The creatures in this world enjoy their individuality; they delight in the fact that they are not divisible into distinct categories. So when another newborn arrives with an esoterically rare chromosomal formation, there is a little celebration: "Aha," they say, "another sign that we are each unique."

These creatures also live with the knowledge that they are born with a vast range of genital formations. Between their legs are tissue structures that vary along a continuum, from clitorises with a vulva through all possible combinations and gradations to penises with a scrotal sac. These creatures live with an understanding that their genitals all developed prenatally from exactly the same little nub of embryonic tissue called a genital tubercle, which grew and developed under the influence of varying amounts of the hormone androgen. These creatures honor and respect everyone's natural-born genitalia—including what we would describe as a microphallus or a clitoris several inches long. What these creatures find amazing and precious is that because everyone's genitals stem from the same embryonic tissue, the nerves inside all their genitals got wired very much alike, so these nerves of touch just go crazy upon contact in a way that resonates completely between them. "My gosh," they think, "you must feel something in your genital tubercle that intensely resembles what I'm feeling in my genital tubercle." Well, they don't exactly *think* that in so many words; they're actually quite heavy into their feelings at that point; but they do feel very connected—throughout all their wondrous variety.

I could go on. I could tell you about the variety of hormones that course through their bodies in countless different patterns and proportions, both before birth and throughout their lives— the hormones that we call "sex hormones" but that they call "individuality inducers." I could tell you how these creatures think about reproduction: For part of their lives, some of them are quite capable of gestation, delivery, and lactation; and for part of their lives, some of them are quite capable of insemination; and for part or all of their lives, some of them are not capable of any of those things—so these creatures conclude that it would be silly to lock anyone into a lifelong category based on a capability variable that may or may not be utilized and that in any case changes over each lifetime in a fairly uncertain and idiosyncratic way. These creatures are not oblivious to reproduction; but nor do they spend their lives constructing a self-definition around their variable reproductive capacities. They don't have to, because what is truly unique about these creatures is that they are capable of having a sense of personal identity without struggling to fit into a group identity based on how they were born. These creatures are quite happy, actually. They don't worry about sorting *other* creatures into categories, so they don't have to worry about whether they are measuring up to some category they themselves are supposed to belong to. . . .

Perhaps you have guessed the point of this science fiction: Anatomically, each creature in the imaginary world I have been describing could be an identical twin of every human being on earth. These creatures, in fact, *are us*—in every way except socially and politically. The way they are born is the way we are born. And we are not born belonging to one or the other of two sexes. We are born into a physiological continuum on which there is no discrete and definite point that you can call "male" and no discrete and definite point that you can call "female." If you look at all the variables in nature that are said to determine human "sex," you can't possibly find one that will unequivocally split the species into two. Each of the so-called criteria of sexedness is itself a continuum—including chromosomal variables, genital and gonadal variations, reproductive capacities, endocrinological proportions, and any other criterion you could think of. Any or all of these different variables may line up in any number of ways, and all of the variables may vary independently of one another.[1]

What does all this mean? It means, first of all, a logical   5 dilemma: Either human "male" and human "female" actually exist in nature as fixed and discrete entities and you can credibly base an entire social and political system on those absolute natural categories, or else the variety of human sexedness is infinite. As Andrea Dworkin wrote in 1974:

> The discovery is, of course, that "man" and "woman" are fictions, caricatures, cultural constructs. As models they are reductive, totalitarian, inappropriate to human becoming. As roles they are static, demeaning to the female, dead-ended for male and female both.[2]

The conclusion is inescapable:

> We are, clearly, a multisexed species which has its sexuality spread along a vast continuum where the elements called male and female are not discrete.[3]

"We are . . . a multisexed species." I first read those words a little over ten years ago—and that liberating recognition saved my life.

All the time I was growing up, I knew that there was something really problematical in my relationship to manhood. Inside, deep inside, I never believed I was fully male—I never believed I was growing up enough of a man. I believed that someplace out there, in other men, there was something that was genuine authentic all-American manhood—the real stuff—but I didn't have it: not enough of it to convince *me* anyway, even if I managed to be fairly convincing to those around me. I felt like an impostor, like a fake. I agonized a lot about not feeling male enough, and I had no idea then how much I was not alone.

Then I read those words—those words that suggested to me for the first time that the notion of manhood is a cultural delusion, a baseless belief, a false front, a house of cards. It's not true.

The category I was trying so desperately to belong to, to be a member of in good standing—it doesn't exist. Poof. Now you see it, now you don't. Now you're terrified you're not really part of it; now you're free, you don't have to worry anymore. However removed you feel inside from "authentic manhood," it doesn't matter. What matters is the center inside yourself—and how you live, and how you treat people, and what you can contribute as you pass through life on this earth, and how honestly you love, and how carefully you make choices. Those are the things that really matter. Not whether you're a real man. There's no such thing. . . .

10   Penises and ejaculate and prostate glands occur in nature, but the notion that these anatomical traits comprise a sex—a discrete class, separate and distinct, metaphysically divisible from some other sex, *the* "other sex"—is simply that: a notion, an idea. The penises exist; the male sex does not. The male sex is socially constructed. It is a political entity that flourishes only through acts of force and sexual terrorism. Apart from the global inferiorization and subordination of those who are defined as "nonmale," the idea of personal membership in the male sex class would have no recognizable meaning. It would make no sense. No one could be a member of it and no one would think they *should* be a member of it. There would be no male sex to belong to. That doesn't mean there wouldn't still be penises and ejaculate and prostate glands and such. It simply means that the center of our selfhood would not be required to reside inside an utterly fictitious category—a category that only seems real to the extent that those outside it are put down. . . .

Male sexual identity is the conviction or belief, held by most people born with penises, that they are male and not female, that they belong to the male sex. In a society predicated on the notion that there are two "opposite" and "complementary" sexes, this idea not only makes sense, it *becomes* sense; the very idea of a male sexual identity produces sensation, produces the meaning of sensation, becomes the meaning of how one's body feels. The sense and the sensing of a male sexual identity is at once mental and physical, at once public and personal. Most people born with a penis between their legs grow up aspiring to feel and act unambiguously male, longing to belong to the sex that is male and daring not to belong to the sex that is not, and feeling this urgency for a visceral and constant verification of their male sexual identity—for a fleshy connection to manhood—as the driving force of their life. The drive does not originate in the anatomy. The sensations derive from the idea. The idea gives the feelings social meaning; the idea determines which sensations shall be sought.

People born with penises must strive to make the idea of male sexual identity personally real by doing certain deeds, actions that are valued and chosen because they produce the desired feeling of belonging to a sex that is male and not female. Male sexual identity is experienced only in sensation and action, in feeling and doing, in eroticism and ethics. The feeling of belonging to a male sex encompasses both sensations that are explicitly "sexual" and those that are not ordinarily regarded as such. And there is a tacit social value system according to which certain acts are chosen because they make an individual's sexedness feel real and certain other acts are eschewed because they numb it. That value system is the ethics of male sexual identity— and it may well be the social origin of all injustice. . . .

So much of most men's sexuality is tied up with gender-actualizing—with feeling like a real man—that they can scarcely recall an erotic sensation that had no gender-specific cultural meaning. As most men age, they learn to cancel out and deny erotic sensations that are not specifically linked to what they think a real man is supposed to feel. An erotic sensation unintentionally experienced in a receptive, communing mode—instead of in an aggressive and controlling and violative mode, for instance—can shut down sensory systems in an instant. An erotic sensation unintentionally linked to the "wrong" sex of another person can similarly mean sudden numbness. Acculturated male sexuality has a built-in fail-safe: Either its political context reifies manhood or the experience cannot be felt as sensual. Either the act creates his sexedness or it does not compute as a sex act. So he tenses up, pumps up, steels himself against the dread that he be found not male enough. And his dread is not stupid; for he sees what happens to people when they are treated as nonmales.

My point is that sexuality does not *have* a gender; it *creates* a gender. It creates for those who adapt to it in narrow and specified ways the confirmation for the individual of belonging to the idea of one sex or the other. So-called male sexuality is a learned connection between specific physical sensations and the idea of a male sexual identity. To achieve this male sexual identity requires that an individual *identify with* the class of males—that is, accept as one's own the values and interests of the class. A fully realized male sexual identity also requires *nonidentification with* that which is perceived to be nonmale, or female. A male must not identify with females; he must not associate with females in feeling, interest, or action. His identity as a member of the sex class men absolutely depends on the extent to which he repudiates the values and interests of the sex class "women."

15   I think somewhere inside us all, we have always known something about the relativity of gender. Somewhere inside us all, we know that our bodies harbor deep resemblances, that we are wired inside to respond in a profound harmony to the resonance of eroticism inside the body of someone near us. Physiologically, we are far more alike than different. The tissue structures that have become labial and clitoral or scrotal and penile have not forgotten their common ancestry. Their sensations are of the same source. The nerve networks and interlock of capillaries throughout our pelvises electrify and engorge as if plugged in together and pumping as one. That's what we feel when we feel one another's feelings. That's what can happen during sex that is mutual, equal, reciprocal, profoundly communing.

So why is it that some of us with penises think it's sexy to pressure someone into having sex against their will? Some of us actually get harder the harder the person resists. Some of us with penises actually believe that some of us without penises want to be raped. And why is it that some of us with penises think it's sexy to treat other people as objects, as things to be bought and sold, impersonal bodies to be possessed and consumed for our sexual pleasure? Why is it that some of us with penises are aroused by sex tinged with rape, and sex commoditized by pornography? Why do so many of us with penises want such antisexual sex?

There's a reason, of course. We have to make a lie seem real. It's a very big lie. We each have to do our part. Otherwise the lie will look like the lie that it is. Imagine the enormity of what we each must do to keep the lie alive in each of us. Imagine the awesome challenge we face to make the lie a social fact. It's a lifetime mission for each of us born with a penis: to have sex in such a way that the male sex will seem real—and so that we'll feel like a real part of it.

We all grow up knowing exactly what kind of sex that is. It's the kind of sex you can have when you pressure or bully someone else into it. So it's a kind of sex that makes your will more important than theirs. That kind of sex helps the lie a lot. That kind of sex makes you feel like someone important and it turns the other person into someone unimportant. That kind of sex makes you feel real, not like a fake. It's a kind of sex men have in order to feel like a real man.

There's also the kind of sex you can have when you force   20
someone and hurt someone and cause someone suffering and humiliation. Violence and hostility in sex help the lie a lot too. Real men are aggressive in sex. Real men get cruel in sex. Real men use their penises like weapons in sex. Real men leave bruises. Real men think it's a turn-on to threaten harm. A brutish push can make an erection feel really hard. That kind of sex helps the lie a lot. That kind of sex makes you feel like someone who is powerful and it turns the other person into someone powerless. That kind of sex makes you feel dangerous and in control—like you're fighting a war with an enemy and if you're mean enough you'll win but if you let up you'll lose your manhood. It's a kind of sex men have *in order to have* a manhood.

There's also the kind of sex you can have when you pay your money into a profit system that grows rich displaying and exploiting the bodies and body parts of people without penises for the sexual entertainment of people with. Pay your money and watch. Pay your money and imagine. Pay your money and get real turned on. Pay your money and jerk off. That kind of sex helps the lie a lot. It helps support an industry committed to making people with penises believe that people without are sluts who just want to be ravished and reviled—an industry dedicated to maintaining a sex-class system in which men believe themselves sex machines and men believe women are mindless fuck tubes. That kind of sex helps the lie a lot. It's like buying Krugerrands as a vote of confidence for white supremacy in South Africa.

And there's one more thing: That kind of sex makes the lie indelible—burns it onto your retinas right adjacent to your brain—makes you remember it and makes your body respond to it and so it makes you believe that the lie is in fact true: You really are a real man. That slavish and submissive creature there spreading her legs is really not. You and that creature have nothing in common. That creature is an alien inanimate thing, but your penis is completely real and alive. Now you can come. Thank god almighty—you have a sex at last.

Now, I believe there are many who are sick at heart over what I have been describing. There are many who were born with penises who want to stop collaborating in the sex-class system that needs us to need these kinds of sex. I believe some of you want to stop living out the big lie, and you want to know how. Some of you long to touch truthfully. Some of you want sexual relationships in your life that are about intimacy and joy, ecstasy and equality—not antagonism and alienation. So what I have to say next I have to say to you.

When you use sex to have a sex, the sex you have is likely to make you feel crummy about yourself. But when you have sex in which you are not struggling with your partner in order to act out "real manhood," the sex you have is more likely to bring you close.

This means several specific things:

1. *Consent is absolutely essential.* If both you and your partner have not freely given your informed consent to the sex you are about to have, you can be quite certain that the sex you go ahead and have will make you strangers to each other. How do you know if there's consent? You ask. You ask again if you're sensing any doubt. Consent to do one thing isn't consent to do another. So you keep communicating, in clear words. And you don't take anything for granted.

2. *Mutuality is absolutely essential.* Sex is not something you do *to* someone. Sex is not a one-way transitive verb, with a subject, you, and an object, the body you're with. Sex that is mutual is not about doing and being done to; it's about being-with and feeling-with. You have to really be there to experience what is happening between and within the two of you—between every part of you and within both your whole bodies. It's a matter of paying attention—as if you are paying attention to someone who matters.

3. *Respect is absolutely essential.* In the sex that you have, treat your partner like a real person who, like you, has real feelings—feelings that matter as much as your own. You may or may not love—but you must always respect. You must respect the integrity of your partner's body. It is not yours for the taking. It belongs to someone real. And you do not get ownership of your partner's body just because you are having sex—or just because you have had sex.

25   For those who are closer to the beginning of your sex lives than to the middle or the end, many things are still changing for you about how you have sex, with whom, why or why not, what you like or dislike, what kind of sex you want to have more of. In the next few years, you are going to discover and decide a lot. I say "discover" because no one can tell you what you're going to

find out about yourself in relation to sex—and I say "decide" because virtually without knowing it you are going to be laying down habits and patterns that will probably stay with you for the rest of your life. You're at a point in your sexual history that you will never be at again. You don't know what you don't know yet. And yet you are making choices whose consequences for your particular sexuality will be sealed years from now.

I speak to you as someone who is closer to the middle of my sexual history. As I look back, I see that I made many choices that I didn't know I was making. And as I look at men who are near my age, I see that what has happened to many of them is that their sex lives are stuck in deep ruts that began as tiny fissures when they were young. So I want to conclude by identifying what I believe are three of the most important decisions about your sexuality that you can make when you are at the beginning of your sexual history. However difficult these choices may seem to you now, I promise you they will only get more difficult as you grow older. I realize that what I'm about to give is some quite unsolicited nuts-and-bolts advice. But perhaps it will spare you, later on in your lives, some of the obsessions and emptiness that have claimed the sexual histories of many men just a generation before you. Perhaps it will not help, I don't know; but I hope very much that it will.

First, you can start choosing now not to let your sexuality be manipulated by the pornography industry. I've heard many unhappy men talk about how they are so hooked on pornography and obsessed with it that they are virtually incapable of a human erotic contact. And I have heard even more men talk about how, when they do have sex with someone, the pornography gets in the way, like a mental obstacle, like a barrier preventing a full experience of what's really happening between them and their partner. The sexuality that the pornography industry needs you to have is not about communicating and caring; it's about "pornographizing" people—objectifying and conquering them, not being with them as a person. You do not have to buy into it.

Second, you can start choosing now not to let drugs and alcohol numb you through your sex life. Too many men, as they age, become incapable of having sex with a clear head. But you need your head clear—to make clear choices, to send clear messages, to read clearly what's coming in on a clear channel between you and your partner. Sex is no time for your awareness to sign off. And another thing: Beware of relying on drugs or alcohol to give you "permission" to have sex, or to trick your body into feeling something that it's not, or so you won't have to take responsibility for what you're feeling or for the sex that you're about to have. If you can't take sober responsibility for your part in a sexual encounter, you probably shouldn't be having it—and you certainly shouldn't be zonked out of your mind *in order* to have it.

Third, you can start choosing now not to fixate on fucking—especially if you'd really rather have sex in other, noncoital ways. Sometimes men have coital sex—penetration and thrusting then ejaculating inside someone—not because they particularly feel like it but because they feel they *should* feel like it: It's expected that if you're the man, you fuck. And if you don't fuck, you're not a man. The corollary of this cultural imperative is that if two people don't have intercourse, they have not had real sex. That's baloney, of course, but the message comes down hard, especially inside men's heads: Fucking is *the* sex act, the act in which you act out what sex is supposed to be—and what sex you're supposed to be. . . .

30   I invite you too to resist the lie. I invite you too to become an erotic traitor to male supremacy.

Endnotes

1. My source for the foregoing information about so-called sex determinants in the human species is a series of interviews I conducted with the sexologist Dr. John Money in Baltimore, Maryland, in 1979 for an article I wrote called "The Multisex Theorem," which was published in a shortened version as "Future Genders" in *Omni* magazine, May 1980, pp. 67–73ff.
2. Dworkin, Andrea. *Woman Hating* (New York: Dutton, 1974), p. 174.
3. Dworkin, *Woman Hating*, p. 183.

Questions for Thought and Writing

1. Stoltenberg argues that there is no "male sex," but "only the idea of it," an idea that "only seems real to the extent that those outside it are put down." Write about the traits and actions you associate with the male sex, then reconsider the things you identified. To what extent are they based on superiority over "nonmales?"
2. In the "science fiction" part of his essay, Stoltenberg's otherworldly creatures believe that it would be "silly" to "spend their

lives constructing a self-definition" around their reproductive capacities. To what extent do you believe men and women in contemporary America engage in this practice? How would your own sense of femininity or masculinity change if you decided not to (or were unable to) have children?

3. According to Stoltenberg, a man's identity "as a member of the sex class men absolutely depends on the extent to which he repudiates the values and interests of the sex class 'women.'" Consider a man you know and admire in terms of this claim. What values and interests does he associate himself with? To what extent does he avoid or discourage being associated with traditionally female values and interests? (If you are a man, you might want to consider yourself in this essay.)

4. What are the differences between sex in which men "act out real manhood" and sex that is "about intimacy and joy, ecstasy and equality"? What actions does Stoltenberg recommend men take in order to be able to "touch truthfully"? Why are these actions so difficult in contemporary culture?

ISSUES

This Issues section opens with Mercedes E. Steedman's "Who's on Top? Heterosexual Practices and Male Dominance During the Sex Act," which highlights the contradictory messages about receptivity and control delivered by contemporary popular culture to women about their sexuality and demonstrates, among other insights, how female sexuality is pervasively viewed through a lens of masculine desires. In "Is There a Muslim Sexuality? Changing Constructions of Sexuality in Egyptian Bedouin Weddings," Lila Abu-Lughod explains that, like American ones, Bedouin weddings work to "produce" sexuality in culturally critical ways. A central element of her argument is a warning about the dangers of "essentializing" sexuality or race in any culture. D. Travers Scott in "Le Freak, C'Est Chic! Le Fag, Quelle Drag!: Celebrating the Collapse of Homosexual Identity" argues that "homosexuality's over." By focusing on widespread gender "border crossings" in dress and behavior, he speculates about how much longer mainstream society will tolerate rigid definitions of sex and gender.

Who's on Top? Heterosexual Practices and Male Dominance During the Sex Act

Mercedes E. Steedman

. . . Recent evidence from anatomical examination of male and female muscle construction in the genital area seems to indicate that the vasocongestion process (the engorgement of genital muscle tissue with blood) affects analogous muscles in the penile shaft and in the vaginal-labial system. The physiological processes of vasocongestion and myotonia (muscle spasm) are actually more similar for the two sexes than different.

Survey evidence has suggested that assertive sexual behaviour is still perceived as unfeminine by many women. As a result, women sacrifice sexual pleasure for fear of being perceived as "cheap." The good girl/bad girl dichotomy perpetuates the ideal of innocence as a component of femininity. Yet innocence and restraint are not effective behaviour if one is seeking to be orgasmic. Only 30 percent of Hite's sample reported orgasm through intercourse alone (Hite, 1976:229), and Seymour Fisher's study of 300 women (1972) reported a corresponding figure of only 20 percent. (Although other surveys show slightly higher figures for coital orgasm, it continues to be a minority response.) (See Fisher, 1973.)

SEXUAL POWER/SOCIAL POWER

Both men and women are asked to accept a code of social passivity for women during the act of coitus. Shere Hite comments on the contradictory message that men give here. "Although many men are very angry with women and suffer profound discomfort due to women's passivity regarding sex—possibly because of buried feelings of guilt and defensiveness, knowing that women are being exploited—most men do not overtly connect this with the need for improving women's status. Most men prefer to think that the problem is simply a lingering vestige of 'Victorian morality'—and prefer to believe that somehow women can be sexually 'free' even though they are not also economically and politically free" (Hite, 1981:736). As long as women remain economically dependent on men, it is risky for them to challenge or threaten men's masculinity in the bedroom. So there is collusion between men and women. Rubin encountered this attitude in her interviews with working-class wives: "One thing I know he likes is that he taught me mostly all I know about sex, so that makes him feel good." Rubin commented: "That seems a strange thing to say when you were married for some years before." The woman replied, "Yeah, I guess you'd think so. Well, you know, he likes to feel that way so why shouldn't he, and why shouldn't I let him?" (Rubin, 1976:142).

In addition, men and women alike continue to feel ambiguous about women's sexual aggression. Few studies have observed the man's reaction to a woman's assertiveness in the bedroom. Hunt's 1974 survey suggests that the norms for women's passivity are changing; he found that women did engage in a greater variety of sexual behaviour than they had some 20 years ago, but their comfort level in doing so seemed closely linked to their education, religiosity, urbanism, income, and age.[1] Allgeier and Fogel's 1978 study of coital positions and sex roles suggests that the changes observed by Hunt remain superficial. Their study of middle-class men and women found that "females rated the woman as dirtier, less respectable, less moral, less good, less desirable as a wife and less desirable as a mother when she was on top than when she was beneath the man during intercourse" (Allgeier and Fogel, 1978:589). Women (but not men) discriminated against the woman-on-top position, despite research evidence that suggests that women enjoy a higher orgasmic response rate when they are on top. A study of American university students conducted by Clinton Jessor (1978) found that women believed men would be "turned off" by women's sexual assertiveness, despite evidence that suggested the opposite to be true (Jessor, 1978:118-28). A woman's femininity is still partly perceived as residing in her receptivity, not in her control. Interestingly, this perception seems to influence women more than men. It would seem that the traditional dictates of appropriate, moral sex behaviour continue to outweigh reason and the dictates of "liberated" sexuality.

The thing is, there is more at stake here than a good orgasm. 5
Men and women alike are caught up in the view that women must remain the standard-bearers for morally correct behaviour in our society, while pornography pushes the opposite view—that women are sexual aggressors and whores. Men and women alike

live with these contradictory conceptions of women's sexuality, and the consequences are often confusing for both. One man said to Lillian Rubin: "It isn't that I mind her letting me know when she wants it, but she isn't very subtle about it. I mean, she could let me know in a nice, feminine way" (Rubin, 1976:143). Referring to oral sex, one respondent stated, "No, Alice isn't that kind of girl. Jesus, you shouldn't ask questions like that. She wasn't brought up to go for all that fancy stuff. . . . There's plenty of women out there to do that kind of stuff with. You can meet them in any bar any time you want to. You don't have to marry those kind" (Rubin, 1976:141). The "liberated" sexuality of the eighties remains a cloak for traditional views of sexuality—and control of women. This control of women is maintained by the active suppression of their sexuality, by the ignoring of their sexuality, or by the rationalization of women's inability to reach orgasm in the traditional sex act, and by a medicalized language that labels women's (and men's) behaviour as "dysfunctional." "Sexual liberation" may have brought in some new rules, but the game remains the same.

Language further confuses the issue. The symbols and verbal clues we use ostensibly communicate real experience, yet they serve to maintain a certain image of sex. For example, the word "foreplay" suggests a prelude to a main event—penetration and orgasm. This language reinforces a conception of the sex act as sequential behaviour. A term such as "impotence" conveys a message about male sexual power (or the lack of it), and links men's power to their ability to maintain an erection. The public representation of the sensual intervenes in the intimate relations of the couple. Masculine dominance is reaffirmed in the erotic imagery of advertising and pornography. As the unreal becomes real, our perceptions of the sexes are distorted. The ad in *Penthouse* magazine for a life-size doll (called "Heaven") epitomizes this fantasy view of sexual experience: "Heaven has only one function in life, to please you, . . . and her only passion is your endless pleasure, your total release!" The ad goes on to say, "In her sultry tones, she'll marvel at your body, plead for mercy when you hurt her, purr from the pleasure you give her and moan with ecstasy the instant she takes your manhood into her warm, willing mouth."[2] The image of feminine sexual submission portrayed here may seem extreme and distorted, but it does reinforce the point that male power is legitimized in popular sexual imagery, and that little room is accorded to female sexual expression.

The masculine dominance of sexual imagery continues to influence our conception of sexual arousal. Sexual images of women are usually constructed for and by the ignorant male observer, to serve as stimulants for solitary sex. As a result they portray women in passive and often vulnerable poses. They present an image of sexual arousal in women that is impossible to duplicate in the actual act of coitus. However, when women's sexual behaviour is perceived as assertive, as in the image of engulfment of the penis by the vagina, it is usually portrayed by pornographic imagery as threatening and castrating. The affirmation of female sexual power remains limited to images constructed by feminist cultural workers, and therefore outside the mainstream. The images that "teach" women what their sexual body language should be are the images of a masculine culture. Pornography, recently challenged by feminists, requires our serious examination for, as Roz Coward so succinctly puts it, "Pornography as a representation of the sexual sets up, reinforces and sexualizes certain behaviors and certain images as erotic and sexual" (Coward, 1982:9–21).

Despite the expectation of intimacy during the sex act, the two sexes remain strangers. Many men remain uncertain of women's behaviour during the sex act; they often misinterpret the signals given by the woman. Hite reports men's accounts of how they know their partner has had an orgasm: "all the women I've ever known have uncontrollable erection of their nipples when they climax"; "she rapidly moves her hips, makes a sound deep in her throat, and smiles"; "she will become short-breathed and many times will dig her fingernails into my shoulders" (Hite, 1981:637–38). While these descriptions may accurately portray arousal stages in women, they in no way represent orgasmic behaviour. . . .

The "discovery" of the female orgasmic potential has not served to free women from sexual repression, for this "discovery" has occurred within a climate of masculine dominance. What this has often meant, in effect, is that a woman's orgasm is used as an indicator of her partner's success as a lover. Given this, it is not surprising that 53 percent of Shere Hite's female informants reported "faking" orgasm at least some of the time (Hite, 1976:257). When a partner's manhood is at stake, a woman does not in fact have ownership of her orgasmic response (any more than she has control over her economic life). Working-class women, more vulnerable to the dictates of men's egos, are quick to assess the significance of this. "I rarely have climaxes. But if it didn't bother my husband it wouldn't bother me. I keep trying to tell him that I know it is not his fault, that he's really a good lover. I keep telling him it's something the matter with me, not with him. But it scares me because he doesn't believe it, and I worry he might leave me for a woman who will have climaxes for him" (Rubin, 1976:152). . . .

Endnotes

1. Hunt (1974:198); see also Petras (1978), for a review of these findings.
2. This ad often appears in *Penthouse,* under the title "Heaven Can't Wait."

Bibliography

Allgeier, Elizabeth Rice, and Arthur F. Fogel. 1978. "Coital Positions and Sex Roles: Responses to Cross Sex Behavior in Bed." *Journal of Consulting and Clinical Psychology* 46 (no. 3):589.

Coward, R. 1982. "Sexual Violence and Sexuality." *Feminist Review* II (summer): 9–21.

Fisher, Seymour. 1973. *Understanding the Female Orgasm.* New York: Bantam.

Hite, Shere. 1976. *The Hite Report: A Nationwide Study on Female Sexuality.* New York: Macmillan.

Hite, Shere. 1981. *The Hite Report on Male Sexuality.* New York: Dell.

Hunt, Morton. 1974. *Sexual Behaviour in the 1970's.* Chicago: Playboy Press.

Jessor, Clinton J. 1978. "Male Responses to Direct Verbal Sexual Initiatives of Females." *Journal of Sex Research* 14 (no. 2):118–128.

Petras, J. 1978. *The Social Meaning of Human Sexuality.* Boston: Allyn and Bacon.

Rubin, Lillian Breslow. 1976. *Worlds of Pain.* New York: Basic Books.

Questions for Thought and Writing

1. Steedman's argument that "a woman's femininity is still partly perceived as residing in her receptivity, not in her control" is based largely on research from the 1970s. To what extent do you believe this circumstance to be true in contemporary culture? What examples from popular media could you use to support your conclusion?
2. What are the contradictory messages women in contemporary culture get sent about their sexuality? What are some of the sources of these messages? Consider your own perceptions about appropriate ways for women to think and behave sexually. Are they influenced by these contradictions?

3. Steedman states that "the images that 'teach' women what their sexual body language should be are the images of a masculine culture" and that even women's own sexual responses are used primarily to gauge not female pleasure but rather male performance. Identify images of or language about women from advertisements that seem to represent masculine ideas of female sexuality. How might a feminist artist revise these materials? If you can, cite some ads with alternate messages.

Is There a Muslim Sexuality? Changing Constructions of Sexuality in Egyptian Bedouin Weddings

Lila Abu-Lughod

The project of defining the nature of Muslim Arab sexuality— what it is or what it should be—has engaged many people with different stakes and interests. Western discourses have tended to contrast the negative sexuality of "the East" with the positive sexuality of the West. French colonial settlers in Algeria depicted Algerian women in pornographic postcards that suggested a fantastic Oriental world of perverse and excessive sexuality (Alloula 1986). Western feminists concerned with global issues dwell on veiling and other practices like clitoridectomy found in the Muslim Arab world as signs of the repressive control over or exploitation of women's sexuality (e.g., Daly 1978).

From the Muslim world itself come other discourses on Arab Muslim sexuality. These include religious and legal texts and pronouncements, but also, more recently, some critical studies by intellectuals and scholars. How different the understandings can be is clear from two important books. One, by a Tunisian scholar with a background in psychoanalytic thought, argues that the misogynist practices of sexuality in the Muslim world are corruptions of the ideals of the Quran and other religious texts (Bouhdiba 1985). The second, by a Moroccan sociologist, argues from a feminist perspective that the legal and sacred texts themselves, like the erotic

texts that flourished in the medieval period, carry negative messages about and perpetuate certain consistent attitudes toward the
bodies and behavior of Muslim women (Sabbah 1984).

What these various discourses on Arab Muslim sexuality, by
outsiders and insiders, defenders and critics, share is the presumption that there is such a thing as a "Muslim sexuality." An
anthropologist like myself, familiar with the tremendous variety
of communities to be found in the regions composing the Muslim
Arab world, would have to question this presumption. Neither Islam nor sexuality should be essentialized—taken as things with
intrinsic and transhistorical meanings. Rather, both the meaning
of Islam and the constructions of sexuality must be understood in
their specific historical and local contexts.[1]

To show why I argue this, I will analyze wedding rituals in a
community of Awlad 'Ali Bedouin in Egypt's Western Desert—a
community I worked in over a period of twelve years. Weddings
are the highlight of social life, awaited with anticipation and participated in with enthusiasm. Each wedding is different. And each
wedding is a personal affair of great moment for the bride and
groom, even if only one dramatic event in what will be their marriage, lasting for years. Yet public rituals in face-to-face societies
are also arenas where people play out their social and political relations. There are other discourses and practices related to sexuality in this Bedouin community but none so powerfully seek to
produce, and are now transforming, people's experiences of sexuality and gender relations as weddings do. Without pretending
that a symbolic analysis exhausts the meaning of weddings for
the individuals involved, I would still insist that such an analysis
of Awlad 'Ali weddings is useful: It reveals both how sexuality is
constructed by the symbols and practices of members of particular communities and how these symbols and practices themselves
are open to change and political contestation. Islam, it will be
seen, figures not so much as a blueprint for sexuality as a weapon
in changing relations of power.

SEXUALITY AND CULTURAL IDENTITY

In the twelve years between 1978 and 1990 that I had been regularly returning to this community of Arab Muslim sedentarized
herders in Egypt, the same questions had been asked of me,
sometimes even by the same people, as were asked in the first
month of my stay. Usually in the context of a gathering of older
women, one old woman would lean toward me and ask if I were

married. After a short discussion of the fact that I was not, she or another older woman would ask me the next intense question: "Where you come from, does the bridegroom do it with the finger or with 'it'?" The first time they asked me this, I did not know what they meant by "it" and they had a good laugh. The question that followed inevitably in such conversations was, "And do they do it during the daytime or at night?" They were asking about weddings and particularly about the defloration of the virgin bride, which is for them the central moment of a wedding.[2]

In the obsessive concern with whether they do it with the finger or "it," at night or during the daytime, is a clue to one of the things the discourse on this aspect of sexuality has become as the Awlad 'Ali Bedouins have greater contact and interaction with outsiders, primarily their Egyptian peasant and urban neighbors. Whatever its former or current meaning within the community, meanings I will analyze in the following section, the central rite of weddings has now also become a marker of cultural identity—essential to the Awlad Ali's self-defining discourse on what makes them distinctive.

Individuals vary in how they evaluate their differences from their compatriots. When I met the Bedouin representative to the Egyptian Parliament, a sophisticated man in sunglasses whose long contact with other Egyptians showed in his dialect, he assured me that there were a few Bedouin practices that were wrong: One was that they used the finger in the daytime. But he defended the practice by saying that it reminded girls to be careful. Another respected man of the community explained to me that "entering" with the finger was wrong. "We're the only ones who do it this way," he noted. Then he added, "Nothing in our religion says you should." By way of excuse, though, he said, "But the faster the groom does it, the better—the more admired he is because it means he wasn't timid or cowardly." Even women occasionally complained that it was stupid how the female wedding guests waited and waited, just to see that drop of blood. But they too defended the ceremony, saying that the defloration had to take place in the afternoon so that everyone could see and there would be no doubts about the reputation of the girl. Their horror at the idea that the groom would use "it" came from their fear that it would be more painful for the bride.

Besides asking whether they do it with the finger or "it," day or night, the women I knew often asked whether, where I came from, there was anyone with the bride to hold her down. They were surprised to hear that she needed no one and marveled that she wasn't afraid to be alone with the man. Among themselves, they almost always had a few older women, usually aunts or close neighbors of the groom and bride, in the room with the bride when the groom came to her. There in theory to hold the bride, these women also end up giving advice to the groom and making sure that he knew what to do so that everything—the display of the blood on the cloth—would turn out right.

For their part, somewhat like most Europeans and Americans, non-Bedouin Egyptians and assimilated Awlad 'Ali from the agricultural areas find Bedouin weddings scandalous and distasteful. Bedouin women are not unaware of these views and the men discussed previously were probably reacting defensively to them. These outsiders may laugh at some customs but they are embarrassed by others. After one wedding in the community in which I was living, the bride's aunt, who had spent most of her life in a non-Bedouin provincial town, talked about the wedding and some of the customs she had witnessed that made her laugh "until her stomach hurt." She obviously considered her new in-laws backward.[3]

10   What seemed to disturb her most was the public nature of what she felt should be private. She thought it humiliating, for example, that at night, the young men from the community (peers of the bridegroom) hung around the room, listening, shining a flashlight under the door and through the window, and generally being disruptive. More horrible to her was the public display of the blood-stained cloth. "It was incredible," she exclaimed. "After the defloration didn't you hear my son saying to his aunt when she went to hang the cloth on the tent ropes, 'It's shameful, my aunt, it's shameful to put the cloth out for people to see.' " Like other urban and rural Egyptians, she thought that the bride and groom should be brought together at night and left alone.

Although other Egyptians and Americans might feel that such privacy is more civilized, the Awlad 'Ali women I knew did not see it that way. Bedouin women were scandalized by the secrecy of night deflorations, the immediate and explicit link such weddings make between marriage and sexual intercourse, and what they view as either the total vulnerability of the poor bride forced to be alone with a man or, even worse, the bride's immodest desire for a man. They knew that instead of struggling, the Egyptian bride has her photo taken with her husband-to-be, she sits with him at weddings where the sexes mix, and she dresses in make-up and fancy clothes for all to see. Because poorer

Bedouin men sometimes marry young women from peasant areas, whether they are of Egyptian stock or long-sedentarized Bedouin involved in agriculture, the Bedouin women also knew that unmarried sisters accompanied the bride. They interpreted this practice as a shameful attempt to display and "sell" marriageable daughters. They also knew that such brides sometimes arrived bringing a cooked duck or goose to feed a new husband; they took this as a sign of the bride's unseemly eagerness to please the groom.

Egyptian weddings, much like American ones, construct the couple as a separate unit, distinct from families or ties to members of the same gender group. At their center is a sexual joining that is private and intimate. For the Awlad 'Ali, this is a strange thing. The secrecy of private sex, in the dark, behind closed doors, and preferably in the foreign or anonymous setting (for the honeymoon) produces sexuality as something personal, intensely individual, apparently separate from society and social power. It produces sexuality as something belonging in an inviolable private sphere—the bedroom—a sphere in which others cannot interfere with whatever pleasure or violence and coercion accompanies it. One of the consequences of this construction of sexuality is that we, and perhaps Egyptians, come to think there is a part of oneself that is not social or affected by the prevailing power relations in society.[4]

The three crucial elements in the Bedouin discourse on differences between their weddings and those of other groups are (1) whether the defloration is public and participatory, (2) whether it involves sexual intercourse, and (3) whether it is seen as a contest, especially between bride and groom. These elements also had meaning within the local context. In Bedouin weddings the ways in which sexuality is related to power relations and the social order were clear. Marriages have been the occasion for people to collectively enact and reproduce this social order and the individual's place in it. And the individual's place was, until recently, very much a part of the group—whether the kin group or the group defined by gender.

WEDDINGS AS PUBLIC RITES: THE POWER OF KINSHIP AND GENDER

The participants in Awlad 'Ali Bedouin weddings instantiate, by means of a bride and groom, the relations between families or kin groups on the one hand, and the relations between men and women on the other. A symbolic analysis of the central rite, the defloration, enacted in a homologous fashion on the bodies of the bride and groom and on the collective bodies of the gathered kin and friends, reveals that it produces an understanding of sexuality as something public and focused on crossing thresholds, opening passages, and moving in and out. There are no strong messages of mingling or joining or even interchange in a private sexual act. The emphasis is on opening the bride's vagina by breaking the hymen and bringing out or making visible what was in there. And although people say that deflorations should be done during the daytime so everyone can see the cloth, the fact that in the rhythm of daily life morning and daytime generally are times of opening and going out from home or camp, while evening is a time of returning inward, cannot but reinforce the auspiciousness of this time for opening and taking outward.[5]

15   That this opening is a prelude to the insemination which should eventuate in childbirth is suggested by some practices associated with the blood-stained virginity cloth. It is taken out of the room by the groom and thrown to the women gathered just outside. It is said that if the cloth is then brought back into the room without the bride having exited first—if, as they say, the cloth enters upon her—it will block her from conceiving.[6] Young women are told to save their virginity cloths; if they have trouble conceiving, they must bathe in water in which they have soaked the cloth.

    Everything in the rites and the songs that accompany them suggests that the individuals engaged in this opening and being opened, taking out and showing, and having something taken out and shown, embody both their kin groups and their gender groups. The connection to kin, and control by the kin group, is clear in the key role they have in arranging and negotiating marriages and is reflected in the songs the groom's female relatives sing as they go to fetch the bride from her father's household. It is also reinforced in the songs the bride's female kin sing to greet these people. Most of the songs compliment the social standing of the families of the bride and groom.

    Even the practices and movements of the wedding itself perpetuate the identifications with kin groups. Most brides, even today, are brought from their fathers' households completely covered by a white woolen woven cloak (*jard*) that is the essential item of men's dress. The cloak must belong to the girl's father or some other male kinsman. So, protected and hidden by her father's cloak, she is brought out of her father's protected domain and carried to her husband's kin group's domain. There she is rushed, still hidden, into the room (or in the past, the tent) which she will share with her husband. Although nowadays the woven cloak is usually removed once she enters the room, in the past the bride remained under her father's cloak and was not revealed even to the women gathered around her until after the defloration.

The virginity of the bride is also constructed as something inseparable from her family's honor. Although one unmarried girl explained the importance of the blood-stained cloth in terms of her own reputation, she stressed the effect it would have on others.

> For us Bedouins, this is the most important moment in a girl's life. No matter what anyone says afterward, no one will pay attention as long as there was blood on the cloth. They are suspicious of her before. People talk. "She went here, she went there." "She looked at So-and-so." "She said hello to So-and-so." "She went to the orchard," But when they see this blood the talk is cut off. . . . When they see the cloth, she can come and go as she pleases. They love her and everything is fine.

. . .

About the bride a woman might sing: 20

Bravo! She was excellent
she who didn't force down her father's
eyelashes . . .

Given this group investment in the bride's virginity, the central rite of the wedding becomes a drama of suspense and relief that must powerfully shape people's experiences of sexuality as something that belongs to the many, and especially to one's family. The wedding is also, importantly, an occasion when families find themselves in some rivalry, the honor of each at stake. This was more apparent in the past when the young men celebrated all night on the eve of the wedding and expressed the rivalry through singing contests that sometimes broke out into actual fights between lineages.

Kinship is not the only power-laden aspect of social life that finds itself reflected and reinforced in the wedding. The second set of power relations weddings play with are those of gender. The bride and groom in the wedding rite enact the charged relations between men and women as distinct genders in a kind of battle of the sexes. Although most activities in the community are informally segregated by gender, at weddings—in part because there are non-family members present—the sexual segregation is more obvious and fixed, women and men forming highly separate collectivities for nearly all events.

Given this separation of the sexes, the defloration, taking place in the middle of the day when all are gathered in their distinct places, becomes a ritualized and extreme form of encounter between both the bride and groom and the women and men who surround each of them. The movements of the groom and his age-mates as they penetrate the crowd of women surrounding the bride mirror the groom's penetration of his bride, who forms a unit with the women in the room with her. The young men stand just outside the door, sometimes dancing and singing, ready to fire off guns in celebration when the groom emerges. They rush him back away from the women. This mirroring is expressed in the ambiguity of the term used for both moments of this event: the entrance (*khashsha*) refers both to the entry with the finger and the whole defloration process when the groom enters the bride's room, which can be thought of as his kin group's womb.

The encounter between male and female takes the form of a contest. The groom is encouraged to be fearless. He is expected to finish the deed in as short a time as possible. The bride is expected to try valiantly to fight him off. Taking the virginity she has been so careful to guard and thus opening the way for his progeny is the groom's victory; the bride doesn't give it up without a struggle. Calling this, as the literature often does, a virginity test is a misnomer in that it misses this combative dimension of the ritualized act. The way people describe what happens even on the wedding night suggests again that the groom and bride are involved in a contest. The rowdy young men who listen outside the marital chamber want to know "who won." They know this, some adolescent girls informed me, not just by whether the groom succeeds in having intercourse with his bride (a rare event), but by whether the groom succeeds in making his bride talk to him and answer his questions. This is, perhaps, another kind of opening up. . . .

SEXUAL TRANSFORMATIONS

Many Awlad 'Ali claim that their rituals are changing. In this final section, I want to explore how in these changed wedding practices we can begin to track changes in the nature of power and social relations. This is further support for my initial argument that constructions of sexuality cannot be understood apart from understandings of particular forms of social power. Most people talked about changes in weddings over the last twenty years or so in terms of what had been lost. Many said weddings were not fun any more. As far as I could determine, the main element that seems to have been lost is the celebration the night before the wedding (*saamir*). Not only do the young men no longer sing back and forth, but no longer is it even thinkable that a young woman from the community would come out to dance in front of them. This is what used to happen and the change is crucial for Bedouin gender relations.

What happened in the past was that an unmarried sister or cousin of the groom would be brought out from among the women by a young boy. She would dance amidst a semi-circle of young men. Her face veiled and her waist girded with a man's white woven cloak, like the one the bride would come covered in the following day, she danced with a stick or baton in her hands. According to one man who described this to me, the young men tried to "beg" the stick from her, sometimes using subterfuges like pretending to be ill; she would often bestow the stick, he said, on someone she fancied. But according to the women I spoke with, the young men would sometimes try to grab the stick from her and she would, if they were too aggressive, get angry with them and leave.

The young men took turns singing songs that welcomed the dancer and then described her every feature in flattering terms. The standard parts praised in such songs were her braids, her eyes, her eyebrows, her cheeks, her lips, her tattoos, her neck, her breasts, her arms, her hands, and her waist—most of which, it should be remembered, because of the way she was dressed were not actually visible. Thus in a sense the dancer was, through men's songs, made into the ideal woman, attractive object of men's desires.

The dancer must be seen as the bride's double or stand-in, an interpretation supported by the other occasion on which a young woman danced in front of men. In the days before cars, brides were carried from their fathers' households to their husbands' on camel-back, completely cloaked and sitting hidden inside a wooden litter (*karmuud*) covered in red woven blankets. Another woman always preceded her on foot, dancing as young men sang to her and shot off guns near her.

In both cases, the dancer as bride and as ideal womanhood went out before men who complimented and sought her. What is crucial to notice is how the women described the dancer. They attributed to her a special bravery and described her actions as a challenge to the young men. One wedding in which a young woman was accidentally wounded by a poorly aimed gun was legendary. The wedding went on, the story went, as a second dancer who had been near her merely wiped the blood from her forehead and continued to dance. More telling is the ritualized struggle over the stick, which one anthropologist who worked with a group in Libya has argued is associated with virginity (Mason 1975). A woman explained to me, "If the dancer is sharp they can't take the stick from her. They'll be coming at her from all sides but she keeps it."

But perhaps some of the short songs traditionally exchanged between the women (gathered in a tent some distance away from the young men standing in a line near the dancer) and the young men, make clearest the ways in which a challenge between the sexes was central to weddings. One especially memorable competitive exchange was the following. As her sister danced a woman sang of her:

A bird in the hot winds glides
and no rifle scope can capture it . . .

A man responded with the song:

The heart would be no hunter
if it didn't play in their feathers . . .

30   In the loss and delegitimation of this whole section of the wedding ritual, an important piece of the construction of Bedouin sexual relations has disappeared. Today, all that is left in a ritual that was a highly charged and evenly matched challenge between the sexes is the enactment of the men's hunt. The groom is the hunter, the bride his prey. Decked out in her make-up and white satin dress, she is brought from her father's house and her "virginity" taken by her groom in a bloody display.

Wedding songs, only sung by women now, reinforce this construction of the bride as vulnerable prey. They liken the bride to a gazelle. This is a compliment to her beauty but also suggests her innocence and defenselessness. Other songs liken the groom to a falcon or hunter. This is no longer balanced by women's former powers to create desire but elude capture.

The disappearance of the female dancer can thus be seen to have shifted the balance such that women's capacities to successfully challenge men have been de-emphasized. Although the sexes are still pitted against each other, the contest is no longer represented as even.

There is a second important point to be made about the dancer that relates to some transformations in constructions of power and sexuality. For it is not completely true that women no longer dance in front of men at Awlad 'Ali weddings. It has become unacceptable for respectable young kinswomen to dance, but there are now some professional dancers. They accompany musical troupes hired to entertain at weddings of the Bedouin nouveau riche. These women may or may not be prostitutes but they are certainly not considered respectable.[7] In that sense, and in the fact that ordinary women go nowhere near the areas where these musicians and dancers perform, one cannot any longer claim that the dancer represents Woman or enacts women's challenge of men. The opposite may be true. This new kind of wedding may be introducing a new view of women, one quite familiar to us in the United States but quite strange to the Awlad 'Ali: women as sexual commodities stripped of their embeddedness in their kin groups or the homosocial world of women.

The professionalization of weddings as entertainment and spectacle (if spectacles that retain vestiges of the participatory in that young men seize the microphone to sing songs) may also be signaling a fundamental shift in the relationship of the construction of sexuality and the construction of the social order. What seems to be disappearing is the participation of the whole community in the responsibility of ritually reproducing the fundamental social and political dynamics of the community. Does this indicate the emergence of a new kind of power? One that works differently? One whose nexus is perhaps the individual rather than the kin group or gender group? This new form of wedding is not being adopted universally in the Bedouin region since the poor cannot afford it and the respectable condemn it as undignified and inappropriate for pious Muslims. Nevertheless, as a public discourse it must enter and shape the field of sexuality for all. . . .

If, as I have tried to show, in a small Bedouin community in   35 Egypt, sexuality can come to be a crucial marker of cultural identity, and if the construction of sexuality is so closely tied to the organization of kinship and gender and changes as the community is transformed by such broad processes as its incorporation into the wider Egyptian nation and economy, then it seems impossible to assert the existence of a Muslim sexuality that can be read off texts or shared across communities with very different histories and ways of life. Instead, we need to think about specific constructions of sexuality and, in the case of the Muslim Arab world, about the variable role discourses on religion can play in those constructions.

Author's Note: Most of the research in Egypt on which this article is based was supported by an NEH Fellowship for College Teachers and a Fulbright Award under the Islamic Civilization Program. I am grateful to Samia Mehrez for inviting me to present an early version at Cornell University. I am more grateful to the women and men in the Awlad 'Ali community who shared their lives, including their weddings, with me.

Endnotes

1. The literature, especially the feminist literature, on sexuality has become vast in the last decade or two. A helpful early text is Vance (1984). Anthropologists have recently begun to pay more attention to constructions of sexuality and their cross-cultural perspective should contribute to our understanding of the way that sexuality is constructed. For a good introduction to some of that work, see Caplan (1987).
2. For this reason the weddings of divorcees or widows are not celebrated with as much enthusiasm and are considered somewhat ordinary affairs.
3. For example, she described what is known as the *dayra* (the circling). On the evening of the wedding day, they had seated the bride and groom on a pillow, back to back. A neighbor carrying a lamb on his back, holding one foreleg in each of his hands, had walked around and around them—seven times. She mimicked the audience counting: "Hey, did you count that one? One, two, three, four." "Thank God," she said at one point, "there were no outsiders (non-relatives) from back home with us. How embarrassing it would have been."
4. The theorist who has most developed this notion of the effects on subjectivity and sense of individuality of the Western discourses on sexuality is Michel Foucault (1978, 1985).
5. For an analysis of similar kinds of symbolic constructions of gender and sexuality, see Bourdieu's (1977) work on Algerian Kabyles. My analysis of the meaning of this rite differs significantly from that of Combs-Schilling (1989), who worked in Morocco.
6. For more on rituals related to fertility and infertility, see my *Writing Women's Worlds* (1993). Boddy (1989) has analyzed for Muslim Sudanese villagers the extraordinary symbolic stress on women's fertility over their sexuality.
7. As Van Nieuwkerk (1995) has documented, this is generally true about professional dancers in Egypt.

References

Abu-Lughod, Lila. 1993. *Writing Women's Worlds: Bedouin Stories.* Berkeley and Los Angeles: University of California Press.

Alloula, Malek. 1986. *The Colonial Harem.* Myran and Wlad Godzich, trans. Minneapolis: University of Minnesota Press.

Boddy, Janice. 1989. *Wombs and Alien Spirits: Women, Men, and the Zar Cult in Northern Sudan.* Madison, WI: University of Wisconsin Press.

Bouhdiba, Abdelwahab. 1985. *Sexuality in Islam.* London and Boston: Routledge & Kegan Paul.

Bourdieu, Pierre. 1977. *Outline of a Theory of Practice.* Cambridge: Cambridge University Press.

Caplan, Patricia, ed. 1987. *The Cultural Construction of Sexuality.* London and New York: Tavistock Publications.

Combs-Schilling, M.E. 1989. *Sacred Performances: Islam, Sexuality and Sacrifice.* New York: Columbia University Press.

Daly, Mary. 1978. *Gyn/ecology, the Metaethics of Radical Feminism.* Boston: Beacon Press.

Foucault, Michel. 1978. *The History of Sexuality: Volume 1: An Introduction.* New York: Random House.

———. 1985. *The Use of Pleasure.* Vol. 2 of *The History of Sexuality.* New York: Pantheon.

Mason, John. 1975. "Sex and Symbol in the Treatment of Women: The Wedding Rite in a Libyan Oasis Community." *American Ethnologist* 2: 649–61.

Sabbah, Fatna A. 1984. *Woman in the Muslim Unconscious.* New York and Oxford: Pergamon Press.

Vance, Carole. 1984. *Pleasure and Danger: Exploring Female Sexuality.* Boston and London: Routledge & Kegan Paul.

Van Nieuwkerk, Karin. 1995. *"A Trade Like Any Other": Female Singers and Dancers in Egypt.* Austin, TX: University of Texas Press.

Questions for Thought and Writing

1. In describing non-Bedouin Egyptian weddings as "much like American ones," Abu-Lughod explains that weddings work to "produce" sexuality in certain ways. In both non-Bedouin Egyptian and American weddings, for example, sexuality is "produced" as "something personal, intensely individual, apparently separate from society and social power." How does thinking about sexuality as a "product" of social rituals affect your understanding of it? Does the author's use of the word "apparently" suggest that there is a different reality from the overt one?

2. The author explains that weddings are rituals in which kinship and gender relations are acted out publicly. In Bedouin
   weddings, rituals have changed over the years to reflect
   changing perceptions of women's capabilities and strengths
   compared to men. How have weddings in American culture
   changed—or failed to change—in recent decades to reflect
   changes in gender relations? How do these rituals reinforce or
   challenge traditional notions of men and women's sexuality?
3. One of the central premises of Abu-Lughod's article is that
   there is no one "Muslim sexuality;" she argues that "neither
   Islam nor sexuality" should be essentialized, or reduced to a
   rigid set of characteristics and qualities. Identify a social
   group that you think frequently gets "essentialized" in contemporary American culture, and discuss what kind(s) of information you believe most people lack about the variations
   and differences among people within this group.

Le Freak, C'Est Chic!
Le Fag, Quelle Drag!:
Celebrating the Collapse of
Homosexual Identity

D. Travers Scott

My boyfriend and I just moved to the gay ghetto. I've never really
lived in the gay ghetto before. A brief stint near Chicago's
Boystown was spent in a mouse-infested basement apartment whose
floor gave way from the wall, whose toilet never worked, and whose
front window framed hookers' stilettos. There I dated two straight
men and had more sexual incidents with women than fags. So,
despite my physical proximity to the Pride Parade route, the ubiquitous Curl Up & Dye salon, kitchen ceramics boutique, and several
queer commodity outlets, I wasn't really living the gay lifestyle.

I am now.

My boyfriend and I fell into jobs in a new city, returning to
full-time work after years of freelancing. As we prepared to move,
we decided we were fed up with low-rent artists' dives in obscure

neighborhoods where we couldn't get pizza delivered. We wanted some convenience. So we got an overpriced apartment in Seattle's queer/boho Capitol Hill, within quick walking distance to our jobs, plus bookstores, bars, coffee shops, etc. It's nice having neighbors who will look us in the eyes. It's nice not turning off the Christopher Rage video when the building manager drops by. It's nice getting sucked off in the laundry room.

Yes, sex is *very* convenient here. In addition to my dear boyfriend, there's jerk-offs at the YMCA, a dozen bars within arm's length, the ceaselessly cruisey Broadway Ave ("I'm just out to buy toilet paper, okay?! I'm *really* not cruising!"), the adult theater, the johns at the parks, sex clubs A, B or C (D is downtown, and that's *such a hike*), and the aforementioned friendly neighbors.

It's also easy to shop here. Proudly-queer clothes, videos,   5
churches, snacks, meals, coffee, books, mags, and music glare from every shop window, should the preponderance of lust out-lets not serve as reminder enough of one's faggottry. Homo propa-ganda is everywhere, in the form of banners, badges, and posters, like some rainbowed *1984*. And it's all for sale. You have an end-less supply of ready-made identity signifiers: all the mass-pro-duced knick-knacks to show off and celebrate your oh-so-uniquely-*you* Queer Identity. Camp/retro/kitsch fashions and furnishings abound, and Urban Outfitters is so much more con-venient (and smells better) than trudging through Goodwill. *Genre* and *Out* are so kind as to provide handy shopping guides so we don't have to search boutique after boutique to find faux an-tique photo frames, porno screen savers, and rainbow dildo elec-tric toothbrushes. For the first time since I was sixteen, I received a copy of *International Male* in the mail addressed to me, and I didn't even have to order it. It must automatically come to every address in this zip code, like those coupon packs.

I scraped off the mailing label and took it straight to the recy-cling before the neighbors could see.

Don't get me wrong, I'm not totally bashing queer neighbor-hoods. I realize it's a luxury that I even have one to grouse about. I've always said I thought separatism and strength in numbers were good when you needed them. It's a healing and strengthen-ing phase. Some of the rural kids who move here probably des-perately need this validation and support. But achieving a well-accessorized Queer Identity is only a phase, not a destination, end product, or utopia, and it's time we stop treating it as such. Urban gay ghettos may be really comfy and safe little scenes but they are part of a decadent, mannerist, final phase before the movement shifts into something else entirely.

It's already happening. The constant pride, boasting, and reaffirming of Queer Identity all are beginning to seem childishly obvious. You're here, you're queer, we're over it. When even the faggot bible *Genre* runs an article titled "We're So Over the Rainbow," you know something's up. The parades have gone from being revolutionary to boring as shit. Besides, the names are too long: the Gay, Lesbian, Bisexual, Transgendered & Friends Show does not roll trippingly off the tongue. (Don't even try to pull that "lesbigay" shit, our little Esperanto that some well-intentioned fool came up with. And "queer" almost immediately came to mean "saucy fags and dykes," not the radically-sexualized boundary-breaking coalition it was first advertised to be, or we'd have a hell of a lot more heterosexual "queers" in our parades.)

But beyond semantic bitching, there are larger issues at stake. All this Pride and Identity and Culture and Community, frankly, get in the way. They're awkward, clunky albatrosses, limiting concepts which simply don't work anymore. Witness gay men and lesbians coming out of the closet—they're admitting that they've fallen in love with and married heterosexuals of the opposite sex. And many were not bisexuals to begin with. It could happen to even the most devout Kinsey Six: if your hormones were powerful enough to make you break with the norms of a heterosexual society, do you honestly think you could never fall for a person of the opposite sex? To paraphrase Tennessee Williams, "a line is straight, a road may be straight, but the heart curves and curves." Williams was implying everyone can enjoy same-sex relations and fall in love with same-sex partners. A lovely thought when cruising straight trade, but just remember—it works both ways. Love is unpredictable, capricious, and fucking powerful.

10   Let's address those heterosexual fags and dykes for a second. I'm not talking about bisexuals. I'm not talking about some hulking mouth-breather at Hooters "co-opting queer semiotics" by wearing an earring and saying, "Go girl," or some foxy business babe with a flattop. I'm talking about those people we've all met and joked about but don't quite know what to do with: they're predominantly heterosexual, maybe a little variance here and there but nothing major. But they're campy, promiscuous, play good softball, drive a truck, or do whatever queerish behavior you identify with. Or it may not even be that specific: there's just something you can't put your finger on that sends your gaydar screaming. You muse that

maybe they just haven't come out yet, or just haven't met the right person to make them realize their queer potential. They just seem so queer, just like you and me! Substitute straight for queer in that argument and it suddenly sounds all too familiar.

One of my best friends was at times dismissed as a fag hag because she identifies with so much of gay male culture. She's actually far more a fag than a fag hag. We've all heard the line about "a gay man trapped in a woman's body," but I don't mean it here in the usual pejorative sense: sexless and pathetic women, hanging out with gay men they can never have because they're too afraid/ugly to relate to straight men. What a bunch of sexist, internally-homophobic crap. Only psychotic women hang out with fags? Fags are only good enough for second-rate women-friends? Puh-leeze, they are fags, just like the rest of us.

My friend is a stud and a slut. She has no trouble getting men and has had some escapades that put my sexual revolutionary status to shame. She's also never had an unrequited crush on a gay man; it's been the reverse far more frequently. She loves both Pee Wee Herman and Disco Tex and the Sex-o-lettes, and leaped at the chance to go see the Pet Shop Boys in concert with me when all my alterna-fag friends sniffed at the idea. Recently she's gone off and complicated things even more by finding herself this lesbian lover who's a man, but with really sexy femme dyke-type tendencies toward stockings and slips.

Elsewhere on the horizon, the transgender activists are making things even more confusing. How can a rigid Gay Male identity cope with that really cute guy, who used to be a baby butch dyke, and is still involved in a primary relationship with a woman, but considers herself basically a gay man? How do you relate to that foxy dominatrix who's a power femme dyke, but used to be a man? Fuck "relating"—the important issue for a neat 'n' tidy boyfag is: *Which one are you supposed to have sex with?* As it's finally sinking in that if gender is fluid, how can sexual "orientation" not be as well? How can you be rigidly "oriented" toward something that is amorphous, shifting, fluid, tricky, elusive? Basing your identity on sexuality is like building a house on a foundation of pudding.

That's one reason why I think it'd be healthy for many of my fellow fagboys to stop shuddering and wincing at the idea of sex with women, to get over being so neurotically invested in their constructed identity as a Gay Man that the faintest brush of bush threatens them to lengths of misogynist and reactionary overcompensation. I'm not proposing some utopian idealized state of bisexuality here, I'm just suggesting that a little dose of muff might provoke a healthy reassessment of a sex-based identity. But don't give me the "queer sex is better than straight sex" trope some fags use to consider sex with women without threatening their precious queer identity. That's the line where they'll only consider it if they're being fucked by a butch dyke with a strap-on. Could someone please explain to me how this is different from being fucked by a really butch *straight* woman with a strap-on? Think about this, boys: if it's a dyke, she might invite her girlfriend to join in, but a straight woman might get her boyfriend into the act.

15   I'm not the first person to say this, but really, if gay men are such sexual outlaws and pioneers of the erotic imagination, what's so goddamn freaky about a little pussy? We love to crow about how any straight man can be had, and cheer them on when they are. Why are we so threatened by the reverse? What are we afraid of losing but an easy answer, a convenient but outmoded identity?

Fucking is not an answer. More realistically, it's a gateway or lens into even more questions, more exploration, and more insight into oneself and society. That's why I'm far more excited these days by ideas running through the bi, transgender, and S/M and kink movements. Instead of protecting territory, engaging in pissing matches and rigidly policing identity boundaries and definitions, they're doing the opposite. They're asking more questions rather than stamping their feet, claiming that they already have the answers. They're pushing issues further, introducing shades of gray. They're forcing us to question whether identity is something that really boils down to a name, label, tag, or definition. Perhaps it's a range of experience. Perhaps it's not one thing at all but several, simultaneous and contradictory, even.

In exploring the complex, fluid, and contradictory identities found within UK gay skinhead subcultures, Murray Healy points out that rigid identities are part and parcel of a conservative, far-right ideology. "The semiotic fundamentalism of skinhead = fascist only serves to reinforce the far right's project of social homogenization and the fixing of identity boundaries. . . . Fascist ideology is contested by . . . fluid sexualities" (*Gay Skins: Class, Masculinity, and Queer Appropriation*, Cassell, 1996, p. 145). Fixed, strictly-policed identities are a right-wing project, as are the literal use and zealous protection of symbols and signifiers of those identities. This has been evidenced in the United States, for example, by the far right's fervor against flag burning.

A strain of fascism and conservatism runs through sex-based identities—revealed by the shrillness with which their names and

symbols are debated and the vehemence with which their boundaries are policed. However, due to the traditional location of gay
rights within leftist politics, the fascist streak inherent in demanding such fixed identities is obscured. But in gay ghettos
such as my current home, the normalizing project of building a
lesbigay suburban utopia parallel to the sexist, patriarchal original seems apparent. Note what we continue to fight over: perver-
sity; NAMBLA and drag queens in parades; leatherwomen and
transgendereds at womyn's music fests. Polymorphous desire and
the fluid, non-fixed identities they entail do not allow for the
power hierarchies many wish to erect and maintain. Ultimately,
identities based on unrealistically stable concepts of sex and gender play into this project too much for my taste. I don't want to be
identified, named, pinned down, understood. Those are all the
first steps toward manipulation and control.

There are advantages to this fluid alternative, to what must
seem like a morass of instability. If we aren't just helpless slaves
to our identity, it opens up the philosophical playroom for much
more exciting possibilities, such as *choice* and *freedom*. These
ideas, in turn, necessitate exploration and articulation of *values*
and *responsibilities*. And guess where that leads us? To a field of
debate in which we can actually engage the conservative right using their own terms, instead of shrugging our shoulders with a
hapless, "We can't help it, this is who we are!"

Homosexuality's over. It was mainly a twentieth-century   20
thang anyway, so let's leave it there. Time's up, kaput. Page me
when we get our shit together and have a Sex Celebration Parade
or a Take Back the Body March, when we stop dividing and start
joining together with others who recognize Western culture is
royally fucked when it comes to body, sex, spirit, sensuality, pleasure, and gender. "Queers" are not a distinct minority group neatly
parallel to ethnic, religious, or biologically based groups. The issue isn't identity, it's ideology. It's about freedom, responsibility,
and values.

Questions for Thought and Writing

1. Although Scott argues that he is "not totally bashing queer
   neighborhoods," he does have strong reasons for believing
   that they are no longer necessary or even desirable, even
   though he lives in one. What are his reasons? What does he
   believe is happening to the Queer Identity movement?

2. What is Scott attempting to illustrate with the example of his best friend who is "actually far more a fag than a fag hag"? How does he seem to feel about the fact that "elsewhere on the horizon, the transgender activists are making things even more confusing"? What does he think is being confused by both his friend and these activists, and does he believe this is a positive or a negative development? What kinds of gender "border crossings" in dress or behavior can you identify among your peers or in the larger culture? Do these border crossings indicate that the lines between genders are shifting or even fading?

3. Scott ends his essay with the bold claim that "Homosexuality's over. It was mainly a twentieth-century thang anyway, so let's leave it there." What do you think he means by this statement? In an essay that uses examples from popular culture and/or from your own experience to support your conclusion, decide whether you agree or disagree with Scott's assertion and why.

Exploring Connections

1. In both "How Men Have (a) Sex" and "Who's on Top? Heterosexual Practices and Male Dominance During the Sex Act," controlling women's sexuality is discussed as a means of controlling women themselves. According to these authors, what are the strategies used in contemporary culture to control women's sexuality? How might society change if women had greater control over their own sexuality?

2. Both Chesler and Stoltenberg offer specific suggestions to their readers about how to take charge of their own sexual freedoms and responsibilities. How does this kind of approach to sexuality compare to the way you have been conditioned to think about it? Which, if any, of their suggestions would you be willing to take, and why?

3. Lila Abu-Lughod's "Is There a Muslim Sexuality? Changing Constructions of Sexuality in Egyptian Bedouin Weddings" warns of the dangers in "essentializing" people or groups of people by reducing them to a rigid set of characteristics. How does the argument against "gay neighborhoods" in "Le Freak, C'Est Chic! Le Fag, Quelle Drag!: Celebrating the Collapse of Homosexual Identity" point to the same problem?

Gender and Work

CHAPTER 4

OVERVIEW

The Overview articles that follow—"Sex-Role Spillover: Personal, Familial, and Organizational Roles" and "The Second Shift: Working Parents and the Revolution at Home"—are cautious in measuring women's progress in the work force since the 1950s. In the first essay, Rita Mae Kelly challenges the notion that women's progress in the work force is complete. She enumerates the areas that are still mainly delegated to women, such as childcare and housework, suggesting that traditional gender roles still limit women's workplace opportunities. Arlie Russell Hochschild contrasts advertising images of working women with working women's actual experiences. She proposes that although marriage relationships between men and women have been redefined as women have entered the workforce, the working world itself has remained resistant to change.

Sex-Role Spillover: Personal, Familial, and Organizational Roles

RITA MAE KELLY

Americans have traditionally equated the role of "worker" with the roles of breadwinner, father, and husband. As women enter the work force, they have been expected to meet this male-centered

161

standard. At the same time, women also have been expected to follow their traditional roles of wife or girlfriend, mother, daughter, and sex partner/object. The intertwining of women's expanding economic power and less rapidly evolving sex roles has produced the gendered dimension of the U.S. segmented labor market.

In 1986 more than 80 percent of women in the work force were of childbearing age (Hardesty and Jacobs 1986). A large proportion of employed women experienced significant conflicts between their roles as workers, wives, mothers, daughters, and family caretakers, all of which they were expected to play simultaneously (Lewis and Cooper 1988). These concurrent demands caused many women to suffer from two conditions: role overload, which results when a person is expected to fulfill more roles than she or he can handle; and role strain, which results from conflict between two or more roles. . . .

WORKING WOMEN AND THE HOME

The Wife Role (Housekeeper/Homemaker/Hostess)

In the 1950s and 1960s wives employed outside the home to augment their husbands' income gradually gained acceptance in the role of supplemental workers. By the 1980s, middle-class women had become more than just guardians of their family status and lifestyle; many had also launched careers. At the same time, many couples found that both spouses needed to work to maintain a middle-class standard of living (Pleck 1985). Wives were not the only women entering the paid labor force; 45 percent of all employed women were single, separated, or divorced (U.S. Bureau of the Census 1988). Further, 23 percent of all households consisted of nonmarried, single women (Blank 1988). The median weekly earnings in 1989 for a male-supported household without an employed wife were $486. For families with both spouses working, the median earnings were $668; yet, for a female-supported household, median weekly earnings totaled only $334 (U.S. Department of Labor 1989). These statistics indicate that increasing numbers of women have fallen into or have barely escaped poverty.

Regardless of income or marital status, female workers must deal with home and hearth in ways that male workers do not. In *The Second Stage*, Betty Friedan recognized that, while women were pulled into the public realm, men were not enticed into the private domain (Friedan 1981). The resulting lopsided division of familial responsibilities led to a condition Friedan termed the "superwoman" syndrome. While women attempted to excel at both the traditional female sex roles and the male role of paid laborer, men avoided the women's traditional role of housekeeper/homemaker/hostess. Consequently, women entering the paid labor force encountered a Herculean task that only a mythical "superwoman" could have completely fulfilled.

Empirical studies demonstrate the burden this condition places on women. Arlie Hochschild's (1989) study of couples and housework shows that this imbalance of roles requires women to put in a "second shift" as housekeeper, consumer, and care-giver. Skow (1989) reports that working wives spend 15 fewer hours at leisure each week than their husbands, and when faced with scheduling conflicts, women tend to reduce leisure time before reducing time spent on child care. A study reported in *The American Woman* compared married men and women who spend equal hours in the paid work force. This study found that women put in an additional 18 hours per week doing home labor (Blank 1988). Fathers average only 12 minutes per day in primary child care (Blank 1988). Even women who claim to have egalitarian arrangements at home still put in more energy, time, and labor during this second shift than do their spouses (Hochschild 1989; MacCorquodale 1986).

Although custom has decreed that women be more available for family care, this role expectation has not been viewed positively in the workplace. Ten executive men were asked by *Executive Female* magazine to participate in a roundtable discussion about the strengths and weaknesses of female peers. One executive claimed:

> "People have to have families—you can't argue that—but within the business environment, it's a negative. A woman always wants to go home at 5:00 to be with her family. Men have families too, but they don't leave. . . ." (Heller 1983, p. 102)

Men make sacrifices in order to make money and to gain power. These executives suggested that women may be hitting the glass ceiling because they are not ready to make the same sacrifices for their careers.

This perception shifts the blame for women's difficulties in the workplace to women, rather than on recognizing socially institutionalized and individually internalized stereotypes. In addition, reports indicate that this type of perception about women is becoming increasingly inaccurate. A roundtable discussion of ten successful female executives by *Nation's Business* indicates women are not only "ready to make the sacrifice" but also are making the personal concessions necessary for career advancement (Nelton and Berney 1987). One IBM executive found that her 10 to 12 hour workdays made it impossible to keep a commitment to a family evening meal. "I took a close look at that ritual and decided it had to go" (Nelton and Berney 1987, p. 18). Letting go of time-honored practices is one of the many sacrifices women, especially those in the primary labor market, have to make.

To be most competitive, especially in the primary job sector, requires not being a "wife," but actually having an effective substitute. Many careers command complete loyalty and submission to organizational goals with total submersion into corporate culture. Most management and executive careers are project-driven. Deadlines are not flexed to accommodate family or personal schedules. High-powered careers blur the lines between the personal and private realms. Work often takes place with a client over dinner, with the boss at a show, with co-workers on the golf course, and frequently out of town. It is assumed a babysitter is available, that the children are always well, or that there are no children at all.

Companies frequently expect employees will not be burdened with responsibility for cleaning the home, purchasing consumer goods, and caring for children. In addition, the higher level professional is expected to have a partner who serves as hostess to the boss and clients, stands in line to buy the theater tickets, makes reservations for the restaurant, packs the luggage for out-of-town meetings, and drives the higher status spouse (usually the man) to the airport in mid-workday. Without the help of "wives," married career women and career women with children suffer a real disadvantage competing for important contracts, key line positions or out-of-town jobs.

The Mother Role (Childbearing and Child Rearing)

In 1990 more than 70 percent of women age 25 to 34 were in the labor force. In 1950, there were only 35 percent. Lenhoff reports that 80 percent of all women in the workplace are of childbearing age, and 93 percent of them will become pregnant while working

(Lenhoff 1987). Overall, approximately three-fourths of women in the work force will be affected by pregnancy and motherhood. Given that about 50 million women are in the labor force, that means about 37.2 million women will be directly affected by pregnancy and child-care policies. This estimate does not include the millions of children, elderly relatives, and spouses that are indirectly impacted.

The number of working mothers has increased sharply since the 1950s, when only 12 percent of women with children under the age of six worked. In 1988, approximately six of every ten mothers with a child under age six were employed. Half of all married mothers with infants younger than one year were in the labor force. In 1990, fewer than 5 percent of families had a father who worked and a mother who stayed home caring for the children. By 1995 it is estimated that two-thirds of all preschool children will have mothers in the work force, and that four of five school-age children will have employed mothers (U.S. Department of Labor 1988).

Neither U.S. employers nor the government have been quick to respond to these radical changes. In 1987 the Bureau of Labor Statistics estimated that only 2 percent of businesses with 10 or more workers sponsored child-care centers; an additional 3 percent provided financial assistance for day-care services; and only 6 percent offered help in the form of information, referral, or counseling services (Thompson 1988). AT&T reported in 1989 that families juggle up to four different kinds of child-care arrangements each week (Allen 1989). Although the number of day-care centers built in or near the workplace increased from 110 in 1979 to 4,000 in 1989 (Garbarine 1989), most workers have to rely on other family members, neighbors, religious institutions, or personally devised arrangements. In 1989, churches provided one-third of the child-care services (Hochschild 1989). In 1989, only 14 percent of U.S. corporations offered child-care benefits to their employees, arguing that the bottom line costs outweighed benefits.

The options for integrating the roles of mother and career woman have not been great. Women have been expected to fit into the male model of work, which forces them to either avoid being a mother, adopt a "father's" approach to child care, or seek alternative work hours and work forms. . . .

A common solution to the motherhood conflict for ambitious career women has been avoidance. Whereas 90 percent of male executives age 40 and under are fathers, only 35 percent of their female counterparts are mothers (Wallis et al. 1989). As the biological clock ticked close to menopause, more and more career women of the 1980s sought alternative approaches to the work force. Women who put off having children until the last possible moment were not rewarded for their sacrifice. Instead, their choices regarding pregnancy and maternity leave became a test of organizational loyalty (Hardesty and Jacobs 1986). The more seniority and/or responsibility a woman has, the more child-birth is likely to be viewed as an organizational disruption. Employers often want reassurance that the motherhood role will not supersede the employee role.

15   Large numbers of women, especially those with well-paying jobs, addressed the stress of role overload and role strain due to motherhood as single working fathers have previously done. They hire other women to assist in mothering and family chores. This "fatherly" approach to child care, house care, and family consumption is a major factor in the rise of the service economy and self-employment of women in the peripheral sector of the labor market (Beattie 1984).

Although the need for child care has led to more jobs for women and greater flexibility for women owners and managers of such services, the resulting businesses and jobs have also contributed to pay inequities and employment of women in jobs that lack career growth potential. Although nearly one-half of all day-care teachers have bachelor degrees or at least some college training, the average salary of these professionals—mostly women—was only $5.35 per hour in 1988, a salary that amounts to about $9,363 a year. This sum is less than the $9,431 federally defined poverty level for a family of three (Lewin 1989). As the need for day care increased in the 1980s, the average salary of day-care teachers declined by 27 percent from 1977 to 1988 (Lewin 1989).

The low salaries reflect a dilemma facing U.S. women. Day care services bear large price tags. In 1986, the estimated cost of purchasing in-home care was $8,000 per year, $5,000 for day care per year, and $2,500 for a year of full-time preschool tuition—costs comparable to college tuition (Elrich 1986). Women who must hire other women to watch their children typically do not earn salaries high enough to pay day-care providers higher wages.

Working women still earn only 74 cents to every working man's dollar (Blank 1988). Even the highest level executive women suffer dramatic pay gaps. According to the U.S. Chamber of Commerce in May 1987, "corporate women at the vice-presidential level and above earn 42 percent less than their male peers" (Wallis et al. 1989, p. 85).

In addition to the burden of affordability, a shortage of licensed day-care centers makes it unlikely that a good center will be conveniently located. Many centers cater to those who work a regular day shift. Women who work odd shifts, who are going to school, or who often have after-hour meetings find themselves struggling to find additional home care and solutions to the restrictive drop-off and pick-up hours at the day-care center. And those few centers that can accommodate parents after 6:00 p.m. often charge an additional fee for these "off hours."

Many licensed day-care centers have age restrictions preventing enrollment of young babies. Often maternity or pregnancy leaves are not long enough to meet the age requirements for enrollment. In addition, care for physically challenged or sick children is rare and very expensive. In 1987, approximately 67 percent of all child care still took place in a home (Blank 1988). 20

School-age children pose additional problems. While public schools dismiss students in early afternoon, the average workday ends at 5:00 p.m. Lack of transportation to a care center or prohibitive costs of two to three hours of care per child often results in children caring for themselves after school.

Family work alternatives . . . put women—especially mothers—on a separate "Mommy Track." This Mommy Track reinforces the superiority of the present male career model, preventing married women and mothers from developing a more appropriate female work model. These alternatives relieve the conflict between work and home but typically become formidable barriers to long-term career success.

AT THE WORKPLACE: WORKERS AS SURROGATE DAUGHTERS, WIVES, GIRLFRIENDS, AND SEX PARTNERS/OBJECTS

Career women suffer role stress in two directions. Not only does the public role of worker create overload and conflict within the home, but the spillover of traditional sex-role expectations into the workplace is a critical career barrier to women (Gutek 1985). Unlike their male peers, women are often perceived in the limited roles of surrogate daughters, wives, or mothers rather than as workers. Working women may find that they are judged by their presence, attractiveness, and attitudes rather than their talents and skills as professionals. One reason for this spillover may be that institutions adhere to a family model. In fact, with divorce so prevalent, the corporation may be a more stable institution than marriage (Berstein 1985).

For a man, the apprenticeship role may be the first of many stages in his career. For a woman, however, the novice role may be the "end of the line." As "daddy's little girl" female proteges are granted the privileged inequality of the little girl, a privilege their male peers don't have—to fail and to lean on someone. However, "as long as her need for approval is stronger than her need for self-expression, a woman may always be trapped in this subordinate daughter role" (Berstein 1985, p. 139), also called the "office daughter syndrome." A study of 18 California families owning businesses found that none of the fathers of daughters had planned on their daughters succeeding them (*Wall Street Journal* 1990). Unexpected events led to the daughters entering the business. Once in the business, 44 percent felt obliged to be nurturing of their fathers as well as of the business. The daughters reported feeling it necessary to kiss their dad and to continue being "daddy's little girl." Most daughters helped their fathers remain at the head of the company longer, rather than pushing him out as soon as possible, as sons often do. So few fathers assume their daughters will take over that almost no studies have been done on the topic. In one study reported in 1990, 78 percent of the fathers interviewed "had difficulty handling their daughters' dual family and business roles—as did 89 percent of the daughters. Unlike sons, daughters find themselves competing at work in their fathers' eyes with male managers from outside the family" (*Wall Street Journal* 1990, p. B12). One woman interviewed shared that her father would not listen to her evidence regarding the behavior of the hired male manager.

25   The difficulties daughters have with their own fathers often carry over to male mentors. With less than 10 percent of top executive positions being held by women, it is rare that an aspiring woman finds a female mentor. Therefore, a woman's mentor will more likely be a man. Executive men who adhere to using a family model for relating to their co-workers may hesitate to invest in females as proteges because "daughters" have a tendency to grow up, go away, get married, and have babies. The organizational "sons" are viewed as a better bet to become the "heir apparent."

In addition to the daughter role, significant numbers of women also must cope with the girlfriend role. In 1980, Mary

Ann Cunningham made the headlines of all the major newspapers, not because she was a graduate of Harvard and the executive vice president of a Fortune 500 corporation, but rather because she was perceived by her male co-workers to be "sleeping her way to the top." Interestingly enough, she never denied having sex with the president but rather insisted they were "truly in love" (Cunningham 1984).

The occasional headlines about office romances reflect a change that occurred in the 1980s. The office became a place for professionals and career-oriented individuals to "meet, date, and relate." Workplaces, not unlike the sex-segregated dormitories of the 1960s, had become "co-ed."

Being a successful professional often means working long hours under tight deadlines, being available on an on-call basis, and working long stints out of town. The same institutions that afford little time for house and child care make it equally difficult for singles to develop and nurture romantic relationships. According to Lisa A. Maniero's latest report on office romance, the sexual revolution that exploded on college and university campuses in the 1960s and 1970s had moved to the workplace in the 1980s (Maniero 1989). Although Maniero finds romance at work a positive influence on worker morale and productivity, Barbara Gutek (1985) finds that sex in the workplace actually reduces productivity and is generally detrimental to women workers.

Perhaps the most central traditional role for women is that of sex partner (or sex object) and procreator. When this role supersedes appropriate worker roles, the work environment becomes "eroticized." *Playboy* pin-ups in the workplace, off-color graffiti, teasing and flirting behaviors, and physical touching are all manifestations of the spillover of inappropriate sex-role expectations into the workplace.

Women in such workplaces may be accused of capitalizing on their abilities as sex partners/objects rather than as creative employees. Like Mary Ann Cunningham, they may be charged with sleeping their way to the top. Gutek suggests that one may use her "feminine wiles" to get a better typewriter, a free out-of-town excursion, a car phone, or an office with a window, but Cunningham's notoriety stands testament to the fact that sex will not necessarily take you to the top.

The spillover of sex roles into the business environment can become the career woman's nightmare—sexual harassment. Survey research has indicated that from 45 percent to 90 percent of

30

all working women experience sexual harassment (Stambaugh 1989). This wide margin in estimating the prevalence of sexual harassment is due to an inability of the scientific, business, and legal communities to reach a consensus on a precise definition of this problem. Although it is true that harassers can be of either sex, reports of female harassment of males is rare. According to a recent study of Arizona upper-level government employees (grades 23–30), only 7 percent of the males surveyed had experienced requests for sexual favors—contrasted with 21 percent of the women (Hale and Kelly 1989). Women at lower levels experience higher rates of harassment. Probably the most famous sexual harassment case of the 1980s has been the Jim Bakker-Jessica Hahn affair. In this case, both Bakker and Hahn claim to be victims of harassment.

Fifteen years of case law indicates three conditions that must be proved before sexual harassment is charged: (1) the behavior must be *unwelcomed*, (2) it must be *repetitive*, and (3) it must be considered *offensive* by the subject of the action (Cohen 1987).

Typically, male victims assert that they are targets of a much younger, provocatively dressed, attractive "girl" (Backhouse and Cohen 1981). In these cases, the young women refuse to take a "hint"; the "victims" of sexual harassment typically see to it that the young women are transferred or dismissed. The most prevalent sexual harassment cases, however, involve male superiors who press female subordinates for sexual favors.

A more subtle form of harassment stems not from any one person's behavior but from a *hostile environment*. Hostile behaviors often develop at office parties, picnics, and other "fun" activities where drinking and unprofessional behavior are encouraged. Workplaces where flirting and sexual touching are accepted are highly "eroticized" and are more likely to harbor sexual harassers than environments free of sexual expectations (Gutek 1985).

35   Such sexual harassment of women in traditional male careers by co-workers may be the result of the defensive posture of the men. Sexual harassment is used to remind the invading women that their primary role is that of a sex object, not of a professional.

There is evidence that sexual harassment occurs across all industries, including the Fortune 500 companies (Sandroff 1988). Employees in all occupations are harassed—supervisors have been harassed by their staff (Clarke 1986) and teachers often endure harassment by their students (Herbert 1989). It is prevalent in the military (Reily 1980), in the government (U.S. Merit Systems Protection Board 1987), and in academic institutions (Dziech and Weiner 1984). The scope of the problem is difficult to assess because most cases go unreported (Markunas and Joyce-Brady 1987). This fact may reflect a fear held by victims that nothing will be done to address the problem adequately. One case that has become an important exception to this rule occurred in Arizona. Leta Ford, a manager for Revlon, brought suit against her employer (*Ford v. Revlon* 1987). The courts ruled in Ford's favor because she was able to produce a "paper trail" of complaints and grievances over a 13-month period and to demonstrate that Revlon had not taken action to stop the harassment.

The 1986 Supreme Court opinion in the case of *Meritor Savings Bank v. Vinson* has been widely used by organizations to formulate their sexual harassment policy (Cohen 1987). In the *Vinson* decision, victims of sexual harassment won the battle but lost the war. In the first year after *Vinson,* the courts ruled against the plaintiff and in favor of employers in 20 of 31 federal district court cases (Bureau of National Affairs, Inc. 1988). The majority of appeals court decisions have also favored the employer (Bureau of National Affairs, Inc. 1988). Therefore, it appears that the judicial opinions on sexual harassment have served to create effective sexual harassment policies that *avoid liability.* However, it is not clear to what degree these policies actually prevent sexual harassment.

In October of 1989, the House Ethics Committee found representative Jim Bates (D-Calif.) guilty of sexually harassing two members of his staff (Associated Press 1989). The women claimed his behavior created a hostile environment. Bates apologized to the two women but stated: "Times are changing. Members of Congress are going to be scrutinized for their personal and professional behavior . . . sexual harassment is very serious and not to be taken lightly. *I did not know what sexual harassment means until this came up*" (Associated Press 1989, p. A13).

It is clear from Rep. Bates's last remark that, even though sexual harassment has been a long-standing problem for women and a political issue for more than ten years, many still are not aware of the basic dimensions of the problem: (1) of what sexual harassment is, (2) that it is harmful, and (3) that the consequences can be harsh. Increased media attention would do much to increase the public's awareness of the problem.

CONCLUSION

Establishing a successful career in the 1990s requires integrating one's private and public lives. The task is much more than an individual or even an organizational matter. It involves a reconceptualization of sex-role ideology; the acceptance of this new ideology by both men and women; and the adoption of this way of thinking by the nation's political, economic, and judicial institutions.

References

Allen, R. E. 1989. "It pays to invest in tomorrow's workforce." *The Wall Street Journal*, 6 November: A16.

Associated Press. 1989. "Lawmaker harassed two women on staff, is rebuked by panel." *Arizona Republic*, 19 (October):A13.

Backhouse, C., and L. Cohen. 1981. *Sexual Harassment on the Job*. Toronto: Prentice-Hall.

Beattie, L. E. 1984. "Battling another bias in business lending." *Business Week*, 31 (October):14–16.

Berstein, P. 1985. "Family ties, corporate bonds." *Working Women*, 10(S) (May):85–87; 138–139.

Blank, R. M. 1988. "Women's paid work, household income and household well-being." In S. E. Rix (ed.), *The American Woman 1988–1989*. New York: W. W. Norton.

Bureau of National Affairs, Inc. 1988. "Sexual harassment." In *Corporate Affairs, Nepotism, Office Romance and Sexual Harassment*. Washington, D.C.: Bureau of National Affairs.

Clarke, L. W. 1986. "Women supervisors experience sexual harassment, too." *Supervisory Management*, 31(4) (April):35–36.

Cohen, C. F. 1987. "Implications of *Meritor Savings Bank, FSB v. Vinson et al.*" *Labor Law Journal*, 38 (April):243–247.

Cunningham, M. 1984. *Power Play*. New York: Simon & Schuster.

Dziech, B. W., and L. Weiner. 1984. *The Lecherous Professor*. Boston: Beacon.

Elrich, E. 1986. "Child care, the private sector cannot do it alone." *Business Week*, (October):52–53.

Ford v. Revlon. 1987. Arizona State Supreme Court.

Friedan, B. 1981. *The Second Stage*. New York: Summit.

Garbarine, R. 1989. "Building workplace centers to reduce turnover." *New York Times*, 15 (October):32.

Gutek, B. A. 1985. *Sex and the Workplace*. San Francisco: Jossey-Bass.

Hale, M. M., and R. M. Kelly. 1989. *Gender, Bureaucracy and Democracy*. Westport, CT: Greenwood.

Hardesty, S., and N. Jacobs. 1986. *Success and Betrayal: The Crisis of Women in Corporate America*. New York: Franklin Watts.

Heller, L. 1983. "The last of the angry men." *Executive Female*, (September/October):33–38.

Herbert, C. 1989. *Talking of Silence: The Harassment of School Girls.* New York: Palmer.

Hochschild, A. 1989. *The Second Shift.* New York: Wiley.

Lenhoff, D. 1987. "Family medical leave act." In L. Tarr-Whelan and L.C. Isensee (eds.), *The Women's Economic Justice Agenda: Ideas for the States.* Washington, D.C.: Center for Policy Alternatives.

Lewin, T. 1989. "Study finds high turnover in child care workers." *New York Times,* 18 October:A10.

Lewis, S. N. C., and C. L. Cooper. 1988. "Stress in dual-earner families." In B. Gutek, A. Stromberg, and L. Larwood (eds.), *Women and Work, An Annual Review,* Vol. 3, Newbury Park, CA: Sage.

MacCorquodale, P. 1986. "The economics of home and family." In J. Monk and A. Schelgle (eds.); *Women in the Arizona Economy.* Tucson: University of Arizona Press.

Maniero, L. A. 1989. *Office Romance: Love, Power and Sex in the Workplace.* New York: Rawson of McMillan.

Markunas, P. V., and J. M. Joyce-Brady. 1987. "Underutilization of sexual harassment procedures." *Journal of the National Association for Women Deans,* (Spring):27–32.

Nelton, S., and K. Berney. 1987. "Women: The second wave." *Nation's Business,* (May):18–22.

Pleck, Joseph H. 1985. *Working Wives, Working Husbands.* Beverly Hills, CA: Sage.

Reily, P. J. 1980. "Sexual harassment in the Navy." Unpublished master's thesis. U.S. Navy Post Graduate School, Monterey, CA.

Sandroff, R. 1988. "Sexual harassment in the Fortune 500." *Working Woman,* (December):69–73.

Skow, J. 1989. "The myth of male housework." *Time,* (August):62.

Stambaugh, P. 1989. "Sexual harassment: The politics of discourse." Unpublished paper, School of Justice Studies, Arizona State University, Tempe, Arizona.

Thompson, R. 1988. "Caring for the children." *Nation's Business,* 76 (May):20.

U.S. Bureau of the Census. 1988. *Current Population Survey Report.* Washington, D.C.: U.S. Government Printing Office.

U.S. Department of Labor. 1988. *Child Care: A Work Force Issue,* Table B-21. Washington, D.C.: U.S. Government Printing Office.

U.S. Department of Labor. 1989. *Handbook of Labor Statistics.* Washington, D.C.: U.S. Government Printing Office.

U.S. Merit Systems Protection Board, 1987. *Sexual Harassment in the Federal Workplace: Is It a Problem?* Washington, D.C.: U.S. Government Printing Office.

Wallis, C., S. Brown, M. Ludtke, and M. Smiligis. 1989. "Onward women!" *Time,* 4 (December):80–89.

Wall Street Journal. 1990. "A daughter heir apparent isn't heir." *Wall Street Journal,* 9 February:B12.

Questions for Thought and Writing

1. In the *Executive Female* interview discussed in the article, 10 executive men suggested that women hit "the glass ceiling" because they are less willing than men to make personal sacrifices for their careers. How does the author of the study interpret this conclusion? In an essay that explains Kelly's position, decide whether you agree with her and why or why not.

2. Kelly argues that although women's presence in the labor force has increased from 35 percent in the 1950s to over 70 percent in the 1990s, "options for integrating the roles of mother and career woman have not been great." Women in the work force, she claims, have been forced "to either avoid being a mother, adopt a 'father's' approach to child care, or seek alternative work hours and work forms." In your own experience, what is a "father's" approach to child care? How did your own family compare to the model described by Kelly in this section?

3. According to Kelly's study, one of the barriers women face in the workplace is being "perceived in the limited roles of surrogate daughters, wives, or mothers rather than as workers." What does Kelly believe are the long-term disadvantages for women that result from these perceptions? Discuss this idea in terms of the work environments you have experienced. Have you seen these perceptions at work? How would the expectations to which you are held at work change if your gender changed?

The Second Shift: Working Parents and the Revolution at Home

ARLIE RUSSELL HOCHSCHILD WITH ANN MACHUNG

CHAPTER 1: A SPEED-UP IN THE FAMILY

She is not the same woman in each magazine advertisement, but she is the same idea. She has that working-mother look as she strides forward, briefcase in one hand, smiling child in the other. Literally and figuratively, she is moving ahead. Her hair, if long, tosses behind her; if it is short, it sweeps back at the sides, suggesting mobility and progress. There is nothing shy or passive about her. She is confident, active, "liberated." She wears a dark tailored suit, but with a silk bow or colorful frill that says, "I'm really feminine underneath." She has made it in a man's world without sacrificing her femininity. And she has done this on her own. By some personal miracle, this image suggests, she has managed to combine what 150 years of industrialization have split wide apart—child and job, frill and suit, female culture and male.

When I showed a photograph of a supermom like this to the working mothers I talked to in the course of researching this book, many responded with an outright laugh. One daycare worker and mother of two, ages three and five, threw back her head: "Ha! They've got to be *kidding* about her. Look at me, hair a mess, nails jagged, twenty pounds overweight. Mornings, I'm getting my kids dressed, the dog fed, the lunches made, the shopping list done. That lady's got a maid." Even working mothers who did have maids couldn't imagine combining work and family in such a carefree way. "Do you know what a baby *does* to your life, the two o'clock feedings, the four o'clock feedings?" Another mother of two said: "They don't show it, but she's whistling"—she imitated a whistling woman, eyes to the sky—"so she can't hear the din." They envied the apparent ease of the woman with the flying hair, but she didn't remind them of anyone they knew.

The women I interviewed—lawyers, corporate executives, word processors, garment pattern cutters, daycare workers—and most of their husbands, too—felt differently about some issues: how right it is for a mother of young children to work a full-time job, or how much a husband should be responsible for the home. But they all agreed that it was hard to work two full-time jobs and raise young children.

How well do couples do it? The more women work outside the home, the more central this question. The number of women in paid work has risen steadily since before the turn of the century, but since 1950 the rise has been staggering. In 1950, 30 percent of American women were in the labor force; in 1986, it was 55 percent. In 1950, 28 percent of married women with children between six and seventeen worked outside the home; in 1986, it had risen to 68 percent. In 1950, 23 percent of married women with children under six worked. By 1986, it had grown to 54 percent. We don't know how many women with children under the age of one worked outside the home in 1950; it was so rare that the Bureau of Labor kept no statistics on it. Today half of such women do. Two-thirds of all mothers are now in the labor force; in fact, more mothers have paid jobs (or are actively looking for one) than non-mothers. Because of this change in women, two-job families now make up 58 percent of all married couples with children.[1]

5   Since an increasing number of working women have small children, we might expect an increase in part-time work. But ac-tually, 67 percent of the mothers who work have full-time jobs— that is, thirty-five hours or more weekly. That proportion is what it was in 1959.

If more mothers of young children are stepping into full-time jobs outside the home, and if most couples can't afford household help, how much more are fathers doing at home? As I began ex-ploring this question I found many studies on the hours working men and women devote to housework and childcare. One na-tional random sample of 1,243 working parents in forty-four American cities, conducted in 1965–66 by Alexander Szalai and his coworkers, for example, found that working women averaged three hours a day on housework while men averaged 17 minutes; women spent fifty minutes a day of time exclusively with their children; men spent twelve minutes. On the other side of the coin, working fathers watched television an hour longer than their working wives, and slept a half hour longer each night. A compar-ison of this American sample with eleven other industrial coun-tries in Eastern and Western Europe revealed the same difference between working women and working men in those countries as well.[2] In a 1983 study of white middle-class families in greater Boston, Grace Baruch and R. C. Barnett found that working men married to working women spent only three-quarters of an hour longer each week with their kindergarten-aged children than did men married to housewives.[3]

Szalai's landmark study documented the now familiar but still alarming story of the working woman's "double day," but it left me wondering how men and women actually felt about all this. He and his coworkers studied how people used time, but not, say, how a father felt about his twelve minutes with his child, or how his wife felt about it. Szalai's study revealed the visible surface of what I discovered to be a set of deeply emotional is-sues: What should a man and woman contribute to the family? How appreciated does each feel? How does each respond to sub-tle changes in the balance of marital power? How does each develop an unconscious "gender strategy" for coping with the work at home, with marriage, and, indeed, with life itself? These were the underlying issues.

But I began with the measurable issue of time. Adding together the time it takes to do a paid job and to do housework and childcare, I averaged estimates from the major studies on time use done in the 1960s and 1970s, and discovered that women worked roughly fifteen hours longer each week than men. Over a year, they worked an *extra month of twenty-four-hour days a year.* Over a dozen years, it was an extra year of twenty-four-hour days. Most women without children spend much more time than men on housework; with children, they devote more time to both housework and childcare. Just as there is a wage gap between men and women in the workplace, there is a "leisure gap" between them at home. Most women work one shift at the office or factory and a "second shift" at home.

Studies show that working mothers have higher self-esteem and get less depressed than housewives, but compared to their husbands, they're more tired and get sick more often. In Peggy Thoits's 1985 analysis of two large-scale surveys, each of about a thousand men and women, people were asked how often in the preceding week they'd experienced each of twenty-three symptoms of anxiety (such as dizziness or hallucinations). According to the researchers' criteria, working mothers were more likely than any other group to be "anxious."

In light of these studies, the image of the woman with the flying hair seems like an upbeat "cover" for a grim reality, like those pictures of Soviet tractor drivers smiling radiantly into the distance as they think about the ten-year plan. The Szalai study was conducted in 1965–66. I wanted to know whether the leisure gap he found in 1965 persists, or whether it has disappeared. Since most married couples work two jobs, since more will in the future, since most wives in these couples work the extra month a year, I wanted to understand what the wife's extra month a year meant for each person, and what it does for love and marriage in an age of high divorce. . . .

10

Inside the Extra Month a Year

The women I interviewed seemed to be far more deeply torn between the demands of work and family than were their husbands. They talked with more animation and at greater length than their husbands about the abiding conflict between them. Busy as they were, women more often brightened at the idea of yet another interviewing session. They felt the second shift was *their* issue and most of their husbands agreed. When I telephoned one husband to arrange an interview with him, explaining that I wanted to ask him about how he managed work and family life, he replied genially, "Oh, this will *really* interest my *wife.*"

It was a woman who first proposed to me the metaphor, borrowed from industrial life, of the "second shift." She strongly resisted the *idea* that homemaking was a "shift." Her family was her life and she didn't want it reduced to a job. But as she put it, "You're on duty at work. You come home, and you're on duty. Then you go back to work and you're on duty." After eight hours of adjusting insurance claims, she came home to put on the rice for dinner, care for her children, and wash laundry. Despite herself her home life *felt* like a second shift. That was the real story and that was the real problem.

Men who shared the load at home seemed just as pressed for time as their wives, and as torn between the demands of career and small children. . . . But the majority of men did not share the load at home. Some refused outright. Others refused more passively, often offering a loving shoulder to lean on, an understanding ear as their working wife faced the conflict they both saw as hers. At first it seemed to me that the problem of the second shift was hers. But I came to realize that those husbands who helped very little at home were often indirectly just as deeply affected as their wives by the need to do that work, through the resentment their wives feel toward them, and through their need to steel themselves against that resentment. Evan Holt, a warehouse furniture salesman . . . did very little housework and played with his four-year-old son, Joey, at his convenience. Juggling the demands of work with family at first seemed a problem for his wife. But Evan himself suffered enormously from the side effects of "her" problem. His wife did the second shift, but she resented it keenly, and half-consciously expressed her frustration and rage by losing interest in sex and becoming overly absorbed with Joey. One way or another, most men I talked with do suffer the severe repercussions of what I think is a transitional phase in American family life.

One reason women take a deeper interest than men in the problems of juggling work with family life is that even when husbands happily shared the hours of work, their wives felt more *re-*

sponsible for home and children. More women kept track of doctors' appointments and arranged for playmates to come over. More mothers than fathers worried about the tail on a child's Halloween costume or a birthday present for a school friend. They were more likely to think about their children while at work and to check in by phone with the baby-sitter.

Partly because of this, more women felt torn between one sense of urgency and another, between the need to soothe a child's fear of being left at daycare, and the need to show the boss she's "serious" at work. More women than men questioned how good they were as parents, or if they did not, they questioned why they weren't questioning it. More often than men, women alternated between living in their ambition and standing apart from it.

As masses of women have moved into the economy, families have been hit by a "speed-up" in work and family life. There is no more time in the day than there was when wives stayed home, but there is twice as much to get done. It is mainly women who absorb this "speed-up." Twenty percent of the men in my study shared housework equally. Seventy percent of men did a substantial amount (less than half but more than a third), and 10 percent did less than a third. Even when couples share more equitably in the work at home, women do two-thirds of the *daily* jobs at home, like cooking and cleaning up—jobs that fix them into a rigid routine. Most women cook dinner and most men change the oil in the family car. But, as one mother pointed out, dinner needs to be prepared every evening around six o'clock, whereas the car oil needs to be changed every six months, any day around that time, any time that day. Women do more childcare than men, and men repair more household appliances. A child needs to be tended daily while the repair of household appliances can often wait "until I have time." Men thus have more control over *when* they make their contributions than women do. They may be very busy with family chores but, like the executive who tells his secretary to "hold my calls," the man has more control over his time. The job of the working mother, like that of the secretary, is usually to "take the calls."

Another reason women may feel more strained than men is that women more often do two things at once—for example, write checks and return phone calls, vacuum and keep an eye on a three-year-old, fold laundry and think out the shopping list. Men more often cook dinner *or* take a child to the park. Indeed, women more often juggle three spheres—job, children, and housework—while most men juggle two—job and children. For women, two activities compete with their time with children, not just one.

15

Beyond doing more at home, women also devote *proportionately more* of their time at home to housework and proportionately less of it to childcare. Of all the time men spend working at home, more of it goes to childcare. That is, working wives spend relatively more time "mothering the house"; husbands spend more time "mothering" the children. Since most parents prefer to tend to their children than clean house, men do more of what they'd rather do. More men than women take their children on "fun" outings to the park, the zoo, the movies. Women spend more time on maintenance, feeding and bathing children, enjoyable activities to be sure, but often less leisurely or "special" than going to the zoo. Men also do fewer of the "undesirable" household chores: fewer men than women wash toilets and scrub the bathroom.

As a result, women tend to talk more intently about being overtired, sick, and "emotionally drained." Many women I could not tear away from the topic of sleep. They talked about how much they could "get by on" . . . six and a half, seven, seven and a half, less, more. They talked about who they knew who needed more or less. Some apologized for how much sleep they needed—"I'm afraid I need eight hours of sleep"—as if eight was "too much." They talked about the effect of a change in baby-sitter, the birth of a second child, or a business trip on their child's pattern of sleep. They talked about how to avoid fully waking up when a child called them at night, and how to get back to sleep. These women talked about sleep the way a hungry person talks about food.

20　　　All in all, if in this period of American history, the two-job family is suffering from a speed up of work and family life, working mothers are its primary victims. It is ironic, then, that often it falls to women to be the "time and motion expert" of family life. Watching inside homes, I noticed it was often the mother who rushed children, saying, "Hurry up! It's time to go," "Finish your cereal now," "You can do that later," "Let's go!" When a bath is crammed into a slot between 7:45 and 8:00 it was often the mother who called out, "Let's see who can take their bath the quickest!" Often a younger child will rush out, scurrying to be first in bed, while the older and wiser one stalls, resistant, sometimes resentful: "Mother is always rushing us." Sadly enough, women are more often the lightning rods for family aggressions aroused by the speed-up of work and family life. They are the "villains" in a process of which they are also the primary victims. More than the longer hours, the sleeplessness, and feeling torn, this is the saddest cost to women of the extra month a year.

CHAPTER 2: MARRIAGE IN THE STALLED REVOLUTION

Each marriage bears the footprints of economic and cultural trends which originate far outside marriage. A rise in inflation which erodes the earning power of the male wage, an expanding service sector which opens up jobs for women, new cultural images—like the woman with the flying hair—that make the working mother seem exciting, all these changes do not simply go on *around* marriage. They occur *within* marriage, and transform it. Problems between husbands and wives, problems which seem "individual" and "marital," are often individual experiences of powerful economic and cultural shock waves that are not caused by one person or two. Quarrels that erupt, as we'll see, between Nancy and Evan Holt, Jessica and Seth Stein, Anita and Ray Judson result mainly from a friction between faster-changing women and slower-changing men, rates of change which themselves result from the different rates at which the industrial economy has drawn men and women into itself.

There is a "his" and "hers" to the economic development of the United States. In the latter part of the nineteenth century, it was mainly men who were drawn off the farm into paid, industrial work and who changed their way of life and their identity. At that point in history, men became more different from their fathers than women became from their mothers. Today the economic arrow points at women; it is women who are being drawn into wage work, and women who are undergoing changes in their way of life and identity. Women are departing more from their mothers' and grandmothers' way of life, men are doing so less.*

Both the earlier entrance of men into the industrial economy and the later entrance of women have influenced the relations *between* men and women, especially their relations within marriage. The former increase in the number of men in industrial work tended to increase the power of men, and the present growth in the number of women in such work has somewhat increased the power of women. On the whole, the entrance of men into industrial work did not destabilize the family whereas *in the absence of other changes*, the rise in female employment has gone with the rise in divorce. . . .

---

*This is more true of white and middle-class women than it is of black or poor women, whose mothers often worked outside the home. But the trend I am talking about—an increase from 20 percent of women in paid jobs in 1900 to 55 percent in 1986—has affected a large number of women.

The exodus of women into the economy has not been accompanied by a cultural understanding of marriage and work that would make this transition smooth. The workforce has changed. Women have changed. But most workplaces have remained inflexible in the face of the family demands of their workers and at home, most men have yet to really adapt to the changes in women. This strain between the change in women and the absence of change in much else leads me to speak of a "stalled revolution."

25   A society which did not suffer from this stall would be a society *humanely* adapted to the fact that most women work outside the home. The workplace would allow parents to work part time, to share jobs, to work flexible hours, to take parental leaves to give birth, tend a sick child, or care for a well one. As Delores Hayden has envisioned in *Redesigning the American Dream*, it would include affordable housing closer to places of work, and perhaps community-based meal and laundry services. It would include men whose notion of manhood encouraged them to be active parents and share at home. In contrast, a stalled revolution lacks social arrangements that ease life for working parents, and lacks men who share the second shift.

If women begin to do less at home because they have less time, if men do little more, if the work of raising children and tending a home requires roughly the same effort, then the questions of who does what at home and of what "needs doing" become key. Indeed, they may become a source of deep tension in the marriage. . . .

As I drove from my classes at Berkeley to the outreaching suburbs, small towns, and inner cities of the San Francisco Bay to observe and ask questions in the homes of two-job couples, and back to my own two-job marriage, my first question about who does what gave way to a series of deeper questions: What leads some working mothers to do all the work at home themselves—to pursue what I call a supermom strategy—and what leads others to press their husbands to share the responsibility and work of the home? Why do some men genuinely want to share housework and childcare, others fatalistically acquiesce, and still others actively resist?

How does each husband's ideas about manhood lead him to think he "should feel" about what he's doing at home and at work? What does he really feel? Do his real feelings conflict with what he thinks he should feel? How does he resolve the conflict? The same questions apply to wives. What influence does each person's consequent "strategy" for handling his or her feelings and actions with regard to the second shift affect his or her children, job, and marriage? Through this line of questioning, I was led to the complex web of ties between a family's needs, the sometime quest for equality, and happiness in modern marriage, the real topic of this book.

We can describe a couple as rich or poor and that will tell us a great deal about their two-job marriage. We can describe them as Catholic, Protestant, Jewish, black, Chicano, Asian, or white and that will tell us something more. We can describe their marriage as a combination of two personalities, one "obsessive compulsive," say, and the other "narcissistic," and again that will tell us something. But knowledge about social class, ethnicity, and personality takes us only so far in understanding who does and doesn't share the second shift, and whether or not sharing the work at home makes marriages happier.

When I sat down to compare one couple that shared the second shift with another three that didn't, many of the answers that would seem obvious—a man's greater income, his longer hours of work, the fact that his mother was a housewife or his father did little at home, his ideas about men and women—all these factors didn't really explain why some women work the extra month a year and others don't. They didn't explain why some women seemed content to work the extra month, while others were deeply unhappy about it. When I compared a couple who was sharing and happy with another couple who was sharing but miserable, it was clear that purely economic or psychological answers were not enough. Gradually, I felt the need to explore how *deep* within each man and woman gender ideology goes. I felt the need to understand the ways in which some men and women seemed to be egalitarian "on top" but traditional "underneath," or the other way around. I tried to sensitize myself to the difference between shallow ideologies (ideologies which were contradicted by deeper feelings) and deep ideologies (which were reinforced by such feelings). I explored how each person reconciled ideology with his or her own behavior, that of a partner, and with the other realities of life. I felt the need to explore what I call loosely "gender strategies."

The Top and Bottom of Gender Ideology

A gender strategy is a plan of action through which a person tries to solve problems at hand, given the cultural notions of gender at play. To pursue a gender strategy, a man draws on beliefs about manhood and womanhood, beliefs that are forged in early child-hood and thus anchored to deep emotions. He makes a connection between how he thinks about his manhood, what he feels about it, and what he does. It works in the same way for a woman.

A woman's gender ideology determines what sphere she *wants* to identify with (home or work) and how much power in the marriage she wants to have (less, more, or the same amount). I found three types of ideology of marital roles:—traditional, tran-sitional, and egalitarian. Even though she works, the "pure" tradi-tional wants to identify with her activities at home (as a wife, a mother, a neighborhood mom), wants her husband to base his at work and wants less power than he. The traditional man wants the same. The "pure" egalitarian, as the type emerges here, wants to identify with the same spheres her husband does, and to have an equal amount of power in the marriage. Some want the couple to be jointly oriented to the home, others to their careers, or both of them to jointly hold some balance between the two. Between the traditional and the egalitarian is the transitional, any one of a variety of types of blending of the two. But, in contrast to the tra-ditional, a transitional woman wants to identify with her role at work as well as at home. Unlike the egalitarian, she believes her husband should base his identity more on work than she does. A typical transitional wants to identify *both* with the caring for the home, and with helping her husband earn money, but wants her husband to focus on earning a living. A typical transitional man is all for his wife working, but expects her to take the main respon-sibility at home too. Most men and women I talked with were "transitional." At least, transitional ideas came out when I asked people directly what they believed. . . .

Gender Strategies

When a man tries to apply his gender ideology to the situations that face him in real life, unconsciously or not he pursues a gender strategy.[4] He outlines a course of action. He might become a "su-perdad"—working long hours and keeping his child up late at night to spend time with him or her. Or he might cut back his hours at work. Or he might scale back housework and spend less time with his children. Or he might actively try to share the second shift.

The term "strategy" refers both to his plan of action and to his emotional preparations for pursuing it. For example, he may require himself to suppress his career ambitions to devote himself more to his children, or suppress his responsiveness to his children's appeals in the course of steeling himself for the struggle at work. He might harden himself to his wife's appeals, or he might be the one in the family who "lets" himself see when a child is calling out for help.

In the families I am about to describe, then, I have tried to be sensitive to the fractures in gender ideology, the conflicts between what a person thinks he or she ought to feel and what he or she does feel, and to the emotional work it takes to fit a gender ideal when inner needs or outer conditions make it hard.   35

As this social revolution proceeds, the problems of the two-job family will not diminish. If anything, as more couples work two jobs these problems will increase. If we can't return to traditional marriage, and if we are not to despair of marriage altogether, it becomes vitally important to understand marriage as a magnet for the strains of the stalled revolution, and to understand gender strategies as the basic dynamic of marriage.

The Economy of Gratitude

The interplay between a man's gender ideology and a woman's implies a deeper interplay between his gratitude toward her, and hers toward him. For how a person wants to identify himself or herself influences what, in the back and forth of a marriage, will seem like a gift and what will not. If a man doesn't think it fits the kind of "man" he wants to be to have his wife earn more than he, it may become his "gift" to her to "bear it" anyway. But a man may also feel like the husband I interviewed, who said, "When my wife began earning more than me I thought I'd struck gold!" In this case his wife's salary is the gift, not his capacity to accept it "anyway." When couples struggle, it is seldom simply over who does what. Far more often, it is over the giving and receiving of gratitude.

Family Myths

As I watched couples in their own homes, I began to realize that couples sometimes develop "family myths"—versions of reality that obscure a core truth in order to manage a family tension.[5] Evan and Nancy Holt managed an irresolvable conflict over the distribution of work at home through the myth that they now "shared it equally." Another couple unable to admit to the conflict came to believe "we aren't competing over who will take responsibility at home; we're just dreadfully busy with our careers." Yet another couple jointly believed that the husband was bound hand and foot to his career "because his work demanded it," while in fact his careerism covered the fact that they were avoiding each other. Not all couples need or have family myths. But when they do arise, I believe they often manage key tensions which are linked, by degrees, to the long hand of the stalled revolution.

After interviewing couples for a while, I got into the practice of offering families who wanted it my interpretations of how they fit into the broader picture I was seeing and what I perceived were their strategies for coping with the second shift. Couples were often relieved to discover they were not alone, and were encouraged to open up a dialogue about the inner and outer origins of their troubles.

40   Many couples in this book worked long hours at their jobs and their children were very young: in this way their lot was unusually hard. But in one crucial way they had it far easier than most two-job couples in America: most were middle class. Many also worked for a company that embraced progressive policies toward personnel, generous benefits and salaries. If *these* middle-class couples find it hard to juggle work and family life, many other two-job families across the nation—who earn less, work at less flexible, steady, or lucrative jobs, and rely on poorer day-care—are likely to find it much harder still.

Anne Machung and I began interviewing in 1976, and accomplished most of our interviews in the early 1980s. I finished in 1988. About half of my later interviews were follow-up contacts with couples we'd talked to earlier; the other half were new.

How much had changed from 1976 to 1988? In practical terms, little: most women I interviewed in the late 1980s still do the lion's share of work at home, do most of the daily chores and take responsibility for running the home. But something was different, too. More couples *wanted* to share and imagined that they did. Dorothy Sims, a personnel director, summed up this new blend of idea and reality. She eagerly explained to me that she and her husband Dan "shared all the housework," and that they were "equally involved in raising their nine-month-old son Timothy." Her husband, a refrigerator salesman, applauded her career and "was more pleased than threatened by her high salary"; he urged her to develop such competencies as reading ocean maps, and calculating interest rates (which she'd so far "resisted learning") because these days "a woman should." But one evening at dinner, a telling episode occurred. Dorothy had handed Timothy to her husband while she served us a chicken dinner. Gradually, the baby began to doze on his father's lap. "When do you want me to put Timmy to bed?" Dan asked. A long silence followed during which it occurred to Dorothy—then, I think, to her husband—that this seemingly insignificant question hinted to me that it was *she*, not he, or "they," who usually decided such matters. Dorothy slipped me a glance, put her elbows on the table, and said to her husband in a slow, deliberate voice, "So, what do *we* think?"

When Dorothy and Dan described their "typical days," their picture of sharing grew even less convincing. Dorothy worked the same nine-hour day at the office as her husband. But she came home to fix dinner and to tend Timmy while Dan fit in a squash game three nights a week from six to seven (a good time for his squash partner). Dan read the newspaper more often and slept longer.

Compared to the early interviews, women in the later interviews seemed to speak more often in passing of relationships or marriages that had ended for some other reason but of which it "was also true" that he "didn't lift a finger at home." Or the extra month alone did it. One divorcee who typed part of this manuscript echoed this theme when she explained, "I was a potter and lived with a sculptor for eight years. I cooked, shopped, and cleaned because his art 'took him longer.' He said it was fair because he worked harder. But we both worked at home, and I could see that if anyone worked longer hours I did, because I earned less with my pots than he earned with his sculpture. That was *hard* to live with, and that's really why we ended."

Some women moved on to slightly more equitable arrangements in the early 1980s, doing a bit less of the second shift than the working mothers I talked to in the late 1970s. Comparing two national surveys of working couples, F. T. Juster found the male slice of the second shift rose from 20 percent in 1965 to 30 percent in 1981, and my study may be a local reflection of this slow national trend.[6] But women like Dorothy Sims, who simply add to their extra month a year a new illusion that they aren't doing it, represent a sad alternative to the woman with the flying hair—the woman who doesn't think that's who she is.

45

Endnotes

1. U.S. Bureau of Labor Statistics, *Employment and Earnings, Characteristics of Families: First Quarter* (Washington, D.C.: U.S. Department of Labor, 1988).
2. Alexander Szalai, ed., *The Use of Time: Daily Activities of Urban and Suburban Populations in Twelve Countries*, p. 668, Table B. Another study found that men spent a longer time than women eating meals

(Shelley Coverman, 626). With regard to sleep, the pattern differs for men and women. The higher the social class of a man, the more sleep he's likely to get. The higher the class of a woman, the less sleep she's likely to get. (Upper-white-collar men average 7.6 hours sleep a night. Lower-white-collar, skilled and unskilled men all averaged 7.3 hours. Upper-white-collar women average 7.1 hours of sleep; lower-white-collar workers average 7.4; skilled workers 7.0 and unskilled workers 8.1.) Working wives seem to meet the demands of high-pressure careers by reducing sleep, whereas working husbands don't. For more details on the hours working men and women devote to housework and childcare, see the Appendix of this book.

3. Grace K. Baruch and Rosalind Barnett, pp. 80–81. Also see Kathryn E. Walker and Margaret E. Woods.
4. The concept of "gender strategy" is an adaptation of Ann Swidler's notion of "strategies of action." Swidler focuses on how the individual uses aspects of culture (symbols, rituals, stories) as "tools" for constructing a line of action. Here, I focus on aspects of culture that bear on our ideas of manhood and womanhood, and I focus on our emotional preparation for and the emotional consequences of our strategies.
5. For the term *family myth* I am indebted to Antonio J. Ferreira, 186–225.
6. F. T. Juster, 1986.

Works Cited

Barnett, R. C., and Baruch, Grace. "Correlates of Fathers' Participation in Family Work: A Technical Report." Working Paper No. 106. Wellesley, Ma: Wellesley College Center for Research on Women, 1983.

Coverman, Shelley. "Gender, Domestic Labor Time and Wage Inequality." *American Sociological Review* 48 (1983).

Ferreira, Antonio J. "Psychosis and Family Myth." *American Journal of Psychotherapy* 21 (1967).

Hayden, Dolores, *Redesigning the American Dream*. New York: W.W. Norton, 1984.

Huber, Joan, and Glenna Spitze. *Sex Stratification: Children, Housework and Jobs*. New York: Academic Press, 1983.

Juster, F. T., and Frank P. Stafford (eds). *Time, Goods, and Well-Being*. Ann Arbor, MI: Survey Research Center, Institute for Social Research, University of Michigan, 1985.

Swidler, Ann. "Culture in Action—Symbols and Strategies." *American Sociological Review* 51 (1986).

Szalai, Alexander. *The Use of Time: Daily Activities of Urban and Suburban Populations in Twelve Countries*. The Hague, Netherlands: Mouton, 1972.

Thoits, Peggy. "Multiple Identities: Examining Gender and Marital Status Differences in Distress." *American Sociological Review* 51 (1986): 259–72.

Walker, Kathryn E., and Margaret E. Woods. *Time Use: A Measure of Household Production of Goods and Services*. Washington, D.C.: American Home Economics Association, 1976.

Questions for Thought and Writing

1. The study discusses the conflict between advertising images of the "working mother" and the actual experiences of working mothers. Identify images of working women in the culture around you. To what extent have your ideas about work and family been influenced by these images? What kind of balance between work and family do you envision for yourself in the future? Based on the experiences of the study participants, do you think your expectations are realistic?

2. The article argues that marriage relationships between men and women have been strained by the fact that while women's roles have dramatically changed since the 1950s, the workforce into which they have entered has *not* changed. What are the changes that the authors believe would make for a "humane" society in which both men and women worked outside the home? What would you add to or subtract from society in order to make it more "humane"? Why?

3. What are the three categories of "gender strategies" that the article determines are used by men and women in their attempts to deal with changing gender roles and family/work conflicts? Which of the three strategies is closest to your own in terms of the family life you imagine for yourself? Why?

ISSUES

Roberta Praeger opens this Issues section with "A World Worth Living In," which shares her wrenching, personal history in an effort to put a sympathetic face on women on welfare. She asks the reader to reconsider pernicious stereotypes about welfare recipients and points to the economic disadvantages particular to poor women. Kim Allen's polemical essay, "The 3rd WWWave: Who We Are, and Why We Need to Speak," introduces readers to the mindset of a contemporary

generation of feminists and focuses on the differences between women "having it all" and "doing it all"; that is, adding
work for wages to their traditional homecare-childcare responsibilities. She argues that contemporary U.S. culture af-
fords little respect for either women or men who organize
their lives around stereotypically feminine pursuits. Anita
Hill's "Sexual Harrassment: The Nature of the Beast" describes sexual harassment as "an equal opportunity" phenomenon that cuts across lines of race and class. She argues that a
deeply rooted fear of women in the workplace drives sexual
harassment at work.

A World Worth Living In
Roberta Praeger

As an impoverished woman I live with the exhaustion, the frustration, the deprivation of poverty. As a survivor of incest I
struggle to overcome the emotional burden. One thing has led to
another in my life as the causes of poverty, of incest, of so many
issues have become increasingly clear. My need to personalize has
given way to a realization of social injustice and a commitment to
struggle for social change.

LIVING ON WELFARE

I live alone with my four-year-old child, Jamie. This state (Massachusetts) allocates $328 a month to a family of two living on Aid
to Families with Dependent Children (AFDC). This sum places us,
along with other social service recipients, at an income 40 percent below the federal poverty line. In today's economy, out of this
sum of money, we are expected to pay for rent, utilities, clothing
for two, child-care expenses, food not covered by food stamps,
and any other expenses we may incur.

My food stamps have been cut to the point where they barely
buy food for half the month. I have difficulty keeping up with the
utility bills, and my furniture is falling apart. Furniture breaks,

and there is no money to replace it. Things that others take for granted, such as sheets and towels, become irreplaceable luxuries.

Chaos exists around everything, even the most important issues, like keeping a roof over one's head. How are people expected to pay rent for their families on the shameful amount of income provided by the Welfare Department? The answer, in many cases, is reflected in the living conditions of welfare recipients. Some of us live in apartments that should be considered uninhabitable. We live with roaches, mice, sometimes rats, and floors about to cave in. I live in subsidized housing. It's that or the street. My rent without the subsidy is $400 a month, $72 more than my entire monthly income. It took over a year of red tape between the time of my first application to the time of final acceptance into the program, all the while watching the amount of my rent climb higher and higher. What becomes of the more than 80 percent of AFDC recipients who are not subsidized because there isn't enough of this housing available?

Emergencies are dealt with in the best way possible. One   5
cold winter day, Jamie broke his ankle in the day-care center. It was the day my food stamps were due to arrive. With no food in the house, I had to take him, on public transportation, to the hospital emergency room and then walk to the supermarket with my shopping cart in a foot of snow. This was not an unusual event in my life. All AFDC mothers get caught up in situations like this, because we are alone, because we have few resources and little money.

Ronald Reagan's war on the poor has exacerbated an already intolerable situation. Human service programs have been slashed to the bone. Regulations governing the fuel assistance program have been changed in ways that now make many of the impoverished ineligible. Energy assistance no longer pays my utility bills. For some these changes have meant going without needed fuel, thereby forcing people to endure freezing temperatures.

The food stamp situation has gone from bad to worse. The amount of money allocated for the program has been drastically reduced. My situation reflects that of most welfare recipients. Last year, my food stamps were cut back from $108 to $76 a month, barely enough to buy food for two weeks. Reagan doesn't even allow us to work to supplement our meager income. His reforms resulted in a law, the Omnibus Budget Reconciliation Act, that, in one fell swoop, instituted a number of repressive work-related changes. Its main impact came when it considerably lowered the amount of money a recipient can earn before the termination of benefits. Under this new law even a low-paying, part-time job can make a person no longer eligible for assistance.

The complexity of our lives reaches beyond economic issues. Monday through Friday, I work as an undergraduate student at the University of Massachusetts. On weekends, when in two-parent families, one parent can sometimes shift the responsibility to the other, I provide the entertainment for my child. All the household chores are my responsibility, for I have no one to share them with. When Jamie is sick I spend nights awake with him. When I am sick, I have no one to help me. I can't do things others take for granted, such as spend an evening out at the movies, because I don't have enough money to pay both the admission fee and for child care. Even if I did, I would be too exhausted to get out the front door. Often I wind up caught in a circle of isolation.

What kind of recognition do I and other welfare mothers get for all this hard work? One popular image of welfare recipients pictures us as lazy, irresponsible women, sitting at home, having babies, and living off the government. Much of society treats us like lepers, degrading and humiliating us at every turn, treating us as if we were getting something for nothing. One day I walked into a small grocery store wearing a button that read "Stop Reagan's War on the Poor." The proprietor of the store looked at my button and said to me, "You know, all those people on welfare are rich." Most welfare recipients would say anything rather than admit to being on welfare because of the image it creates. My brother-in-law had the audacity to say to me in conversation one day, "People are poor because they're lazy. They don't want to work."

10   And the Welfare Department shares this image of the recipient with the general public. From the first moment of contact with the department, the client is treated with rudeness, impatience, mistrust, and scorn. She is intimidated by constant redeterminations, reviews, and threats of being cut off. Her life is controlled by a system wracked with ineptness and callous indifference. Two years ago, unable to pay my electric bill, I applied for emergency assistance. It took the Welfare Department so long to pay the bill that the electric company turned the power off. We lived for two days without electricity before my constant badgering of the Welfare Department and the utility company produced results.

The department gives out information that is misleading and/or incomplete. The recipient is made to feel stupid, guilty, and worthless, a "problem" rather than a person. When I first applied I had to answer all sorts of questions about my personal life time and again. Many of my replies were met with disbelief. I sat there for hours at a time, nine months pregnant, waiting to be interviewed. And that was just the beginning of hours and hours of waiting, of filling in forms for the programs that keep us and our children alive.

THE PERSONAL IS POLITICAL

For most women in this situation, suffering is nothing new. Poverty is seldom an isolated issue. It's part of a whole picture. Other issues complicate our lives. For myself, as for many of us, suffering is complicated by memories, the results of trauma brought forward from childhood. Under frilly pink dresses and little blue sailor suits lay horror stories shared by many. The memories I bring with me from my childhood are not very pretty.

I was born in a Boston neighborhood in 1945. My father was a linoleum installer, my mother a homemaker. I want to say that my childhood was colored by the fact that I was an abused child. It's still difficult for me to talk about some things to this day.

My mother didn't give me a life of my own. When I was an infant she force-fed me. At age nine, she was still spoon-feeding me. Much of the time she didn't let me out of her sight. She must have seen school as a threat to her control, for she kept me home half the time. In me she saw not a separate person but an extension of herself. She felt free to do as she wished with my body. Her attempts to control my elimination process have had a lasting impact on my sexuality. The methods she used have been documented for their use in cases of mother-daughter incest. She had an obsessive-compulsive desire to control what went into me, to control elimination, to control everything about me. I had no control over anything. I couldn't get out from under what was happening to me psychologically. Powerlessness, frustration, and emotional insecurity breed a chain of abuse as men abuse women and children and women abuse children.

In the face of all the adverse, perverted attention received 15 from my mother, I turned to my father for love and affection. We became close. In time, though, it became clear he knew as little about child rearing as my mother. His own deprived childhood had taught him only bitterness.

Throughout the years I knew him, he had gambled literally thousands of dollars away at the horse track. He left me alone outside the track gate at age five or six when the sign read "No children allowed." When I was twelve, he set fire to our house. He had run out of money for gambling purposes, and the house was insured against fire. When the insurance money arrived, my mother somehow managed to intercept it and bought new furniture. When my father found out what she had done, he went on a rampage. I had a knick-knack shelf, charred from the fire. He threw it across the room, splinters of glass flying everywhere, and then he hit my mother. This was not an uncommon scene in my childhood.

By the time I reached eleven, my father was beginning to see me in a different light. At this point, the closeness that had developed between him and me still existed. And he proceeded to take advantage of it.

My mother belonged to a poker club, and once a week she would leave the house to go to these sessions. On these occasions my father would come over to me and remove both my clothes and his. He would then use my body to masturbate until he reached orgasm. He attempted to justify these actions by saying, "A man has to have sex and your mother won't." This occurred a number of times when I was between the ages of eleven and thirteen. I cried the last time he did this and he stopped molesting me sexually. In incestuous situations there doesn't have to be any threat; very often there isn't, because parents are in a position of trust, because parents are in a position of power, and because the child needs love. Children are in a developmental stage where they have no choice.

I went to public school and did very well. When I was sixteen, the school authorities told me that no matter how well I did, no matter how high my grades were, they could not keep me in school if I appeared only half the time. So I dropped out. I just spent the whole time sitting in front of the television until my mother died.

20   I didn't understand the extent of my mother's sickness in her treatment of me. Fear that if my mother knew what my father was doing she would kill him seemed realistic to me at the time. And so, I kept silent. I looked at my parents, as all children do, as authority figures. Longing for a way out of the situation, I felt trapped. In the face of all this I felt overwhelmed, afraid, and isolated. I retreated from reality into a world of fantasy. For only

through my imagination could I find any peace of mind or semblance of happiness. The abuse I had taken all these years began to manifest itself in psychosomatic symptoms. Periodically, I started suffering intense abdominal pain. Once I fainted and fell on the bathroom floor. There were three visits to the hospital emergency room. My doctor had misdiagnosed the symptoms as appendicitis.

When I was seventeen, my father, after a major argument with my mother, moved out. Without money to pay the rent, with no job training or other resources, we rented out a room. Ann, the young woman renting the room, was appalled at the situation she discovered. She began to teach me some basic skills such as how to wash my own clothes. For the first time in my life I related positively to someone. My father moved back two months later. For two years this is how the situation remained, my mother, father, Ann, and I all living together.

In 1965 my mother was diagnosed as having lung cancer. Three months later she was dead. I felt nothing, no sorrow, no anger, no emotion. I had long ago learned how to bury my emotions deep down inside of me. I packed my belongings and moved out with Ann, in the midst of my father's ranting and raving.

Living in an apartment with Ann made things seem to improve on the surface. My life was quieter. I held a steady job for the first time. There was a little money to spend. I could come and go as I pleased. It felt good, and I guess, at that point I thought my life had really changed. It took me a long time to realize what an adult who has had this kind of childhood must still go through. I had nightmares constantly. There were times when I went into deep depressions. I didn't know what was going on, what was happening to me, or why.

After holding my first job for three years, I went through a series of jobs in different fields: sales, hairdressing, and, after a period of training, nursing. It seemed I was not functioning well in any area. I fell apart in any situation where demands were made of me. I had no tolerance for hierarchy. I discovered that I performed best when I was acting as charge nurse. Unfortunately, in my role as a Licensed Practical Nurse, I usually wound up low person on the totem pole, generally having to answer to someone else. In time, it became clear to me, that control was a major factor in a variety of situations that I encountered.

My self-confidence and self-esteem were abysmally low. 25 Every time something went wrong my first thought was, "There must be something wrong with me." I didn't know then, what I know now. Children never blame their parents for the wrong that is done. They blame themselves. This feeling carries on into adulthood until it is difficult not to blame oneself for everything that does not go right.

I was depressed, suicidal, frightened out of my wits, and completely overwhelmed by life. After a series of failed relationships and a broken marriage, I wound up alone, with a small child, living on welfare. The emotional burden I carried became complicated by the misery and exhaustion of poverty.

Why have I survived? Why am I not dead? Because I'm a survivor. Because I have Jamie and I love him more than words can say. In him I see the future, not the past.

A MAJOR CHANGE

I survived because in the midst of all this something happened, something that was to turn out to be the major guiding force in my life. In 1972 the owner of my building sent out notices threatening eviction if the tenants did not pay a huge rent increase. Everyone in the building was aghast at the prospect and so formed a tenant union to discuss alternatives. Through my activities with the union, I learned of an organization that did community work throughout the city. Cambridge Tenants Organizing Committee (CTOC) was a multifaceted organization involved in work around issues such as tenants' rights, welfare advocacy, antiracist work, and education concerning sexism in society. I began working with a group of people unlike any that I had been exposed to in the past. They treated me as a person capable of assuming responsibility and doing any job well. My work with CTOC included organizing tenant unions throughout the city, counseling unemployed workers, and attending countless demonstrations, marches, picketings, and hearings. As a group we organized and/or supported eviction blocking, we helped defend people against physical racist attacks, and we demonstrated at the state house for continuation of rent control. I wasn't paid for my work. What I earned was far more important than money. I learned respect for myself as a woman. I learned the joys and pitfalls of working collectively and began assimilating more information than I had at any other time of my life.

And I flourished. I went to meeting after meeting until they consumed almost all of my nonwork time. Over the years I joined other groups. One of my major commitments was to a group that presented political films. My politics became the center of my life.

Through counseling and therapy groups with therapists who   30
shared my political perspective, the guilt I had shouldered all these
years began to lessen. Within a period of three years, through groups
and conventions, I listened to and/or spoke with more than three
hundred other survivors of incest. I heard stories that would make
your hair stand on end. New learning led to making connections. Although the true extent of incest is not known, owing to the fact that
sexual abuse within families usually goes unreported, various statistics estimate that 100,000 to 250,000 children are sexually molested
each year in the United States. Other studies show that one out of
every three to four women in this country is a victim of sexual abuse
as a child. Incest Resources, my primary resource for group counseling, believes these statistics heavily underestimate the extent of actual abuse. So do I. Although the guilt for the abuse lies with the
abuser, the context of the problem reaches far beyond, beyond me or
my parents, into society itself as power and inequality surround us.

Connections with other people have become part and parcel of
my life as my life situation has led me into work surrounding the
issue of poverty. Although I had known for years of the existence of
the Coalition for Basic Human Needs (CBHN)—a progressive
group composed almost totally of welfare recipients—my political
work, reflecting my life situation, had led me in other directions.
Now I found myself alone with a toddler, living on AFDC. When
Jamie was two, I returned to school to acquire additional skills. My
academic work led me into issues concerning poverty as I became
involved in months of activity, along with students and faculty and
a variety of progressive women's groups, constructing a conference
on the issue of women and poverty. Members of CBHN were involved in work on the conference, and we connected.

Social change through welfare-rights struggles became a major focus in my life as I began working with CBHN. Collectively, we
sponsored legislative bills that would improve our lives financially
while, at the same time, we taught others how we actually live.
Public education became intertwined with legislative work as I
spoke at hearings on the reality of living on AFDC. Political support
became intertwined with public education as I spoke on the work
of CBHN to progressive groups and their constituencies, indicting
this country's political system for the impoverishment of its people.

CBHN is composed of chapters representing various cities and
towns across Massachusetts. Grass-roots organizing of welfare recipients takes place within local chapters, while the organization as
a whole works on statewide issues. We mail out newsletters, hold
press conferences, and initiate campaigns. We are currently in-

volved in our most ambitious effort. Whereas in the past our work has been directed toward winning small goals such as a clothing allowance or a small increase in benefits, this time we have set about to bring welfare benefits up to the poverty level, a massive effort involving all of our past strategies and more. We have filed a bill with the state legislature. Public education has become concentrated in the campaign as we plan actions involving the work of welfare-rights groups and individuals throughout the state.

The courage we share as impoverished women has been mirrored throughout this effort. At a press conference to announce the campaign a number of us gave truth to the statement that we and our children go without the basic necessities of life. One woman spoke of sending her child to school without lunch because there was no food in the house. Others had no money for winter jackets or shoes for their children. Sharing the reality of living at 40 percent below the poverty level brings mutual support as well as frustration and anger. In mid-April hundreds of welfare recipients—women carrying infants, the disabled, and the homeless—came from all over Massachusetts to rally in front of the state house along with our supporters and testify to the legislature in behalf of our "Up to the Poverty Level" bill. Courage and determination rang out in statements such as this:

> Take the cost of implementing this program and weigh it, if it must be weighed at all; then weigh it against the anguish suffered by the six-month-old twins who starved to death in a Springfield housing project.
>
> The day that the state legislature has to scrape the gilt off the dome of the state house and sell it for revenue is the day that this state can answer to us that there is not the means to do this.

35   The complexity of the situation comes home to me again and again as I sit in the CBHN office answering the telephone and doing welfare advocacy work. I've spoken with women on AFDC who have been battered to within an inch of their lives, some who are, like myself, survivors of child abuse, and others who are reeling from the effects of racism as well as poverty.

In this society so many of us internalize oppression. We internalize the guilt that belongs to the system that creates the conditions people live in. When we realize this and turn our anger outward in an effort to change society, then we begin to create a world worth living in.

The work isn't easy. Many of us become overwhelmed as well as overextended. It takes courage and fortitude to survive. For we live in a society laden with myths and an inequality that leads to human suffering. In order to alleviate the suffering and provide the equality each and every one of us deserves, we must effect social change. If we are to effect social change, then we must recognize social injustice and destroy the myths it creates. Little did I realize, years ago, when I first began this work how far it reached beyond my own survival. For those of us involved in creating a new society are doing the most important work that exists.

Questions for Thought and Writing

1. In describing her painful experience as a working student/mother on welfare, the author explains that "emergencies are dealt with in the best way possible," which usually means difficult sacrifices for her on behalf of her child. Consider the last time you were faced with an "emergency." How much of a role did money play in your attempts to resolve it? How would having a child have complicated your decisions?
2. The author describes being "treated with rudeness, impatience, mistrust, and scorn" by employees of the Welfare Department. What are the stereotypes about people on welfare that seem to inspire this kind of treatment? How does your knowledge of the author's childhood and personal circumstances affect your perception of what leads people to welfare?
3. The author describes our society as one "laden with myths and an inequality that leads to human suffering." What are the most damaging "myths" and "inequalities" that she has had to contend with? How might her overall life experience have been different if she had been a man?

The 3rd WWWave: Who We Are, and Why We Need to Speak

Kim Allen

FOR THE SECOND WAVE: WE ARE NOT YOU (AND THAT'S NOT A BAD THING)

The spiral goes on. A new generation of women is emerging into the adult world, the first generation who knew about the ERA and "Women's Lib" from early childhood. Many of our mothers went back to school to get higher degrees that were postponed when they had children; many worked outside the home; many were divorced or separated. We grew up hearing "you can be anything you want to be," and yet we knew also that the world didn't welcome high-achieving girls as it did boys. We knew women had the right to have any job that a man could have, and yet we saw few female auto mechanics, engineers, and athletes. We heard about valuing everyone for their contributions—including stay-at-home dads as well as career women—but nonetheless we observed men going to work, pooh-poohing the concept of raising kids, and women either staying at home exclusively or holding a job *and* doing all the housework on top of that.

Clearly feminism is not "finished" now that women have moved into the workplace and everyone knows to say "chairperson" instead of "chairman."

And yet even though a majority of women support the *goals* of feminism, a majority of those will not call themselves "feminist." Feminism has a problem. It has come to be associated with the academic feminists of the university Women's Studies departments. It has come to represent a rigid "agenda" and a fixed set of beliefs which more and more women are not comfortable adhering to. Feminism used to have so many faces, but now only one is considered "legitimate."

What about women who want to get married and have children even though they believe strongly in equal opportunity for men and women? Have they bowed down to the patriarchy? Can they really claim to be feminists?

What about women who want to make money? Who work hard for that promotion, manage their money in the stock market, and use their financial power to get things they want? Have they bowed down to the evil capitalist empire? Can they really claim to be feminists?

What about women who like to shoot guns, who write pornographic short stories, who use the Internet instead of sending out hand-written flyers? Do they "qualify" as feminists?

Yes. If they want to.

We proudly call ourselves feminists, and we are! It seems that young women these days are getting a lot of criticism from old-guard feminists who call their efforts puny and invalid. Our main crime seems to be that we are not replicas of the 60's activists who started the second wave. Some of feminism's image problem is being *created* by second-wave feminists themselves! It is a shame to disown people from your own movement just because they don't conform to your exact model. Times have changed; we need new strategies. We are happy to learn from what you did, but we also need to move on to new efforts that fit the way women live *today*.

Maybe you just need the question asked in a different way: Do you think the suffragists of the first wave would have enthusiastically supported the 1960's counterculture and the sexual revolution as a logical extension of their feminist efforts? No? So why do you want us to be just like you?

The third wave is gearing up. We know it's unfair that women work just as hard as men outside the home (indeed, *harder* than men just to be considered competent), then come home to do 75% of the housework. We sense that our very value system still rewards men's achievements simply because they are done by men, and that women will never "measure up" on the male yardstick. There's plenty more to do in the name of feminism. We of the third wave are more hard-boiled than the second, lacking the idealism of the 1960's. But we are just as angry, and in a better financial position. Don't underestimate our drive and clout.

Now don't get me wrong. I for one am very grateful to the second wave for helping me get to this point. I have opportunities my mother never did. I am protected by laws that it took sweat, blood, and tears to pass 30 years ago. I will never suffer through some of the humiliating and painful experiences that members of the second wave endured to bring women the rights and priviledges they have now. I am not taking you for granted. But I *am* champing at the bit to fly off in my own direction with these wings you helped me gain! Don't tell me where to fly!

And don't lament the loss of your "Movement"! It's not dead; it's been reborn in a new form appropriate for the 90's. It is moving off in new directions that you couldn't have anticipated 30 years ago. We are not you, and that's not a bad thing. (Are you just like *your* mother?) The third wave has arrived.

FOR THE WOMEN: "BUT ISN'T FEMINISM A THING OF THE PAST?"

I hear this all the time from career women. These are smart women, with college degrees or beyond, often in the midst of a tricky balancing act between job, children, and personal pursuits. They landed a decent job, got a promotion in a couple years, had a family. They "have it all," just like the magazines promised they

would. Who needs feminism? Aren't feminists just a bunch of angry man-haters who see sexism in everything and want to add
new pronouns like "hir" to the English language?

Sigh. No.

Did you ever ask yourself, why do I get up at 5:30 am so I can
get the kids dressed and pack their lunches and send them off to
school, then rush off to my job from 8 to 6, then rush home to
cook dinner, do a couple hours of cleaning, catch up on reading
for work, then collapse in bed? Is this "having it all," or is it
merely "doing it all"?

We don't deny that you have much more than your mother
did. A better education, a higher-paying job, more laws protecting
your rights—all these things are crucial advances that we have
made because of second wave feminism. But it's a very different
thing to say that feminism is over, that it's finished, that nothing
more needs to be done, or that everything will "work itself out"
now that the first bricks have been laid.

There are questions you can ask yourself. Why do women
who hold outside jobs still do 75% of the housework? Didn't feminism enlighten all the men to regard sharing a home as genuine
sharing? Why do most high school kids still learn that history is a
series of wars, kings, pacts, and economic movements? Didn't
feminism enlighten educators to the existence of important
women and their impact on culture? Where are the female athletes, scientists, auto mechanics, and construction workers that
feminism was supposed to create by showing that "girls were as
good as boys"? Where are the househusbands who no longer tie
their egos to supporting a family, but find joy instead in raising
children while their wives work? Where is the *respect* for women
or men who choose stereotypically female pursuits?

The last question is the key. Feminism has not broken the
gender stereotypes that imprison men and women in fundamentally unequal roles. It has allowed very specific women to gain respect because they follow certain rules. Let me say loudly and
clearly that I am **not** criticizing these women—heck, I'm one of
them!—and that I firmly believe our recently gained economic
freedom from men is the best advance we've made.

But the stereotypes *persist.* Part of the problem is that the
Reagan years reentrenched these gender roles like a tick diving
back down under flesh. When it comes right down to it, men do
pretty much the same things that they ever did: get an education,
get a job, have a family, earn money. The difference now is that

women have broken into the job arena. But we still do the lion's share of housework, emotional upkeep in relationships, raising children, caring for elderly family members, and supporting men psychologically.

This was not the goal of the second wave, nor is it especially good for women. Do you really like spending all that money on daycare, rushing around to ten places at once—all so your boss can pay you less overtime, decide that you aren't as "committed" to your career as a man, and subtley decrease your earnings compared to men over the long haul? Do you really think that the male lifestyle of sacrificing personal development and relationships for a career is the *only* lifestyle worthy of rewards and respect? Do you get the feeling America has no concept of "healthy balance"?

Some people are starting to decide that feminists are to blame for this situation. Women say, "I'm not a feminist," by which they mean, "Don't worry—I won't be out there waving a sign that might hurt my position in the company. And by the way, I have to leave at 4 to pick up Bobby from daycare." Translation: feminists are troublemakers and who has time for that anyway when I'm booked 20 hours out of 24? Men say, "Feminism failed. My wife is miserable with all the stress from her job and then having to take care of the kids on top of that." Translation: why can't you women just stay home like you're supposed to? (*Share* the childcare? What does that mean?)

If you're unhappy with the way work and family balance (or fail to balance) for women, that's a clue that feminism is not "a thing of the past." The working world has grudgingly allowed us to enter, but we haven't had a say in the rules! Why can't we have more flexible work schedules, more on-site child care, more telecommuting? Why can't we respect men who want to stay home? Why can't we respect women who want to stay home? People are shifting around in the worlds of work and family, but somehow, the old edifice remains in place. The old values, the old structures. Feminism of the 90's—or at least part of it—is about making new structures that fit the way women live now, not the way men lived in the 1950's.

It will mean that men have to change too. We address that in other parts of this site. The point is, feminism isn't a "thing of the past." It's here now, from the present into the future, in a new form than you remember it. And it can help answer all those nagging questions we asked above. The third wave has arrived.

FOR THE MEN: HOW DOES THIRD-WAVE FEMINISM RELATE TO YOU?

Too many men get 100% of their emotional support from women. Sure, you've got your buddies and your coworkers and your on-line friends. But when you are nervous about an upcoming job interview, unhappy with your boss, or concerned about your mother's health, you turn *exclusively* to your wife or girlfriend. When was the last emotional, vulnerable, heart-to-heart talk you had with another man?

You get *all* your support from us, and almost none from other men. This is an incredible burden to place on another human, and it isn't fair. We have our own emotions to manage, and it is downright tiring to manage yours too. Everyone needs support from their friends and relatives, and of course we care about you as lovers and friends, but please don't ask us to be the only person in your life who fulfills that role. So many men are absolutely *cut adrift* when their relationships break up. Suddenly you have no one you can talk to because you *only* talked to your girlfriend!

I believe this is why men are so often compared to children. You are emotionally needy. I think it is also why so many murders are committed by men who have just broken up with their girl-friends or wives. Losing that special person makes you absolutely despondent and isolated because you have no other close connec-tions. It is unhealthy to structure your life that way.

Many years ago, women were totally dependent on men fi-nancially, which in some sense "balanced" the total dependence of men on women emotionally. (Obviously, it was an unstable equilibrium). Now we are learning to support ourselves money-wise. We can't count on a lifelong income from our husbands—and we can't even count on alimony or child support. We have jobs. We work to live, just like you. (And I happen to think this is a good thing!)

Now you must do your share. Learn not to depend on us for 100% of your emotional support. We just can't do that for you anymore. It's too exhausting when we are trying to deal with our own jobs and lives at the same time.

The third wave of feminism is about helping women learn to use their freedom, power, money, and influence wisely and for the common good. We have no desire to leave our brothers, boyfriends, husbands, and male friends behind because we care about our relationships with you. But we will not do your work for you. We cannot be your surrogate Mom now that you are all grown up. Run alongside us! And please start helping *each other.*

Questions for Thought and Writing

1. Author Kim Allen argues that many people who support the goals of feminism nonetheless resist being called "feminist." To what does she attribute this circumstance? In an essay that explains what you believe are the goals of feminism, explain why you do or do not consider yourself "feminist."
2. One of the important tasks left for third-wave feminists, Allen believes, is clarifying the difference between women "having it all" and women "doing it all." How have the freedoms women have gained inadvertently caused them to have to work harder? What are some of the ways Allen believes this situation could be changed? Can you identify other possibilities?
3. Allen claims that we as a society have little "respect" for people—either women or men—who "choose stereotypically female pursuits" including the role of the homemaker. To what extent do you agree with this assessment? Would you personally be comfortable assuming the role of homemaker and childcare provider for your own family? Why or why not?
4. According to Allen, most men "get 100% of their emotional support from women." Why does she see this as problematic for both the men and the women involved in relationships? How does this assessment compare to your own experience of relationships between men and women?

Sexual Harassment: The Nature of the Beast
Anita F. Hill

The response to my Senate Judiciary Committee testimony has been at once heartwarming and heart-wrenching. In learning that I am not alone in experiencing harassment, I am also learning that there are far too many women who have experienced a range of inexcusable and illegal activities—from sexist jokes to sexual assault—on the job.

My reaction has been to try to learn more. As an educator, I always begin to study an issue by examining the scientific data—the articles, the books, the studies. Perhaps the most compelling lesson is in the stories told by the women who have written to me. I have learned much; I am continuing to learn; I have yet ten times as much to explore. I want to share some of this with you.

"The Nature of the Beast" describes the existence of sexual harassment, which is alive and well. A harmful, dangerous thing that can confront a woman at any time.

What we know about harassment, sizing up the beast:

Sexual harassment is pervasive . . .

1. It occurs today at an alarming rate. Statistics show that anywhere from 42 to 90 percent of women will experience some form of harassment during their employed lives. At least one percent experience sexual assault. But the statistics do not fully tell the story of the anguish of women who have been told in various ways on the first day of a job that sexual favors are expected. Or the story of women who were sexually assaulted by men with whom they continued to work.
2. It has been occurring for years. In letters to me, women tell of incidents that occurred 50 years ago when they were first entering the workplace, incidents they have been unable to speak of for that entire period.
3. Harassment crosses lines of race and class. In some ways, it is a creature that practices "equal opportunity" where women are concerned. In other ways it exhibits predictable prejudices and reflects stereotypical myths held by our society.

5   *We know that harassment all too often goes unreported for a variety of reasons . . .*

1. Unwillingness (for good reason) to deal with the expected consequences;
2. Self-blame;
3. Threats or blackmail by coworkers or employers;
4. What it boils down to in many cases is a sense of powerlessness that we experience in the workplace, and our acceptance of a certain level of inability to control our careers and professional destinies. This sense of powerlessness is particularly troubling when one observes the research that says individuals with graduate education experience more harassment than do persons with less than a high school diploma. The

message: when you try to obtain power through education, the beast harassment responds by striking more often and more vehemently.

That harassment is treated like a woman's "dirty secret" is well known. We also know what happens when we "tell." We know that when harassment is reported the common reaction is disbelief or worse . . .

1. Women who "tell" lose their jobs. A typical response told of in the letters to me was: I not only lost my job for reporting harassment, but I was accused of stealing and charges were brought against me.

2. Women who "tell" become emotionally wasted. One writer noted that "it was fully eight months after the suit was conducted that I began to see myself as alive again."

3. Women who "tell" are not always supported by other women. Perhaps the most disheartening stories I have received are of mothers not believing daughters. In my kindest moments I believe that this reaction only represents attempts to distance ourselves from the pain of the harassment experience. The internal response is: "It didn't happen to me. This couldn't happen to me. In order to believe that I am protected, I must believe that it didn't happen to her." The external response is: "What did you do to provoke that kind of behavior?" Yet at the same time that I have been advised of hurtful and unproductive reactions, I have also heard stories of mothers and daughters sharing their experiences. In some cases the sharing allows for a closer bonding. In others a slight but cognizable mending of a previously damaged relationship occurs.

What we are learning about harassment requires recognizing this beast when we encounter it, and more. It requires looking the beast in the eye.

We are learning painfully that simply having laws against harassment on the books is not enough. The law, as it was conceived, was to provide a shield of protection for us. Yet that shield is failing us: many fear reporting, others feel it would do no good. The result is that less than 5 percent of women victims file claims of harassment. Moreover, the law focuses on quid pro quo, but a recent New York *Times* article quoting psychologist Dr. Louise Fitzgerald says that this makes up considerably less than 5 percent of the cases. The law needs to be more responsive to the reality of our experiences.

As we are learning, enforcing the law alone won't terminate the problem. What we are seeking is equality of treatment in the workplace. Equality requires an expansion of our attitudes toward workers. Sexual harassment denies our treatment as equals and replaces it with treatment of women as objects of ego or power gratification. Dr. John Gottman, a psychologist at the University of Washington, notes that sexual harassment is more about fear than about sex.

10   *Yet research suggests two troublesome responses exhibited by workers and by courts. Both respond by . . .*

1. Downplaying the seriousness of the behavior (seeing it as normal sexual attraction between people) or commenting on the sensitivity of the victim.
2. Exaggerating the ease with which victims are expected to handle the behavior. But my letters tell me that unwanted advances do not cease—and that the message was power, not genuine interest.

We are learning that many women are angry. The reasons for the anger are various and perhaps all too obvious . . .

1. We are angry because this awful thing called harassment exists in terribly harsh, ugly, demeaning, and even debilitating ways. Many believe it is criminal and should be punished as such. It is a form of violence against women as well as a form of economic coercion, and our experiences suggest that it won't just go away.
2. We are angry because for a brief moment we believed that if the law allowed for women to be hired in the workplace, and if we worked hard for our educations and on the job, equality would be achieved. We believed we would be respected as equals. Now we are realizing this is not true. We have been betrayed. The reality is that this powerful beast is used to perpetuate a sense of inequality, to keep women in their place notwithstanding our increasing presence in the workplace.

What we have yet to explore about harassment is vast. It is what will enable us to slay the beast.

Research is helpful, appreciated, and I hope will be required reading for all legislators. Yet research has what I see as one shortcoming: it focuses on our reaction to harassment, not on the harasser. How we enlighten men who are currently in the workplace about behavior that is beneath our (and their) dignity is the challenge of the future. Research shows that men tend to have a narrower definition of what constitutes harassment than do women. How do we expand their body of knowledge? How do we raise a generation of men who won't need to be reeducated as adults? We must explore these issues, and research efforts can assist us.

What are the broader effects of harassment on women and the world? Has sexual harassment left us unempowered? Has our potential in the workplace been greatly damaged by this beast? Has this form of economic coercion worked? If so, how do we begin to reverse its effects? We must begin to use what we know to move to the next step: what we will do about it.

How do we capture our rage and turn it into positive energy?   15
Through the power of women working together, whether it be in the political arena, or in the context of a lawsuit, or in community service. This issue goes well beyond partisan politics. Making the workplace a safer, more productive place for ourselves and our daughters should be on the agenda for each of us. It is something we can do for ourselves. It is a tribute, as well, to our mothers— and indeed a contribution we can make to the entire population.

I wish that I could take each of you on the journey that I've been on during all these weeks since the hearing. I wish that every one of you could experience the heartache and the triumphs of each of those who have shared with me their experiences. I leave you with but a brief glimpse of what I've seen. I hope it is enough to encourage you to begin—or continue and persist with—your own exploration. And thank you.

This article is based on remarks delivered by Anita Hill (professor of law, University of Oklahoma) as part of a panel on sexual harassment and policy-making at the National Forum for Women State Legislators convened by the Center for the American Woman and Politics (CAWP) late last year. Other panel members were Deborah L. Rhode, professor of law at Stanford; Susan Deller Ross, professor of law and director of the Sex Discrimination Clinic at Georgetown University Law School; and Kimberle Williams Crenshaw, professor of law at UCLA. A transcript of the entire proceedings (the largest meeting of elected women ever held) is available from CAWP, Eagleton Institute of Politics, Rutgers University, New Brunswick, New Jersey 08901.

Questions for Thought and Writing

1. Hill suggests that sexual harassment "practices 'equal opportunity' where women are concerned" and ignores lines of race and class. In fact, she states that "individuals with graduate education experience more harassment than do persons with less than a high school diploma." Why do you think this is the case? How does this assertion compare to stereotypical images of where and to whom sexual harassment is most likely to occur?

2. One of the ways victims of harassment are doubly traumatized, according to Hill, is when they are not supported or believed by other women. To what does Hill attribute some women's inability to "look the beast in the eye"? What do women risk when they support other women's claims of harassment? What do men risk by giving support?

3. If "sexual harassment is more about fear than about sex," what are the fears underlying this criminal behavior? What are the reasons that some men—and some women—are threatened by the presence of women in the workplace?

4. Hill states that "men tend to have a narrower definition of what constitutes harassment than do women," and asks, "How do we expand their body of knowledge?" In an essay in which you offer your own definition of sexual harassment, attempt to respond to Hill's question.

Exploring Connections

1. In both "Sex-Role Spillover: Personal, Familial, and Organizational Roles" and "The Second Shift: Working Parents and the Revolution at Home" professional women are acknowledged to be facing "the glass ceiling" or limitations to their ability to professionally and financially progress. In the first article, ten executives at top firms claim that this is because women are not as committed to or willing to sacrifice for their careers as men are. What is the alternative explanation, as offered by the second article?

2. Considering the major pitfalls resulting from gender relations in the workplace that are described in these readings, devise a new set of guidelines for expected behaviors that would promote an equitable atmosphere for all. Be sure to consider age, race, ethnicity, and sexual orientation in devising your guidelines, and refer to the readings in defense of your positions.

CHAPTER 5

Gender and Global Perspectives

OVERVIEW

In the Overview articles that follow—"Empathy Among Women on a Global Scale" and "The Global Human Rights Movement"—the reader is asked to consider women's oppression in patriarchal systems around the world as human rights issues. Mahnaz Afkhami suggests the need for feminists to dismantle the binary of East-West thinking to approach women's empowerment in repressive regimes more globally. The excerpt from the Human Rights Watch Global Report on Women's Human Rights proposes that a definition of "human rights" that ignores private, family relationships is dangerous for women around the globe.

Empathy Among Women on a Global Scale

MAHNAZ AFKHAMI

The history of Iranian women is bound inextricably to the history of Shii Islam and to the myths that emotionally and intellectually sustain it. As a practical philosophy of life, contemporary Shii Islam is a product of a historical process and, like all historical processes, has gone through many changes. The ruling clerics, however, present it as timeless dogma. By presenting it ahistorically, they suggest that Islam is qualitatively different from other religions. Islam, they argue, defines all aspects of

211

life and the Quran, as God's Word, prescribes for all time the proper pattern of relationships within and among all social institutions. Furthermore, what Islam has prescribed as the word of God, they say, corresponds to the order of nature.[1] This is particularly stressed in the case of women and their position relative to men in the household and in society. Major Islamic 'myths'—the *sunna* or the custom of the Prophet and the *hadith,* the compiled sayings of the Prophet and Imams[2]—were designed to uphold this particular interpretation of 'reality' and in the course of time the interpretation itself, as content and process, was established as the center of historical reality. Consequently, Shiism is now what the Shii clerics who dispose of political and moral power say it is.

The ulema defined early and, over the years, precisely the proper place of woman in Iranian society. The late Ayatollah Morteza Motahhari (d. 1979), one of the more enlightened Iranian Shii clerics and probably the foremost authority on contemporary Shii jurisprudence regarding women, provides a modern example of the Shii formulation of woman's proper place. He argues the *naturalness* of the differences between the sexes and the conformity of Islamic law with the purpose of divine (natural) creation.[3] From the idea of purpose and order in the process of divine creation he deduces, among others, formally structured criteria of justice and beauty and concludes what amounts to the proposition that God, in His encompassing wisdom and justice, formally wills woman's subordinate position in accordance with the requirements of nature.

This 'natural' position for women has been asserted by all patriarchal religions throughout history. Indeed, the process of the subjugation of women appears remarkably similar in all cultures. The originary myth usually treats man and woman more equitably, but once the historical process begins, woman is reduced to a vehicle of procreation—the axis around which woman's history as myth or religion is organized.[4]

The theology of procreation emphasizes the family. Within the family, woman achieves value primarily as mother, and secondarily as wife, daughter, or sister. The more society grows, differentiates, and becomes structured, the more the originary concepts yield to systems of mores and regulations that define woman's subordinate place in increasing detail. In time, her contact with the larger society is totally mediated by man.

5   In the originary Zoroastrian sources, for example, the *Gatha,* the *Yashts* and other early religious texts as well as in parts of the

Matikan-e Hazar Datastan (The Digest of a Thousand Points of Law), a later text compiled during the Sasanian period, woman is treated with respect, if not quite as an equal of man.[5] Women in Iranian epics—Sindokht, Rudabeh, Tahmineh, Gordafarid, Manijeh, and a host of others whose names are perpetuated in the *Shahnameh*—are invariably brave, aggressive, and full of initiative.[6] By the middle of the Sasanian period, however, under a dominant Zoroastrian clergy, women had lost many of their rights and privileges.[7]

Abrahamic religions also accord woman an important position in originary sources. Genesis, in fact, seems to treat Eve as the more resourceful of the first pair, man and woman, created in God's image. If human history is said to have begun with the fall of Adam, then Eve, in the act of leading Adam to the forbidden fruit, may be said to have taken upon herself the burden of a civilizing mission. In the Talmudic tradition, however, the laws apply only to men because in the course of time the Israelite woman was relegated to 'a dependent existence derived from that of her father or her husband.'[8] In the Gospels, the very 'idea' of Christ suggests a leveling of inequities that to be meaningful must have included women. After Paul, however, Christianity steadily moved toward the affirmation of patriarchy and by the second Christian century the patriarchal interpretation had become, for all practical purposes, established dogma.[9]

This pattern is repeated in Islam. . . .

The universality of the feminine condition at present suggests the possibility of empathy among women on a global scale—a humanizing process that to succeed must be empowered to travel over time and space, as all successful discourses have historically done. Zoroastrianism, Buddhism, Judaism, Christianity, and Islam moved over many countries across many centuries, nourishing and receiving nourishment from the cultures they encountered. Saint Augustine was a Manichaean at first; Thomas Aquinas received Aristotle's teachings through the intermediary of Muslim scholars. During the nineteenth and twentieth centuries, as we have seen, secular ideas derived from the European Enlightenment traveled east and south. Each transmission produced contradiction, agony, and despair as well as hope. New and unfamiliar ideas broke into established systems and clashed with tradition, merging with indigenous thought, energizing it to overcome intellectual inertia and to produce new form and content that challenged and often changed the established norms and values.

Waging their struggle in the colonial environment, Third World feminist thinkers have achieved a multicultural ethical and intellectual formation and a plethora of experience relevant to the development of an internationally valid and effective discourse addressing women's condition on a global scale. The question is whether this foundation can become a springboard for a global discourse. By definition, such a discourse must transcend the boundaries of Christian, Jewish, Muslim, Buddhist, socialist, capitalist, or any other particular culture. It will be feminist rather than patriarchal, humane rather than ideological, balanced rather than extremist, critical as well as exhortatory.[10] The global feminist discourse recognizes that the problem of women constitutes an issue in its own right, not as a subsidiary of other ideologies, no matter how structurally comprehensive or textually promising they might seem to be. It insists in relating concepts to the historical contexts in which they are embedded.[11] Since 'traditional' concepts are by definition founded in patriarchal discourse, global feminism must be skeptical of propositions that present them as liberating. This feminism is not anti-man; rather, it sees the world in humane terms, that is, it seeks a redefinition of social, economic, and political principles of societal organization on the basis of non-paternalistic models. Realizing that such a feat cannot be accomplished without or against men's participation, it does not hesitate to engage men politically in favor of the feminist cause. On the other hand, given the present effects of the historical process, feminism will be critically aware of and fight against patriarchal structures and institutions.[12]

10   The global feminist discourse rejects the notion that 'East' and 'West' constitute mutually exclusive paradigms; rather, it looks at life as evolving for all and believes that certain humane and morally defensible principles can and should be applied in the West and in the East equally. The point is not that Iranian women should forget the problems that are obviously 'Iranian' and intensely present. It is, rather, that unless Iranian feminists think globally, they will neither be able to mobilize world opinion for their cause, nor succeed in breaking out of the boundaries of patriarchal discourse on their own, and, therefore, they will likely fail to address their problems in a way that will lead to their solution.[13]

At present, of course, reality belies the potential. The disparity in physical and material power between the developed and less-developed countries forces Third World women to withdraw to reactive positions, formulating their discourse in response to the West and its challenge. Consequently, they fail to think globally, that is, to move beyond the indigenous culture they have objectively outgrown. Their discourse remains nationalistic, parochial, fearful, tradition-bound, and rooted in the soil of patriarchy. The world, however, is undergoing a qualitative change, an important aspect of which may be the tumbling of nation-states qua culture boundaries. In the process, women may gain a chance to promote on a world scale the kinds of ideas that are applicable to women everywhere. If they do, Third World women will be able to critique women's condition in the West from a vantage point that transcends the cultures of Abraham, Buddha, and Confucius and thus will help the women of all 'worlds of development,' including Iran.

I am not suggesting therefore that the West be taken as the standard for the evaluation of women's conditions in Iran. On the contrary, it seems to me that there are significant issues of commission and omission in the western discourse that can be addressed profitably only from the global feminist position. The virtue of the global position is that it partakes of the wisdom of all cultures and that it accommodates differences in the levels of economic and social development without succumbing to either the normlessness of cultural relativism or the self-righteous parochialism of any particular culture.

The heightened awareness of female human rights that exists today throughout the world makes possible a more unified and effective approach to the global feminist movement. Western feminists can help this process but only to an extent, because they are burdened by two severe handicaps. First, they carry the onus of historical western hegemony, even though they themselves are the victims of a taxing patriarchal order.[14] Second, their problems as women are often of a different order than the problems of women in Third World countries. Consequently, they appear alternately as self-righteous promoters of their own western culture, when they advocate principles and rights that differ with the tenets of Third World societies, or as self-deprecating defenders of atrociously anti-feminist conditions, when they explain away oppressive behavior in the developing world on the grounds of cultural relativism.

Non-western feminists can be instrumental in the development of a viable global feminism despite their historical handicap. As the world moves from a disjointed society of nation-states to an increasingly interconnected economic and technological

system, and as the symmetry of the enclaves of poverty and back-
wardness in the developed and developing countries is increasingly apparent, it becomes easier for Third World feminists to develop a sense of empathy with their sisters in other parts of the
globe. Indeed, unless such empathy is effected and expanded, patriarchal norms, for all practical purposes, will not be tran-
scended and feminism, global or otherwise, will not fully succeed.

15   It is from this vantage point that the originary myth in the
Shii lore may be successfully engaged. Here is a chance for Iranian women to transcend the parochial discourse. By showing at
once the similarity in the historical treatment of women in all societies and the need for women to deny the legitimacy of the patriarchal order in all cultures, Iranian women can challenge the
claim that there is something unique in Islam that separates it
from other human experiences. The goal is to contest the right
and legitimacy of Iran's patriarchal clerical order to be the sole
interpreters of the values, norms, and aesthetic standards of Shii
Islam—a religion that lies at the core of Iranian culture. The truth
is that there is nothing sacred about a limited and highly protected discourse, developed over centuries by a society of zealous
men in order to produce and maintain a regime of control, a major function of which is to keep women in bondage—for ever.

Endnotes

Author's note: I wish to thank Guity Nashat, Miriam Cooke, Shahla
Haeri and Seyyed Vali Reza Nasr for reading an earlier version of this
paper. Their comments have been of great help to me.

1. The correspondence between Divine Law (*Jus Divine*) and Natural
    Law (*Jus Naturale*) is a commonplace of most religions, including
    the Abrahamic. For a general discussion of the essentials of Shii Is-
    lam see Allameh Sayyid Muhammad Husain Tabataba'i, *Shiite Islam*,
    trans S. H. Nasr (Houston: Free Islamic Literature, 1979). For a dis-
    cussion of women in Islam see Morteza Motahhari, *The Rights of
    Women in Islam* (Tehran: World Organization for Islamic Services,
    1981) part vii; John L. Esposito, *Women in Muslim Family Law*
    (Syracuse: Syracuse University Press, 1982).
2. The theory of *hadith,* or tradition, did not take definite shape until
    late in the second century after Islam. Since its inception, its
    method and authority have been matters for disagreement among
    Muslim scholars as well as others in terms of the reliability of its
    raconteurs and continuity of chains of transmission. Furthermore,
    there has always been a conflict among the various Sunni and Shii

schools. Thus, the time factor involved and the differences between the compilers on the authenticity of the sayings or the chains opens the validity of much of the *hadith* to serious doubt even among Muslim ulema. For Shiis, perhaps the most celebrated compiler of tradition is Mohammad Baqer Majlesi, a *mojtahed* of the Safavid era. For the meaning and a concise discussion of the theory and development of *hadith* see J. Robson's article in *The Encyclopaedia of Islam* (Leiden: E. J. Brill, 1971), vol 3, pp 23–9. For a brief history of imamite jurisprudence, particularly a survey of important Shii jurists, see A. A. Sachedina, *The Just Ruler in Shiite Islam: The Comprehensive Authority of the Jurist in Imamite Jurisprudence* (Oxford: Oxford University Press, 1988), pp 9–25. For a Marxist discussion see I. P. Petrushevski, *Islam in Iran* (Albany: State University of New York Press, 1985), pp 101ff.

3. Motahhari: *Rights of Women in Islam.*
4. See Yvonne Yazbeck Haddad and Ellison Banks Findly (eds) *Women, Religion and Social Change* (Albany: State University of New York Press, 1985); also chapters by Denise L. Carmody, Rosemary R. Ruether and Jane I. Smith on Judaism, Christianity and Islam respectively in Arvind Sharma (ed.), *Women in World Religions* (Albany: State University of New York Press, 1987).
5. See the *Laws of Ancient Persians As Found in the Matikan-i Hazar Datastan or the Digest of A Thousand Points of Law,* trans S. J. Bulasara (Tehran: Imperial Organization for Social Services, 1976), first published by Hoshang T. Anklesaria, Bombay, 1937.
6. For women in *Shahnameh* see Khojasteh Kia, *Sokhanan-e Sezavar-e Zanan dar Shahnameh-ye Pahlavani (Words Deserving of Women in the Epic Shahnameh)* (Tehran: Nashr-e Fakhteh, 1371). For a comparative rendition of Iranian and non-Iranian female character see Saidi Sirjani, *Sima-ye Do Zan (A Portrait of Two Women)* (Tehran: 1367), where an Iranian and non-Iranian woman as portrayed in Nezami's *Khamseh* are compared.
7. See A. Perikhanian, "Iranian Society and Law," in *The Cambridge History of Iran,* vol 3 (2), ed. Ehsan Yarshater (Cambridge: Cambridge University Press, 1983), particularly pp 646–55.
8. Judith Baskin, "The Separation of Women in Rabbinic Judaism," in Haddad and Findly: *Women, Religion and Social Change,* pp 3–18 and Denise L. Carmody in Sharma: *Women in World Religions,* p 192.
9. Rosemary R. Ruether in Sharma: *Women in World Religions,* p. 209.
10. I realize that these terms are problematic. The function of a global discourse is to define and clarify the concepts invoked by these terms in a way that is suitable to the requirements of an equitable system of gender relations in the twenty-first century, if not earlier in the so-called "new world order." For a critique of approaches to feminism, patriarchy, and Islam see Deniz Kandiyoti, "Islam and Patriarchy: A Comparative Perspective," in Nikkie R. Keddie and Beth Baron (eds.), *Women in Middle Eastern History: Shifting*

Boundaries in Sex and Gender (New Haven: Yale University Press, 1991), pp 23–42.

11. For a relevant critique see Christine Delphy, "Protofeminism and antifeminism," in Moi: *French Feminist Thought*, pp 80–109. See also Linda Kauffman (ed), *Gender and Theory: Dialogues on Feminist Criticism* (New York: Basil Blackwell, 1989).

12. For some possibilities of what might constitute a discourse that has a chance of transcending fixed sexual polarities see Julia Kristeva, "Woman's Time," in The Feminist Reader: Essays in Gender and the Politics of Literary Theory, Eds. Catherine Belsey and Jane Moore. Oxford, Blackwell Publishers, 1997 (pp. 198–217).

13. What appear as obstacles to the development of a global approach to a feminist social and literary criticism, namely, the contemporary emphasis in universities on cultural relativism, on one hand, and on textual and deconstructionist analysis, on the other, may prove a positive force for the future involvement of Third World women in the construction of a global discourse. The transition from parochial/relativistic to a global approach is already taking place as more and more feminist positions are advanced mutually through intellectual representatives of western and non-western cultures.

14. Nupur Chaudhuri and Margaret Strobel (eds), *Western Women and Imperialism: Complicity and Resistance* (Bloomington: Indiana University Press, 1992).

Questions for Thought and Writing

1. According to Afkhami, one of the techniques used by clerics in Iran to cement the inferior position of their women is to present Shii Islam "as a timeless dogma" rather than as something that has changed throughout history. Explain how this works. How would an understanding of religion as a changeable phenomenon work to women's advantage?

2. In patriarchal systems, women are typically associated with "nature" and men with "culture." What are the dangers for women in being linked with the "natural" or with "nature"? What limitations do such an association potentially place on women's experience of the "larger society"? Identify images from contemporary American culture in which women are associated with "nature." What does this association encourage viewers to believe about women's priorities, skills, and desires?

3. The author admits that "Western feminists" carry at least two burdens with them that make it difficult for them to effectively help women in Third World countries. What are these burdens? What strategies can you identify that might help to ease them?

The Global Women's Human Rights Movement

HUMAN RIGHTS WATCH

INTRODUCTION

Few movements have made so large an impact in so short a time as the women's human rights movement. Working across national, cultural, religious and class lines, advocates promoting the human rights of women have waged a campaign to ensure respect for women's rights as fundamental human rights. The movement's emergence and growth over the past decade have, to a large extent, also transformed the way human rights issues are understood and investigated, both by intergovernmental bodies and by nongovernmental human rights organizations. The result has been to turn the spotlight on—and to place at the center of the social and political debates at the United Nations and between governments—the role that human rights violations play in maintaining the subordinate status of the world's women. Their impact was powerfully apparent at the World Conference on Human Rights in Vienna in 1993, when governments recognized women's rights as "an inalienable, integral and indivisible part of universal human rights."

Clearly the international women's human rights movement has raised the visibility of abuses against women, and the international community has made welcome statements supporting women's human rights. But the gap between government rhetoric and reality is vast. The challenge now is to ensure that governments that should be combatting violations of women's rights do not get credit for deploring abuse when they do nothing to stop it.

The Range and Severity of Abuse

In 1990 Human Rights Watch began working with colleagues in the human rights and women's movements around the world to apply the fact-finding and advocacy tools of the international human rights movement to documenting violations of women's human rights and seeking remedies for such abuse. We have exposed state-directed and state-approved violence against women;

violence against women by private actors that is legally endorsed; violence against women by private actors that is illegal but is tolerated by the state through discriminatory enforcement of the law; and discriminatory laws and practices. We have explored abuses that are gender-specific either in their form—such as forced pregnancy and forced virginity exams—or in that they target primarily women—such as rape and the forced trafficking of women for purposes of sexual servitude.

Rampant abuses against women have traditionally been excused or ignored. Rape in situations of conflict by combatants is prohibited under international humanitarian law but until recently was dismissed as part of the inevitable "spoils of war." Domestic violence was regarded as a "private" matter only, not as a crime that the state must prosecute and punish. To the extent that control of women's sexuality and physical integrity is regarded as a matter of family or community honor rather than personal autonomy and individual rights, women in much of the world still face enormous obstacles in their search for redress when they have suffered abuse committed in the name of custom or tradition. Throughout the world, women are still relegated to second-class status that makes them more vulnerable to abuse and less able to protect themselves from discrimination.

5   As the country studies in this report show, governments often are directly implicated in abuses of women's human rights. Prison guards in many countries—studies in this report include the United States, Pakistan and Egypt—sexually assault women prisoners and detainees. Rape of women by combatants is frequently tolerated by commanding officers in the course of armed conflict and by abusive security officials in the context of political repression, as the examples of Kashmir, Bosnia-Hercegovina, Peru, Somalia, and Haiti illustrate. And, as our investigations of the trafficking of women and girls into forced prostitution have demonstrated, this ostensibly private commercial trade in human beings would be impossible without the active involvement of government officials, such as corrupt border guards and police who alternate between raiding brothels and profiting from them. Refugee and displaced women, in zones where U.N. or governmental protection is inadequate, are robbed and raped by security forces and camp officials, as described in the case study on Burmese women in this report.

Governments also have imposed, or refused to amend, laws that discriminate against women. In Pakistan, discriminatory evidentiary standards not only deny rape survivors access to justice, but also result in their arbitrary detention and thus expose them to further sexual violence by their jailers. As mothers or potential mothers, women face *de jure* discrimination in many countries. For example, Botswana men who marry foreigners have the right to pass Botswana citizenship on to their children; Botswana women do not.[1] In Russia, women are routinely turned away from public sector jobs because they are considered less productive workers on account of their maternal responsibilities.

In other situations, governments apply gender-neutral laws in discriminatory ways or fail to enforce constitutional and other guarantees of non-discrimination. In Thailand, laws that penalize both prostitution and procurement are applied in a discriminatory manner resulting in the arrest of female prostitutes but impunity for their predominately male agents, pimps, brothel owners, and clients. The Brazilian constitution, in another example, guarantees women equality before the law yet courts in Brazil have exonerated men who kill their allegedly adulterous wives in order to protect their honor.

The women's human rights movement has prompted investigation into another important area of human rights abuse: violence against women carried out by private actors that is tolerated or ignored by the state. As intractable as state-perpetrated violence against women is, women's health and lives are equally endangered by abuse at the hands of husbands, employers, parents, or brothel owners. Domestic violence, for example, is a leading cause of female injury in almost every country in the world and is typically ignored by the state or only erratically punished, as the studies of Brazil, Russia, and South Africa in this report reveal. In Kuwait, employers assault Asian women domestic workers, driving hundreds of women to flee to their embassies each year. Yet only a handful of abusive employers are investigated or prosecuted. To fulfill their international obligations, states are required not only to ensure that women, as victims of private violence, obtain equal protection of the law, but also that the conditions that render women easy targets for attack—including sex discrimination in law and practice—are removed.

Women's lack of social and economic security has compounded their vulnerability to violence and sex discrimination. We have found, for example, that numerous Burmese, Nepali, and Bangladeshi women and girls, seeking to escape poverty at home, accept fraudulent job or marriage offers that result in their being trafficked into forced prostitution. In South Africa, women's lack of access to alternative housing is one reason why some of them hesitate to report domestic violence. At the same time, the lack of access to political power and to equal justice—through the right to organize, to express opinions freely, to participate in the political process, and to obtain redress for abuse—is a central obstacle to women seeking to improve their social and economic status within their societies. At the International Conference on Population and Development in Cairo in 1994, governments recognized that "advancing gender equality and equity and the empowerment of women, and the elimination of all kinds of violence against women, and ensuring women's ability to control their own fertility, are cornerstones of population and development-related programs." Similarly, the stated goals of the Fourth World Conference on Women in Beijing—peace, equality and development—suggest that protection of women's human rights is inextricably connected to the improvement of women's status more generally.

Silence and Impunity

Silence about abuses against women hides the problems that destroy, and sometimes end, women's lives. Governments excuse and fail to take action against soldiers and prison guards who rape, police officers who forcibly traffick women, immigration officials who assault, judges who exonerate wife-murderers, and husbands who batter. They accept and defend domestic laws that discriminate on their face or in practice. Until recently, local and international human rights organizations, the United Nations and regional human rights bodies have approached human rights advocacy by focusing on a narrow interpretation of politically motivated abuse, while often failing to respond to the repression of women even when they challenge existing legal, political or social systems. Also neglected by governments and international organizations have been the range of abuses that women suffer because many of these violations did not conform to standard ideas of what constitutes human rights abuse. Thus, "Nada," a Saudi woman who sought political asylum in Canada in 1992, initially was denied refuge because persecution for her feminist views on the status of women in her country and her activities flowing from those beliefs—attempting to study in the field of her choice, to refuse to wear the veil, and to travel alone—was not deemed political. Similarly, in a notorious case in 1988, a U.S. immigration judge denied political asylum to Catalina Mejia, a Salvadoran woman who was raped by soldiers. In the judge's opinion, Mejia's rape by a Salvadoran soldier, who accused her of being a guerrilla, was not an act of persecution but rather the excess of a soldier acting "only in his own self-interest."[2]

The lack of documentation of violations of women's rights reinforces governments' silence; without concrete data, governments have been able to deny the fact of and their responsibility for gender-based abuse. Where human rights violations against women remain undocumented and unverified, governments pay no political or economic price for refusing to acknowledge the problem and their obligation to prevent and remedy abuse. One of the first challenges faced by the women's human rights movement has been to transform women's experiences of violence and discrimination into fact-based proof of the scale and nature of such abuse and governments' role in its perpetuation.

Just as human rights groups historically have been the primary force in ensuring accountability for politically motivated human rights abuse, women's rights advocates are the vanguard in the fight for justice for gender-based violations. Thus, for example, they have won recognition that traditional notions of the political actor must be modified to acknowledge the political nature of women's efforts to challenge their subordinate status and the violence and discrimination that reinforce it. Women's rights advocacy has rejected the argument that governments bear no responsibility for the wide range of abuses perpetrated by private actors and argued to the contrary that governments must remedy and prevent such acts.

By building regional and international linkages that extend across cultural religious, ethnic, political, class, and geographic divides, women have developed effective political and legal strategies that strengthen their work domestically. Women's ability to secure their rights domestically is always subject to their countries' laws and willingness to enforce those laws. By calling upon the protections of the international human rights system, women are claiming rights that are not only morally desirable but also legally enforceable. Thus, for example, women's rights groups combating rape in custody in Pakistan cast the abuse not only as a criminal act under domestic law, but also as torture, a gross violation of international human rights norms. This strategy helped them to secure legal reform in Pakistan and to influence the approach of the international human rights community to the problem of custodial rape in their country.

In the past, absent support from their domestic legal systems, human rights organizations, and intergovernmental agencies, women often chose not to seek redress rather than risk reprisal and social ostracism in cultures that often blame the victim. As the international human rights system becomes more responsive to gender-based human rights violations, women who have previously been silent about their experiences of abuse are speaking up. Their testimonies add to the evidence of the scale and prevalence of abuses against women that the international community simply cannot afford to ignore.

The Challenge Ahead

The global women's human rights movement has won important battles in the international arena as well as on the home front. In March 1993 the U.N. Commission on Human Rights adopted for the first time a resolution calling for the integration of the rights of women into the human rights mechanisms of the United Nations. Later that year, governments participating in the World Conference on Human Rights declared:

> the human rights of women and of the girl-child are an inalienable, integral and indivisible part of universal human rights. The full and equal participation of women in political, civil, economic, social and cultural life, at the national, regional and international levels, and the eradication of all forms of discrimination on grounds of sex are priority objectives of the international community.
>
> Gender-based violence and all forms of sexual harassment and exploitation, including those resulting from cultural prejudice and international trafficking, are incompatible with the dignity and worth of the human person, and must be eliminated.[3]

This declaration was a milestone for the women's human rights movement because governments around the world had for a long time refused to acknowledge that women, too, are entitled to enjoy their fundamental human rights. In December 1993 the General Assembly took another key step toward integrating women into the U.N.'s human rights work by adopting the Declaration on Violence Against Women. With this declaration, the U.N. member states recognized explicitly that states are obliged to fight specific forms of violence against women and called on governments to exercise due diligence to prevent, investigate, and punish acts of violence against women.

With the appointment in 1994 of a Special Rapporteur on Violence against Women, its Causes and Consequences, the U.N. recognized the need to address the gender-specific aspects of violence against women.[4] The special rapporteur was given the authority to investigate violence against women, to recommend measures to eliminate this violence, and to work closely with other special rapporteurs, special representatives, working groups, and independent experts of the Commission on Human Rights and the Sub-Commission on Prevention of Discrimination and Protection of Minorities and treaty bodies to combat violence against women.

Despite such indicators of progress in promoting women's rights, the dismal record on preventing abuse persists. Even those governments that profess a strong commitment to promoting human rights in general have balked at fulfilling their obligation to protect women's rights. On the international level, the Special Rapporteur on Violence against Women lacks sufficient technical and financial support from the U.N. to carry out her work. Similarly, despite the strengths of the Committee on the Elimination of Discrimination Against Women, its effectiveness in promoting women's rights remains severely compromised by inadequate technical and financial resources and its inability to consider individuals' complaints against states. Moreover, the U.N. has failed to integrate women's human rights into its treaty-based and non-treaty-based bodies' system-wide work on human rights. International financial institutions are also in a position to influence the governmental response to abuses against women, yet they generally have refused to address the discriminatory barriers to women's participation in development, or gross violations of women's human rights.

In far too many cases—many of them documented in this report—overwhelming evidence of human rights violations goes unheeded by repressive governments with the tacit acceptance of other governments and international institutions. In very few instances has the international community denounced abuses against women and pressured abusive governments to prevent and remedy them. Thus, in Peru, President Alberto Fujimori has not prosecuted one soldier accused of rape in the context of the counterinsurgency offensive; instead he declared an amnesty for all security forces that makes it legally impossible to investigate the many egregious abuses, including rape by soldiers and police, committed over the past fifteen years. In the United States, the federal government has failed to use its authority to stop torture and other cruel and inhuman treatment of women prisoners in state prisons. In Turkey, the government has yet to investigate police and state doctors for forcing women and girls to undergo virginity exams; indeed the government tried recently to adopt regulations specifically endorsing such exams. And, in the former Yugoslavia, Serbian forces reportedly have renewed their campaign of massive human rights abuse, including rape, to drive non-Serbs out of so-called safe areas. . . .

RECOMMENDATIONS

[In conclusion,] we present a series of recommendations for responsible governments and the wider international community—including donor countries, the United Nations and other intergovernmental bodies—to end impurity and to prevent future abuse. More generally, the challenge to the women's rights and human rights movements, and to governments that support the goal of gender equality, is to insist that women's human rights be continually integrated into all official programs, legislation, and discourse related to human rights.

Governments should review national legislation and practices in order to eliminate discrimination on the basis of sex and adopt necessary legislation for promoting and protecting women's right to be free from sex discrimination in all spheres. This requires governments to amend criminal, civil, family, and labor laws that discriminate on the basis of sex, including pregnancy and maternity. Governments further should eliminate gender bias in the administration of justice and particularly discriminatory laws and practices that contribute to the wrongful incarceration of women. All victims of discrimination on the basis of sex should be afforded an appropriate forum to challenge the practice and obtain an effective remedy.

As a matter of urgency, governments should protect women's human rights and fundamental freedoms regardless of whether such abuses are attributed to tradition or custom. In countries where customary and/or religious law co-exist with statutory law, governments should ensure that each legal regime is in full compliance with international human rights norms, with particular attention to matters of family and personal status law.

Governments should also implement existing laws and policies that protect women from and guarantee them remedies for gender-based violence. States must guarantee women equal protection of the law through rigorous enforcement of criminal laws prohibiting violence against women, and reform legislation and practices that mischaracterize domestic violence, marital rape and wife-murder as private matters or crimes of honor, and thus allow perpetrators to receive lenient treatment or to go unpunished altogether. Governments should exercise their obligations to investigate and prosecute alleged instances of torture or other forms of cruel, inhuman and degrading treatment, including rape, that occur within their territories and to exercise jurisdiction over torturers who enter their territories.

Governments should promote the universal ratification of the International Covenant on Civil and Political Rights, the International Covenant on Economic, Social and Cultural Rights, the Convention against Torture and Other Cruel, Inhuman or Degrading Treatment or Punishment, and the Convention on the Elimination of All Forms of Discrimination Against Women (CEDAW). Governments should further withdraw all reservations to these treaties that undermine their object and purpose.

Finally, governments should integrate considerations of women's human rights into bilateral and multilateral foreign policy. To this end, governments should systematically use all available leverage to combat violations of women's rights, including bilateral, diplomatic, trade, and military relations; their voice and vote at international and regional financial institutions; and the stigma of public condemnation of abusive governments. 25

The international community should also do more to promote and protect women's human rights. Member states of the U.N. should adopt and ratify a protocol to CEDAW that would allow women whose domestic legal systems have failed them to submit complaints directly to the Committee on the Elimination of Discrimination Against Women. The committee's current inability to consider individual communications or complaints against states severely limits its effectiveness in promoting the rights embodied in CEDAW. Further, countries that are parties to CEDAW should include information in their periodic reports on efforts to combat all forms of abuse identified in this report.

The international community further should integrate women's human rights into the system-wide activities of the United Nations' treaty-based and non-treaty-based bodies on human rights. Member states should seek to ensure that existing thematic and country-specific special rapporteurs, working

groups, and special representatives consistently address violations of women's human rights that fall within their mandates. In
this regard, the international community should ensure adequate
support for the work of the Special Rapporteur on Violence
against Women and renew her mandate beyond the first term of
three years.

United Nations agencies, particularly the U.N. Development
Program and the U.N. Population Fund, donor governments, and
regional and multilateral development banks should seek to ensure that population programs and policies that they support include safeguards for the protection of basic civil and political
rights. International financial institutions, such as the World
Bank, as well as donor governments should extend the concept of
"good governance" to include a firm commitment to the protection of human rights.

Endnotes

1. Human Rights Watch/Africa and Women's Rights Project,
   "Botswana: Second Class Citizens: Discrimination Against Women
   Under Botswana's Citizenship Act," *A Human Rights Watch Short Report*, vol. 6, no. 7 (September 1994).
2. Susan Forbes Martin, *Refugee Women* (London: Zed Books, Ltd.,
   1991), p. 24.
3. "The Vienna Declaration and Program of Action," adopted by the
   World Conference on Human Rights, June 25, 1993, pp. 33–34.
4. U.N. Commission on Human Rights, Fiftieth Session, Resolution
   1994/45, March 4, 1994. Endorsed by Economic and Social Council,
   decision of 1994/254, July 22, 1994.

Questions for Thought and Writing

1. How do women suffer when "human rights" are defined as
   pertaining solely to relationships between citizens and governments and not to relationships between individuals in
   communities and families? What are the contexts in which
   most abuses against women occur on a global scale?
2. According to the article, how do many governments fail to
   prevent and even outright contribute to the continued denial
   to women of their basic human rights? Explain both the active and passive ways that governments have been documented working against women in this realm.
3. What actions do the authors suggest women can take to force
   their governments to be accountable for human rights viola-

tions against women? What do you think are the greatest
challenges women face in taking these steps? How might citizens in rich countries like the U.S. assist in their efforts?

ISSUES

This Issues section includes "The Internet and the Global
Prostitution Industry," which provides the reader with a window into the ways that Internet technology has worked to
make many women around the globe even more vulnerable to
sexual exploitation and abuse than they already were. In "The
Globetrotting Sneaker," Cynthia Enloe demonstrates how
women in particular are vulnerable to exploitation by multinational corporations such as Nike and Reebok. She argues
against cultural relativity in assessing the conditions of sweat-
shop workers around the world. "The Women's Baths," by Ulfat al-Idlibi, provides readers with a glimpse of Syrian family
culture, and in particular the way in which different generations of Syrian women compete for the role of household
leader. The reader can draw instructive analogies and parallels
in comparing the status of older women in U.S. culture with
those described in the reading.

The Internet and the Global Prostitution Industry

DONNA M. HUGHES

The Internet has become the latest place for promoting the
global trafficking and sexual exploitation of women and children. This global communication network is being used to promote and engage in the buying and selling of women and
children. Agents offer catalogues of mail order brides, with girls
as young as 13. Commercial prostitution tours are advertised.
Men exchange information on where to find prostitutes and
describe how they can be used. After their trips men write reports

on how much they paid for women and children and give porno-graphic descriptions of what they did to them. New technology has enabled an online merger of pornography and prostitution, with videoconferencing bringing live sex shows to the Internet.

SEXUAL EXPLOITATION ON THE INTERNET

Global sexual exploitation is on the rise. The profits are high, and there are few effective barriers at the moment. Because there is little regulation of the Internet, the traffickers and promoters of sexual exploitation have rapidly utilised the Internet for their purposes.

Traffickers and pornographers are the leading developers of the Internet industry. *PC Computing* magasine urges entrepreneurs to visit pornography Web sites. "It will show you the future of on-line commerce. Web pornographers are the most innovative entrepreneurs in the Internet." The pornographers and other promoters of sexual exploitation are the Internet leaders in the developing privacy services, secure payment schemes and online data base management.

The development and expansion of the Internet is an integral part of globalisation. The Internet sex industry has made local, community and even, national standards obsolete. Nichols Negroponte, Director of the Media Laboratory at the Massachusetts Institute of Technology, and founder of *Wired* magazine said, "As we interconnect ourselves, many of the values of a nation-state will give way to those of both larger and smaller electronic communities." The standards and values on the Internet are being set by the sex industry and its supporters and users. This has meant that women are increasingly "commodities" to be bought, sold, traded and consumed.

NEWSGROUPS AND WEB SITES FOR MEN
WHO BUY WOMEN AND CHILDREN

The oldest forum on the Internet for promoting the sexual exploitation of women is the alt.sex.prostitution. Its "aim is to create market transparency for sex-related services." Postings from this newsgroup are archived into a site called The World Sex Guide which provides "comprehensive, sex-related information about every country in the world."

The guide includes information and advice from men who have bought women and children in prostitution. They tell others where and how to find and buy prostituted women and children in 110 countries. . . .

The men buying women and posting the information see and perceive the events only from their self-interested perspective. Their awareness of racism, colonisation, global economic inequalities, and of course, sexism, is limited to how these forces benefit them. A country's economic or political crisis and the accompanying poverty are advantages, which produce cheap readily available women for the men. Often men describe how desperate the women are and how little the men have to pay.

The postings also reveal that men are using the Internet as a source of information in selecting where to go and how to find women and children to buy prostitution. Men describe taking a computer print out of hotels, bar addresses and phone numbers with them on their trips, or describe how they used the Internet search engines to locate sex tours. . . .

This rapid publishing electronic medium has enabled men to pimp and exploit individual women. Now, men can go out at night, buy a woman, go home, and post the details on the newsgroup. By morning anyone in the world with an Internet connection can read about it and often have enough information to find the same woman. For example, in Nevada, one man bought a woman called "Honey" and named the brothel where she could be found. Within a couple of weeks other men went and bought "Honey" themselves and posted their experiences to the newsgroup. Within a short period of time men were having an orgy of male bonding by describing what each of them did to this woman. The men are keeping a special Web site on the Internet for men to post their experiences of buying this one woman. Additional sites have been created for other identifiable women. To my knowledge this is completely unprecedented. The implications for this type of public exchange in a fast-publishing easily accessible medium like the Internet are very serious for the sexual exploitation of women in the future.

PROSTITUTION TOURS

Centers for prostitution tourism are also the sources of women trafficked for purposes of sexual exploitation to other countries. For centers of prostitution in European countries, women from poor countries are imported legally and illegally to fill the brothels. Among the largest sources of trafficked women today are the countries of the former Soviet Union.

Advertisements for prostitution tours to these sites appear on the Internet, usually described as "romance tours" or "introduction tours."

Prostitution tours enable men to travel to "exotic" places and step outside whatever community bounds may constrain them at home. In foreign cities they can abuse women and girls in ways that are more risky or difficult for them in their hometowns.

As prostitution has become a form of tourism for men, it has become a form of economic development for poor countries. Tourism was recommended by the United States advisory boards as a way to generate income and repay debts. Nation-states set their own tourist policies and could, if they chose to do so, prevent or suppress the development of prostitution as a form of tourism. Instead, communities and countries have to rely on the sale of women and children's bodies as their cash crop. As the prostitution industry grows, more girls and women are turned into sexual commodities for sale to tourists. In the bars of Bangkok, women and girls don't have names—they have numbers pinned to their skimpy clothes. The men pick them by numbers. They are literally interchangeable sexual objects.

Prostitution tourism centers in industrialised countries are receiving sites for trafficked women from poor countries. The Netherlands is the strongest international proponent for legalised prostitution. Its capital, Amsterdam, is the leading prostitution tourism center in Europe. In 1997 the Netherlands legalized brothels. The result has been increased trafficking to Amsterdam from all over the world.

BRIDE TRAFFICKING

Mail order bride agents have moved to the Internet as their preferred marketing location. The Internet reaches a prime group of potential buyers—men from Western countries with higher than average incomes. The new technology enables Web pages to be quickly and easily updated; some services claim they are updating their selection of women weekly. The Internet reaches a global audience faster and less expensively than any other media.

15   The agents offer men assistance in finding a "loving and devoted" woman whose "views on relationships have not been ruined by unreasonable expectations." The agencies describe themselves as "introduction services," but a quick examination of

many of the Web sites reveals their commercial interests in bride trafficking, sex tours and prostitution.

The catalogues offer women mostly from Asia, Eastern Europe and Latin America, although in mid-1998 special catalogues of women from Africa appeared. They are called "African Queens," and "Brides of Nubia." Pictures of the women are shown with their names, height, weight, education and hobbies. Some catalogues include the women's bust, waist and hip measurements. The women range in age from 13 to 50. One of the commonly promoted characteristics of women from Eastern Europe is that they "traditionally expect to marry gentlemen that are 10 to 20 years older." The women are marketed as "pleasers," who will make very few demands on the men, and will not threaten them with expectations in their relationships, as women from the U.S. and Western Europe do.

In 1990 the Philippine government banned the operation of prostitution tour and mail order bride agencies in the Philippines. One trafficker lamented this new law, and told his customers that now he was operating out of the United States with his computer. He sent his own Filipina wife back to the Philippines to make contact and recruit women and adolescent girls for his Web site. Another complained that with the ban, the Philippine government is "definitely working against the interests of their own people. These girls want and need to leave that country." The same agent also complained that the U.S. government will not allow his youngest "brides" on offer into the country. "The service itself is not restricted by the American government, although they are real picky about getting your bride into the United States—they won't give a visa to a bride under sixteen." In his catalog of potential brides 19 girls are aged 17 or younger.

The bride traffickers sell addresses to men. Later they offer to arrange tours for the men to go to meet the woman with whom they have been corresponding, or to meet as many women as possible. Men pay for these services over the Internet with their credit cards.

LIVE VIDEO CONFERENCING

The most advanced technology on the Internet is live video conferencing, in which live audio and video are transmitted over the Internet from video recorder to computer. This advanced technology is being used to sell live sex shows over the Internet. Real time communication is possible, so the man can personally direct the live sex show as he is viewing it on his computer.

20   The only limitation on this type of global sex show is the need for high-speed transmission, processing and multimedia capabilities. The software required is free, but the most recent versions of Web browsers have these capabilities built into them. As more men have access to high-speed multimedia computer and transmission equipment, this type of private sex show will grow. There are no legal restrictions on live sex shows that can be transmitted over the Internet. As with all Internet transmissions, there are no nation-state border restrictions. With Internet technology a man may be on one continent, while directing and watching a live strip show, a live sex show, or the sexual abuse of a child on another continent. There have been several documented cases of live transmission of the sexual abuse of children through live video conferencing.

Who buys women over the Internet? According to the Internet Entertainment Group (EIG), the largest pimp on the Web, the buyers for live strip shows are 90 percent male, 70 percent are between the ages of 18 and 40. The buyers are young men in college, and businessmen and professionals who log on from work. This information was obtained from analysis of credit card usage.

GROWTH OF THE COMMERCIAL PROSTITUTION INDUSTRY ON THE INTERNET

The estimated number of pornographic Web sites varies widely. In late 1997, according to Naughty Linx, an online index, there were 28,000 "sex sites" on the Web with about half of them trying to make money selling pornography, videos, or live sex shows. Another study estimated that there were 72,000 pornographic Web sites on the Internet. At the end of 1997, Leo Preiser, the Director of the Center for Technology at National University estimated that 60 percent of the electronic commerce on the Web was pornography.

At the end of 1997, the online sex industry was estimated to be making US$1 billion a year, just in the United States. In findings from a 1997 survey, *Inter@ctive Week* magazine reported that 10,000 sex industry sites were bringing in approximately US$1 billion per year. A midsize site that was accessed 50,000 times per day made approximately US$20,000 each month. Established sex industry sites could expect to make 50 to 80 percent profits.

Forrester Research, an Internet analyst firm, estimated that the Internet sex industry would make close to US$1 billion in 1998. "We know of at least three sites doing more than US$100 million a year. And there are hundreds of sites out there."

REGULATION

The new technologies of the Internet have leapt over national borders and have left lawmakers scrambling to catch up. Internet users have adopted and defend an unbridled libertarianism. Any kind of regulation or restriction is met with hysterics and predictions of a totalitarian society. Even the most conservative restrictions on the transmission of child pornography are greeted with cries of censorship. The December 1996 issue of *Wired*, the leading professional publication on the Internet, stated that a new law in the United States, which made it illegal to transmit indecent materials to minors, was censorship. Internet libertarianism coupled with United States free speech absolutism is setting the standard for Internet communications.

Expressions of concern or condemnation of forms of sexual exploitation of women and children on the Internet are minimized by claims that pornographers have always been the first to take advantage of new technology—first photography, then movies, then VCRs, now the Internet. Those concerned about the use of the Internet for sexual exploitation are chastened with history lectures on new technology and pornography.

The solution that is being promoted is software programs that will screen out sexually explicit material. U.S. President Bill Clinton just announced that he supported a rating system on the Internet, so pornography would be rated and software programs will screen it out. This is seen as a way to protect children. Most adults are only concerned that their children may see pornography on the Internet. They aren't concerned about the women who are being exploited in the making of the pornography. In any search for a solution to pornography and prostitution it is crucial to remember, that sexual exploitation starts with real people and the harm is to real people.

We need international judicial and police co-operation in regulating the Internet and ending the trafficking and prostitution of women and the girls. If it is illegal to run a prostitution tour agency or mail order bride agency in the Philippines, then it should be illegal to advertise these services on a computer in the

USA. The countries that send the men on tours and receive the mail order brides should also ban the operation of such agencies and prohibit the advertisement of these services from computer servers in their country.

The European Union defines trafficking as a form of organised crime. It should be treated the same way on the Internet. All forms of sexual exploitation should be recognised as forms of violence against women and human rights violations, and governments should act accordingly. Although the Internet offers open communication to people throughout the world, it should not be permitted to be dominated and controlled by men's interests or the interests of the prostitution industry, at the expense of women and children.

Questions for Thought and Writing

1. The author quotes Nichols Negroponte as saying that "As we interconnect ourselves, many of the values of a nation-state will give way to those of both larger and smaller electronic communities." Consider this statement in terms of how it might apply to American men in search of prostitution. What "values of the nation-state" might they be able to bypass by using the Internet as a tool in this search?
2. Based on the example of the woman called "Honey," how and why does the Internet make women even more vulnerable to sexual exploitation than they were before its existence? What features of the Internet make it most useful to pimps and other exploiters of women and children?
3. In the section on "Bride Trafficking," the author reports that agents help men find women "whose 'views on relationships have not been ruined by unreasonable expectations.' " What are the implications of this statement? Speculate on how the power relations in such a marriage might differ from those in a traditionally forged marriage.

The Globetrotting Sneaker
CYNTHIA ENLOE

Four years after the fall of the Berlin Wall marked the end of the Cold War, Reebok, one of the fastest-growing companies in

United States history, decided that the time had come to make its mark in Russia. Thus it was with considerable fanfare that Reebok's executives opened their first store in downtown Moscow in July 1993. A week after the grand opening, store managers described sales as well above expectations.

Reebok's opening in Moscow was the perfect post–Cold War scenario: commercial rivalry replacing military posturing; consumerist tastes homogenizing heretofore hostile peoples; capital and managerial expertise flowing freely across newly porous state borders. Russians suddenly had the "freedom" to spend money on U.S. cultural icons like athletic footwear, items priced above and beyond daily subsistence: at the end of 1993, the average Russian earned the equivalent of $40 a month. Shoes on display were in the $100 range. Almost 60 percent of single parents, most of whom were women, were living in poverty. Yet in Moscow and Kiev, shoe promoters had begun targeting children, persuading them to pressure their mothers to spend money on stylish, Western sneakers. And as far as strategy goes, athletic shoe giants have, you might say, a good track record. In the U.S. many inner-city boys who see basketball as a "ticket out of the ghetto" have become convinced that certain brand-name shoes will give them an edge.

But no matter where sneakers are bought or sold, the potency of their advertising imagery has made it easy to ignore this mundane fact: Shaquille O'Neal's Reeboks are stitched by someone; Michael Jordan's Nikes are stitched by someone; so are your roommate's, so are your grandmother's. Those someones are women, mostly Asian women who are supposed to believe that their "opportunity" to make sneakers for U.S. companies is a sign of their country's progress—just as a Russian woman's chance to spend two months' salary on a pair of shoes for her child allegedly symbolizes the new Russia.

As the global economy expands, sneaker executives are looking to pay women workers less and less, even though the shoes that they produce are capturing an ever-growing share of the footwear market. By the end of 1993, sales in the U.S. alone had reached $11.6 billion. Nike, the largest supplier of athletic footwear in the world, posted a record $298 million profit for 1993—earnings that had nearly tripled in five years. And sneaker companies continue to refine their strategies for "global competitiveness"—hiring supposedly docile women to make their shoes, changing designs as quickly as we fickle customers change our tastes, and shifting factories from country to country as trade barriers rise and fall.

5   The logic of it all is really quite simple; yet trade agreements such as the North American Free Trade Agreement (NAFTA) and the General Agreement of Tariffs and Trade (GATT) are, of course, talked about in a jargon that alienates us, as if they were technical matters fit only for economists and diplomats. The bottom line is that all companies operating overseas depend on trade agreements made between their own governments and the regimes ruling the countries in which they want to make or sell their products. Korean, Indonesian, and other women workers around the world know this better than anyone. They are tackling trade politics because they have learned from hard experience that the trade deals their governments sign do little to improve the lives of workers. Guarantees of fair, healthy labor practices, of the rights to speak freely and to organize independently, will usually be left out of trade pacts—and women will suffer. The recent passage of both NAFTA and GATT ensures that a growing number of private companies will now be competing across borders without restriction. The result? Big business will step up efforts to pit working women in industrialized countries against much lower-paid working women in "developing" countries, perpetuating the misleading notion that they are inevitable rivals in the global job market.

All the "New World Order" really means to corporate giants like athletic shoemakers is that they now have the green light to accelerate long-standing industry practices. In the early 1980s, the field marshals commanding Reebok and Nike, which are both U.S.-based, decided to manufacture most of their sneakers in South Korea and Taiwan, hiring local women. L.A. Gear, Adidas, Fila, and Asics quickly followed their lead. In short time, the costal city of Pusan, South Korea, became the "sneaker capital of the world." Between 1982 and 1989 the U.S. lost 58,500 footwear jobs to cities like Pusan, which attracted sneaker executives because its location facilitated international transport. More to the point, South Korea's military government had an interest in suppressing labor organizing, and it had a comfortable military alliance with the U.S. Korean women also seemed accepting of Confucian philosophy, which measured a women's morality by her willingness to work hard for her family's well-being and to acquiesce to her father's and husband's dictates. With their sense of patriotic duty, Korean women seemed the ideal labor force for export-oriented factories.

U.S. and European sneaker company executives were also attracted by the ready supply of eager Korean male entrepreneurs with whom they could make profitable arrangements. This fact was central to Nike's strategy in particular. When they moved their production sites to Asia to lower labor costs, the executives of the Oregon-based company decided to reduce their corporate responsibilities further. Instead of owning factories outright, a more efficient strategy would be to subcontract the manufacturing to wholly foreign-owned—in this case, South Korean—companies. Let them be responsible for workers' health and safety. Let them negotiate with newly emergent unions. Nike would retain control over those parts of sneaker production that gave its officials the greatest professional satisfaction and the ultimate word on the product: design and marketing. Although Nike was following in the footsteps of garment and textile manufacturers, it set the trend for the rest of the athletic footwear industry.

But at the same time, women workers were developing their own strategies. As the South Korean pro-democracy movement grew throughout the 1980s, increasing numbers of women rejected traditional notions of feminine duty. Women began organizing in response to the dangerous working conditions, daily humiliations, and low pay built into their work. Such resistance was profoundly threatening to the government, given the fact that South Korea's emergence as an industrialized "tiger" had depended on women accepting their "role" in growing industries like sneaker manufacture. If women reimagined their lives as daughters, as wives, as workers, as citizens, it wouldn't just rattle their employers; it would shake the very foundations of the whole political system.

At the first sign of trouble, factory managers called in government riot police to break up employees' meetings. Troops sexually assaulted women workers, stripping, fondling, and raping them "as a control mechanism for suppressing women's engagement in the labor movement," reported Jeong-Lim Nam of Hyosung Women's University in Taegu. It didn't work. It didn't work because the feminist activists in groups like the Korean Women Workers Association (KWWA) helped women understand and deal with the assaults. The KWWA held consciousness-raising sessions in which notions of feminine duty and respectability were tackled along with wages and benefits. They organized independently of the male-led labor unions to ensure that their issues would be taken seriously, in labor negotiations and in the prodemocracy movement as a whole.

The result was that women were at meetings with management, making sure that in addition to issues like long hours and low pay, sexual assault at the hands of managers and health care were on the table. Their activism paid off: in addition to winning the right to organize women's unions, their earnings grew. In 1980, South Korean women in manufacturing jobs earned 45 percent of the wages of their male counterparts; by 1990, they were earning more than 50 percent. Modest though it was, the pay increase was concrete progress, given that the gap between women's and men's manufacturing wages in Japan, Singapore, and Sri Lanka actually widened during the 1980s. Last, but certainly not least, women's organizing was credited with playing a major role in toppling the country's military regime and forcing open elections in 1987.

Without that special kind of workplace control that only an authoritarian government could offer, sneaker executives knew that it was time to move. In Nike's case, its famous advertising slogan—"Just Do It"—proved truer to its corporate philosophy than its women's "empowerment" ad campaign, designed to rally women's athletic (and consumer) spirit. In response to South Korean women workers' newfound activist self-confidence, the sneaker company and its subcontractors began shutting down a number of their South Korean factories in the late 1980s and early 1990s. After bargaining with government officials in nearby China and Indonesia, many Nike subcontractors set up shop in those countries, while some went to Thailand. China's government remains nominally Communist; Indonesia's ruling generals are staunchly anti-Communist. But both are governed by authoritarian regimes who share the belief that if women can be kept hard at work, low paid, and unorganized, they can serve as a magnet for foreign investors.

Where does all this leave South Korean women—or any woman who is threatened with a factory closure if she demands decent working conditions and a fair wage? They face the dilemma confronted by thousands of women from dozens of countries. The risk of job loss is especially acute in relatively mobile industries; it's easier for a sneaker, garment, or electronics manufacturer to pick up and move than it is for an automaker or a steel producer. In the case of South Korea, poor women had moved from rural villages into the cities searching for jobs to support not only themselves, but parents and siblings. The exodus of manufacturing jobs has forced more women into the growing "entertainment" industry. The kinds of bars and massage parlors offering sexual services that had mushroomed around U.S. military bases during the Cold War have been opening up across the country.

But the reality is that women throughout Asia are organizing, knowing full well the risks involved. Theirs is a long-term view; they are taking direct aim at companies' nomadic advantage, by building links among workers in countries targeted for "development" by multinational corporations. Through sustained grassroots efforts, women are developing the skills and confidence that will make it increasingly difficult to keep their labor cheap. Many are looking to the United Nations conference on women in Beijing, China, this September [1995], as a rare opportunity to expand their cross-border strategizing.

The Beijing conference will also provide an important opportunity to call world attention to the hypocrisy of the governments and corporations doing business in China. Numerous athletic shoe companies followed Nike in setting up manufacturing sites throughout the country. This included Reebok—a company claiming its share of responsibility for ridding the world of "injustice, poverty, and other ills that gnaw away at the social fabric," according to a statement of corporate principles.

Since 1988, Reebok has been giving out annual human rights awards to dissidents from around the world. But it wasn't until 1992 that the company adopted its own "human rights production standards"—after labor advocates made it known that the quality of life in factories run by its subcontractors was just as dismal as that at most other athletic shoe suppliers in Asia. Reebok's code of conduct, for example, includes a pledge to "seek" those subcontractors who respect workers' rights to organize. The only problem is that independent trade unions are banned in China. Reebok has chosen to ignore that fact, even though Chinese dissidents have been the recipients of the company's own human rights award. As for working conditions, Reebok now says it sends its own inspectors to production sites a couple of times a year. But they have easily "missed" what subcontractors are trying to hide—like 400 young women workers locked at night into an overcrowded dormitory near a Reebok-contracted factory in the town of Zhuhai, as reported last August in the *Asian Wall Street Journal Weekly*.

Nike's cofounder and CEO Philip Knight has said that he would like the world to think of Nike as "a company with a soul that recognizes the value of human beings." Nike, like Reebok, says it sends in inspectors from time to time to check up on work conditions at its factories; in Indonesia, those factories are run largely by South Korean subcontractors. But according to Donald

Katz in a recent book on the company, Nike spokesman Dave Taylor told an in-house newsletter that the factories are "[the subcontractors'] business to run." For the most part, the company relies on regular reports from subcontractors regarding its "Memorandum of Understanding," which managers must sign, promising to impose "local government standards" for wages, working conditions, treatment of workers, and benefits.

In April, the minimum wage in the Indonesian capital of Jakarta will be $1.89 *a day*—among the highest in a country where the minimum wage varies by region. And managers are required to pay only 75 percent of the wage directly; the remainder can be withheld for "benefits." By now, Nike has a well-honed response to growing criticisms of its low-cost labor strategy. Such wages should not be seen as exploitative, says Nike, but rather as the first rung on the ladder of economic opportunity that Nike has extended to workers with few options. Otherwise, they'd be out "harvesting coconut meat in the tropical sun," wrote Nike spokesman Dusty Kidd, in a letter to the *Utne Reader.* The all-is-relative response craftily shifts attention away from reality: Nike didn't move to Indonesia to help Indonesians; it moved to ensure that its profit margin continues to grow. And that is pretty much guaranteed in a country where "local standards" for wages rarely take a worker over the poverty line. A 1991 survey by the International Labor Organization (ILO) found that 88 percent of women working at the Jakarta minimum wage at the time—slightly less than a dollar a day—were malnourished.

A woman named Riyanti might have been among the workers surveyed by the ILO. Interviewed by the *Boston Globe* in 1991, she told the reporter who had asked about her long hours and low pay: "I'm happy working here. . . . I can make money and I can make friends." But in fact, the reporter discovered that Riyanti had already joined her coworkers in two strikes, the first to force one of Nike's Korean subcontractors to accept a new women's union and the second to compel managers to pay at least the minimum wage. That Riyanti appeared less than forthcoming about her activities isn't surprising. Many Indonesian factories have military men posted in their front offices who find no fault with managers who tape women's mouths shut to keep them from talking among themselves. They and their superiors have a political reach that extends far beyond the barracks. Indonesia has all the makings for a political explosion, especially since the gap between rich and poor is widening into a chasm. It is in this setting that the government has tried to crack down on any independent labor organizing—a policy that Nike has helped to implement. Referring to a recent strike in a Nike-contracted factory, Tony Nava, Nike representative in Indonesia, told the *Chicago Tribune* in November 1994 that the "troublemakers" had been fired. When asked about Nike policy on the issue, spokesman Keith Peters struck a conciliatory note: "If the government were to allow and encourage independent labor organizing, we would be happy to support it."

Indonesian workers' efforts to create unions independent of governmental control were a surprise to shoe companies. Although their moves from South Korea have been immensely profitable, they do not have the sort of immunity from activism that they had expected. In May 1993, the murder of a female activist outside Surabaya set off a storm of local and international protest. Even the U.S. State Department was forced to take note in its 1993 worldwide human rights report, describing a system similar to that which generated South Korea's boom 20 years earlier: severely restricted union organizing, security forces used to break up strikes, low wages for men, lower wages for women—complete with government rhetoric celebrating women's contribution to national development.

Yet when President Clinton visited Indonesia last November, 20 he made only a token effort to address the country's human rights problem. Instead, he touted the benefits of free trade, sounding indeed more enlightened, more in tune with the spirit of the post–Cold War era than do those defenders of protectionist trading policies who coat their rhetoric with "America first" chauvinism. But "free trade" as actually being practiced today is hardly *free* for any workers—in the U.S. or abroad—who have to accept the Indonesian, Chinese, or Korean workplace model as the price of keeping their jobs.

The not-so-new plot of the international trade story has been "divide and rule": If women workers and their government in one country can see that a sneaker company will pick up and leave if their labor demands prove more costly than those in a neighbor country, then women workers will tend to see their neighbors not as regional sisters, but as competitors who can steal their precarious livelihoods. Yet it is as essential to international trade politics as is the fine print in GATT.

But women workers allied through the networks like the Hong Kong–based Committee for Asian Women are developing their own post–Cold War foreign policy, which means addressing women's needs: how to convince fathers and husbands that a woman going out to organizing meetings at night is not sexually promiscuous; how to develop workplace agendas that respond to family needs; how to work with male unionists who push women's demands to the bottom of their lists; how to build a global movement.

These women refuse to stand in awe of the corporate power of the Nike or Reebok or Adidas executive. Growing numbers of Asian women today have concluded that trade politics have to be understood by women on their own terms. They will be coming to Beijing this September [1995] ready to engage with women from other regions to link the politics of consumerism with the politics of manufacturing. If women in Russia and Eastern Europe can challenge Americanized consumerism, if Asian activists can solidify their alliances, and if U.S. women can join with them by taking on trade politics—the post–Cold War sneaker may be a less comfortable fit in the 1990s.

Author's Note: This article draws from the work of South Korean scholars Hyun Sook Kim, Seung-kyung Kim, Katherine Moon, Seungsook Moon, and Jeong-Lim Nam.

Questions for Thought and Writing

1. Why does the author use italics in describing the "freedom" that Russians suddenly had in buying expensive sneakers after the fall of the Berlin Wall? As potential targets for the sneaker companies, what do the Russians she discusses have in common with "inner-city boys" from the United States?

2. Why are the women—and not so much the men—in countries like South Korea especially vulnerable to multinational corporations like Nike and Reebok? What conditions and philosophies exist in patriarchal countries that make women particularly well-suited to the purposes of these companies? How have women begun to challenge these conditions?

3. Enloe calls Nike's argument that low-paying factories jobs are better for Indonesians than "harvesting coconut meat in the tropical sun" an "all-is-relative response" that "craftily shifts attention away from reality." What is an "all-is-relative" argument? What is the reality from which she believes Nike is distracting attention? How does Nike's rationale compare to those you may have studied in business classes?

4. Enloe argues that "playing women off against each other" is "essential to international trade politics." What does she mean by this? What do trade organizers and factory managers gain by "playing women off against each other"? How do they do this? Can you identify instances in mainstream American culture where women and members of minority groups are encouraged to see each other as competitors?

The Women's Baths

Ulfat al-Idlibi

Our household was troubled by an unusual problem: my grandmother, who had passed the age of seventy, insisted on taking a bath at the beginning of every month at the public baths, or market baths as she used to call them.

In my grandmother's opinion the market baths had a delicious ambience about them which we, who had never experienced it, could not appreciate.

For our part we were afraid that the old lady might slip on the wet floor of the baths—this has often happened to people who go there—and break her leg, as her seventy years had made her bones dry and stiff; or she might catch a severe chill coming outside from the warm air of the baths and contract a fatal illness as a result. But how could we convince this stubborn old lady of the cogency of these arguments?

It was quite out of the question that she should give up a custom to which she had adhered for seventy years, and she had done so without ever once having been stricken with the mishaps we feared. Grandmother had made up her mind that she would keep up this custom as long as she was able to walk on her own two feet, and her tenacity in clinging to her point of view only increased the more my mother tried to reason with her.

Yet Mother never tired of criticizing her mother-in-law, arguing with her and attempting to demonstrate the silliness of her views, even if only by implication. Whenever the subject of the public baths came up my mother proceeded to enumerate their shortcomings from the standpoints of health, of society, and even of economics.

5

The thing which really annoyed Mother was that my grandmother monopolized our only maid from the early morning onward on the day she went to the baths. She would summon her to her room to help her sweep it and change the sheets and do up the bundles to take to the baths. Then she would set out with her and would not bring her back until around sunset, when our maid would be exhausted and hardly able to perform her routine chores.

In our house I was the observer of a relentless, even though hidden, struggle between mother-in-law and daughter-in-law: between my grandmother, who clung to her position in the household and was resolved under no circumstances to relinquish it, and my mother, who strove to take her place.

Although girls usually side with their mother, I had a strong feeling of sympathy for my grandmother: old age had caught up with her since her husband had died some time before and left her a widow, and little by little her authority in the home shrank as my mother's authority gradually extended. It is the law of life: one takes, then one hands over to another in one's turn. But that does not mean we obey the law readily and willingly.

I used to feel a certain prick of pain when I saw Grandmother retire alone to her room for long hours after being defeated in an argument with Mother. I would sometimes hear her talking bitterly to herself, or I would see her monotonously shaking her head in silence, as though she were rehearsing the book of her long life, reviewing the days of her past, when she was the unchallenged mistress of the house, with the last word. I would often see her vent the force of her resentment on her thousand-bead rosary as her nervous fingers told its beads and she repeated the prayer to herself:

10   "Oh merciful God, remove this affliction!"

And who could this "affliction" be but my mother?

Then little by little she would calm down and forget the cause of her anger. There is nothing like the invocation of God for purifying the soul and enabling it to bear the hardships of life.

One day when I saw my grandmother getting her things ready to go to the market baths I had the idea of accompanying her, thinking that perhaps I might uncover the secret which attracted her to them. When I expressed my wish to accompany her she was very pleased, but my mother did not like this sudden impulse at all, and said, in my grandmother's hearing, "Has the craze for going to the market baths affected you as well? Who knows—you may catch some infection, like scabies or something, and it will spread around the family."

Thereupon my father broke in with the final word: "What is the matter with you? Let her go with her grandmother. All of us went to the public baths when we were young and it never did any of us any harm."

My mother relapsed into a grudging silence, while my grand-   15
mother gave an exultant smile at this victory—my father rarely took her side against my mother.

Then Grandmother led me by the hand to the room where her massive trunk was kept. She produced the key from her pocket and opened the trunk in my presence—this was a great honor for me, for the venerable trunk had never before been opened in the presence of another person—and immediately there wafted out of it a strange yet familiar scent, a scent of age, a smell of the distant past, of years which have been folded up and stored away. Grandmother drew out of the depths of the trunk a bundle of red velvet, the corners of which were embroidered with pearls and sequins.

She opened it in front of me and handed me a wine-colored bathwrap decorated with golden stars. I had never set eyes on a more beautiful robe. She also gave me a number of white towels decorated around the edges with silver thread, saying "All these are brand new; no one has ever used them. I have saved them from the time I was married. Now I'm giving them to you as a present, since you are going to the baths with me. Alas . . . poor me. Nobody goes with me now except the servants."

She gave a deep, heart-felt sigh. Then she called the servant to carry the bundle containing our clothes and towels, and the large bag which held the bowl, the soap, the comb, the sponge-bag, the loofah,[1] the soil of Aleppo,[2] and the henna which would transform my grandmother's white hair to jet black. She put on her shawl, and we made our way toward the baths, which were only a few paces from our house. Times without number I had read the words on the little plaque which crowned the low, unpretentious door as I passed by: "Whoever the Divine Blessing of health would achieve, should turn to the Lord and then to the baths of Afif."

We entered the baths.

The first thing I noticed was the female "intendant." She was   20
a stout woman, sitting on the bench to the right of persons coming in. In front of her was a small box for collecting the day's revenue. Next to it was a *nargileh*[3] decorated with flowers. It had a long mouthpiece which the intendant played with between her

lips, while she looked at those around her with a proprietorial air. When she saw us she proceeded to welcome us without stirring from her place. Then she summoned Umm Abdu, the bath attendant. A woman hastened up and gave us a perfunctory welcome. She had pencilled eyebrows, eyes painted with *kohl*,[4] and was dressed very neatly. She had adorned her hair with two roses and a sprig of jasmine. She was very voluble, and was like a spinning-top, never motionless, and her feet in her Shabrawi clogs made a rhythmic clatter on the floor of the baths. Her function was that of hostess to the bathers. She came up to my grandmother and led her to a special bench resembling a bed. Our maid hastened to undo one of our bundles, drawing out a small prayer rug which she spread out on the bench. My grandmother sat down on it to get undressed.

I was fascinated by what I saw around me. In particular my attention was drawn to the spacious hall called *al-barani*.[5] In the center of it was a gushing fountain. Around the hall were narrow benches on which were spread brightly-colored rugs where the bathers laid their things. The walls were decorated with mirrors, yellowed and spotted with age, and panels on which were inscribed various maxims. On one of them I read, "Cleanliness is part of Faith."

My grandmother urged me to undress. I took off my clothes and wrapped myself in the wine-colored bath-wrap, but as I was not doing it properly Umm Abdu came and helped me. She secured it around my body and then drew the free end over my left shoulder, making it appear like an Indian sari.

Then she helped my grandmother down from her bench, and conducted us toward a small door which led into a dark corridor, calling out at the top of her voice, "Marwah! Come and look after the Bey's mother!"

With a sigh a shape suddenly materialized in the gloom in front of me: it was a grey-haired, emaciated woman of middle age with a face in which suffering had engraved deep furrows. She was naked except for a faded cloth which hung from her waist to her knees. She welcomed us in a nasal tone, prattling on although I could not catch a single syllable of what she was saying, thanks to the babble of discordant voices which filled my ears and the hot thick steam which obstructed my sight; and there was a smell which nearly made me faint, the like of which I had never encountered in my life before. I felt nauseous, and was almost sick, leaning against the maid for support.

Nevertheless, in a few moments I grew accustomed to the 25
odor and it no longer troubled me; my eyes, also, became accustomed to seeing through the steam.

We reached a small hall containing a large stone basin. A number of women circled around in it, chatting and washing at the
same time. I asked my grandmother: "Why don't we join them?"

She replied: "This is the *wastani*;[6] I have hired a cubicle in the
juwani.[7] I am not accustomed to bathing with the herd."

I followed her through a small door to the *juwani,* and found
myself looking with confused curiosity at the scene that presented itself. There was a large rectangular hall, at each corner of
which stood a large basin of white marble. Women sat around
each one, busily engrossed in washing, scrubbing, and rubbing,
as though they were in some kind of race. I raised my eyes to look
at the ceiling, and saw a lofty dome with circular openings, glazed
with crystal, through which enough light filtered to illuminate the
hall. The uproar here was at its worst—there was a clashing of
cans, the splashing of water, and the clamor of children.

My grandmother paused for a moment to greet a friend
among the bathers, while I found myself following a violent quarrel which had arisen between two young women. I understood
from the women around them that they were two wives of a
polygamous marriage, who had met face to face for the first time
at the baths. The furious quarrel led at length to an exchange of
blows with metal bowls. Luckily a spirit of chivalry among some
of the bathers induced them to separate the two warring wives
before they could satisfy their thirst for revenge.

As we advanced a little way the howling of a small child 30
drowned the hubbub of the hall. Its mother had put it on her lap,
twisting one of its legs around her and proceeding to scrub its face
with soap and pour hot water over it until its skin was scarlet red.
I averted my gaze, fearing the child would expire before my eyes.

We reached the cubicle, and I felt a sense of oppression as we
entered it. It consisted of nothing but a small chamber with a
basin in the front. Its one advantage was that it screened those
taking a bath inside from the other women.

We were received in the cubicle by a dark, stout woman with
a pock-marked face and a harsh voice. She was Mistress Umm
Mahmud. She took my grandmother from the attendant Marwah,
who was being assailed by shouts from every direction:

"Cold water, Marwah, cold water, Marwah!"

The poor woman set about complying with the bathers' requests for cold water, dispensing it from two big buckets which

she filled from the fountain in the outer hall. She was so weighed down with the buckets that she aroused pity in those who saw her struggle.

35   I turned back to Grandmother and found her sitting on the tiled floor in front of the basin. She had rested her head between the hands of Umm Mahmud, who sat behind her on a sort of wooden chair which was only slightly raised above the level of the floor. She proceeded to scour Grandmother's head with soap seven consecutive times—not more, not less.

I stood at the door of the cubicle, entertained by the scene presented by the bathers. I watched the younger women coming and going, from time to time going into the outer hall for the sake of diversion, their fresh youthfulness showing in their proud swaying gait. In their brightly colored wraps decorated with silver thread they resembled Hindu women in a temple filled with the fragrance of incense. Little circles of light fell from the dome onto their tender-skinned bodies, causing them to glisten.

I found the sight of the older women depressing: they sat close to the walls chatting with one another, while the cream of henna on their hair trickled in black rivulets along the wrinkles of their foreheads and cheeks, as they waited impatiently for their turn to bathe.

Suddenly I heard shrill exclamations of pleasure. I turned toward their source, and saw a group of women gathered around a pretty young girl, loudly expressing their delight at some matter.

Mistress Umm Mahmud said to me: "Our baths are doing well today: we have a bride here, we have a woman who has recently had a child, and we have the mother of the Bey—may God spare her for us!"

40   It was no wonder that my grandmother swelled with pride at being mentioned in the same breath with a bride and a young mother.

I enjoyed standing at the door of the cubicle watching the bride and her companions. Then I caught sight of a fair well-built woman enveloped in a dark blue wrap, giving vent to overflowing joy with little shrieks of delight. I realized from the words she was singing that she must be the bride's mother:

"Seven bundles I packed for thee, and the eighth in the chest
    is stored;
To Thee, Whom all creatures need, praise be, oh Lord!"

A young woman, a relative or friend of the bride, replied:

"Oh maiden coming from the *wastani,* with thy towel all
   scented.
He who at thy wedding shows no joy, shall die an infidel, from
   Paradise prevented!"

The bride's mother continued the song:

"The little birds chirp and flutter among the trellis'd leaves;
How sweet the bride! The bath upon her brow now pearly
   crowns of moisture weaves.
Thou canst touch the City Gate with thy little finger tip, though
   it is so high;
I have waited long, long years for this day's coming nigh!"

But the best verse was reserved for the bridegroom's mother:

"Oh my daughter-in-law! I take thee as my daughter!
The daughters of Syria are many, but my heart only desires and
   wishes for thee!
Pistachios, hazels and dates: the heart of the envious has been
   sore wounded;
Today we are merry, but the envious no merriment shall see!"

The singing finished as the bride and her companions formed
a circle around a tray upon which had been placed cakes of Dam- 45
ascene mincemeat, and a second one filled with various kinds of
fruit. The bride's mother busied herself distributing the cakes
right and left, and one of them fell to my share also!

In a far corner a woman was sitting with her four children
around a large dish piled with *mujaddarah*[8] and pickled turnips,
their preoccupation with their meal rendering them completely
oblivious to what was going on around them in the baths. When
the dish had been emptied of food the mother took from a basket
by her side a large cabbage. Gripping its long green leaves, she
raised it up and then brought it down hard on the tiled floor, until
it split apart and scattered into fragments. The children tumbled
over each other to snatch them up and greedily devoured them,
savoring their fresh taste.

Then my attention was diverted by a pretty girl, about fifteen
or sixteen years old, sitting on a bench along the wall of the
boiler-house. She seemed impatient and restless, as though she
found it hard to tolerate the pervasive heat. She was surrounded
by three women, one of whom, apparently her mother, was fever-
ishly fussing over her. She began to rub over her body a yellow
ointment which exuded a scent of ginger (it was what was called

"strengthening ointment"). My grandmother explained to me that it reinforced the blood vessels of a new mother, and restored her to the state of health she had enjoyed before having her child.

The attendant Umm Abdu came up to us and inquired after our comfort. She brought us both glasses of licorice sherbet as a present from the intendant. Then she lit a cigarette for my grandmother, who was obviously regarded as a patron of distinction.

It was now my turn. My grandmother moved aside, and I sat down in her place, entrusting my head to the attentions of Umm Mahmud for a thorough rubbing. After I had had my seven soapings I sat down before the door of the cubicle to relax a little. I was amused to watch the bath attendant Marwah scrubbing one of the bathers. Her right hand was covered with coarse sacking, which she rubbed over the body of the woman sitting in front of her. She began quite slowly, and then sped up, and as she did so little grey wicks began to appear under the sacking, which quickly became bigger and were shaken to the floor.

50   After we had finished being loofah-ed and rubbed, Umm Mahmud asked me to come back to her to have my head soaped an additional five times. I surrendered to her because I had promised myself that I would carry out the bathing rites through all their stages and degrees as protocol dictated, whatever rigors I had to endure in the process!

I was not finished until Umm Mahmud had poured the last basinful of water over my head, after anointing it with "soil of Aleppo," the scent of which clung to my hair for days afterwards.

Umm Mahmud rose, and standing at the door of the cubicle, called out in her harsh voice: "Marwah! Towels for the Bey's mother!"

With a light and agile bound Marwah was at the door of the *wastani*, calling out in a high-pitched tone, like a cockerel: "Umm Abdu! Towels for the Bey's mother!" Her shout mingled with that of another "Mistress" who was standing in front of a cubicle opposite ours, likewise demanding towels for her client.

Umm Abdu appeared, clattering along in her Shabrawi clogs, with a pile of towels on her arm which she distributed among us, saying as she did: "Blessings upon you . . . Have an enjoyable bath, if God wills!"

55   Then she took my grandmother by the arm and led her to the *barani*, where she helped her to get up onto the high bench, and then to dry herself and get into her clothes.

Grandmother stood waiting her turn to pay her bill. There was a heated argument going on between the intendant and a middle-aged woman who had three girls with her. I gathered from what was being said that the usual custom was for the intendant to charge married women in full, but that widows and single women paid only half the normal fee. The lady was claiming that she was a widow, and her daughters were all single. The intendant listened to her skeptically, and obviously could not believe that the eldest of the girls was single, in that she was an adult and was very beautiful. But at last she was forced to accept what the woman said after the latter had sworn the most solemn oath that what she was saying was the truth.

My grandmother stepped forward and pressed something into the intendant's hand, telling her: "Here's what I owe you, with something extra for the cold water and the attendance."

The intendant peered down at her hand and then smiled; in fact she seemed very pleased, for I heard her say to my grandmother: "May God keep you, Madam, and we hope to see you every month."

Then my grandmother distributed tips to the attendant, the "Mistress," and Marwah, as they emerged from the *juwani* to bid her good-bye.

I have never known my grandmother to be so generous and open-handed as on the day which we spent at the market baths. She was pleased and proud as she listened to the blessings called down on her by those who had received her largesse. Then she gave me an intentionally lofty look, as if to say: "Can you appreciate your grandmother's status now? How about telling your mother about *this*, now that she's begun to look down her nose at me?"

As she left the baths there was a certain air of haughtiness in her step, and she held herself proudly upright, although I had only known her walk resignedly, with a bent back, at home.

Now she was enjoying the esteem which was hers only when she visited the market baths. At last I understood their secret . . .

Endnotes

1. The fibrous pod of an Egyptian plant, used as a sponge.
2. A kind of clay, found around Aleppo, which is mixed with perfume used in washing the hair.
3. An eastern tobacco pipe in which the smoke passes through water before reaching the mouth.
4. A powder, usually of antimony, used in eastern countries to darken the eyelids.
5. The outer hall of a public bath.
6. The middle hall of a public bath.
7. The inner hall of a public bath.
8. A Syrian dish of rice, lentils, onions, and oil.

Questions for Thought and Writing

1. In the author's Syrian culture, there is a high degree of competition between women of different generations for the leadership role in the household. How does this circumstance compare to relationships between mothers and daughters in contemporary U.S. culture? Identify instances from popular culture or from your own experience in which older and younger women consider each other competitors for authority and resources.

2. How much of a role does body image and concern with appearance play in the Syrian bathhouse compared to the role these things might play among a group of women in contemporary U.S. culture? Write about how differently the author's experience might have been had she been American rather than Syrian.

3. The author's grandmother is honored along with a bride and a new mother by the bath Mistress. Why does the Mistress seem to feel the grandmother is worthy of being honored? Compare this circumstance to the way you observe older women being treated in the U.S. Identify examples from popular culture or from your own experience of how the United States equates youth with beauty and worthiness.

Exploring Connections

1. In "The Internet and the Global Prostitution Industry," author Hughes notes how *PC Computing* magazine "urges entrepreneurs to visit pornography Web sites" because they are "the future of on-line commerce. Web pornographers are the most innovative entrepreneurs in the Internet." Similarly, in "The Globetrotting Sneaker," the oppression of women in sneaker factories was explained as part of "The New World Order." Based on these circumstances, what seems to be the relationship between global capitalism and women? How do the essays complicate your perceptions of capitalism as a system?

2. "Empathy Among Women on a Global Scale" explains that in "all patriarchal religions throughout history" women have been confined to the domestic sphere and "reduced to vehicle(s) of procreation." How does this circumstance—which is reflected in "The Women's Baths"—contribute to exaggerated competition and antagonism between women in these societies?

Kim Allen, originally a physicist, now works as a market analyst and strategic consultant.

Lila Abu-Lughod teaches Anthropology and Middle Eastern Studies at New York University and has authored *Writing Women's Worlds: Bedouin Stories* and *Veiled Sentiments: Honor and Poetry in a Bedouin Society*, and has edited *Remaking Women: Feminism and Modernity in the Middle East*.

Mahnaz Afkhami is the president of Women's Learning Partnership for Rights, Development and Peace. Her books include *Claiming Our Rights* (with Haleh Vaziri), *Faith & Freedom* (editor), *Toward a Compassionate Society* (editor), *Women in Exile*, and *Safe and Secure* (with Greta H. Nemiroff and Haleh Vaziri).

Ulfat al-Idlibi is a Syrian short story writer and novelist born in Damascus. She is the author of *Sabriya: Damascus Bitter Sweet* and *My Grandfather's Tale*.

Phyllis Chesler is founder of The Association for Women in Psychology and The National Women's Health Network. Her nine books include *Women and Madness, Letters to a Young Feminist*, and *Patriarchy: Notes of an Expert Witness*.

Eisa Davis is a writer-performer who has received fellowships from the Van Lier Foundation, the Mellon Foundation, and Cave Canem (a workshop/retreat for black poets). She was the MacDowell Colony's Thornton Wilder Fellow for 1999-2000. Her plays include *Umkovu, Bulrusher*, and *Paper Armor*.

Robbie Davis-Floyd is a cultural anthropologist specializing in the anthropology of reproduction, medical anthropology, and ritual and gender studies. A research fellow at the University of Texas at Austin, she published *Cyborg Babies: From Techno-Sex to Techno-Tots*.

Cynthia Enloe is a professor of government and director of the Women's Studies Program at Clark University. She studies the impact of state policies and politics on the lives of women throughout the world. Her most recent publication is *Maneuvers: The International Politics of Militarizing Women's Lives.*

Ellen G. Friedman is Director of the Women's and Gender Studies Program and Professor of English at The College of New Jersey. Her most recent book is *Morality USA* with Corinne Squire.

Anita F. Hill is a law professor at the Heller School for Social Policy and Management at Brandeis University. Hill is the author of *Speaking Truth to Power,* which recounts her experience as a witness in the Senate confirmation hearings of Clarence Thomas for Supreme Court Justice. She is co-editor, with Emma Coleman Jordan, of *Race, Gender and Power in America.*

Arlie Russell Hochschild teaches sociology at the University of California, Berkeley. She is the author of *The Second Shift* and *The Time Bind.*

bell hooks (nee Gloria Watkins) is Distinguished Professor of English at City College in New York. Her recent books include *Bone Black: Memories of Girlhood, Reel to Real: Race, Sex, and Class at the Movies,* and *Wounds of Passion: A Writing Life.*

Donna M. Hughes holds the Eleanor M. and Oscar M. Carlson Endowed Chair at the University of Rhode Island. She writes on trafficking, sexual exploitation, violence against women, women's organized resistance to violence, religious fundamentalism and women's rights, and on issues related to women, science and technology.

Human Rights Watch is an independent, nongovernment organization supported by contributions from private individuals and foundations worldwide.

Nan D. Hunter is a law professor at Brooklyn Law School in New York City. She served as Deputy General Counsel for the Department of Health and Human Services in the Clinton Administration. Her books include *Sexuality, Gender and the Law* (with W. Eskridge), *Sex Wars: Sexual Dissent and Political Culture* (with L. Duggan), and *The Rights of Lesbians and Gay Men.*

Sut Jhally is the author of *The Codes of Advertising: Fetishism and the Political Economy of Meaning in the Consumer Society, Enlightened Racism: The Cosby Show,* and *Audiences and the Myth of the American Dream.* He teaches communications at the University of Massachusetts.

Rita Mae Kelly is Dean of Social Sciences at the University of Texas at Dallas. Her books include *Gender Power, Leadership, and Governance* and *The Gendered Economy: Work, Careers, and Success.*

Jennifer D. Marshall is a doctoral candidate in English at Lehigh University in Bethlehem, Pennsylvania. She teaches Rhetoric and Gender and Popular Culture at The College of New Jersey. Her doctoral dissertation explores issues of space in cultural studies composition.

Roberta Praeger is an activist who has worked on housing, welfare, and women's issues.

Lillian B. Rubin teaches sociology at Queens College, C.U.N.Y, and is Senior Research Associate at the Institute for the Study of Social Change at the University of California, Berkeley. She is the author of *The Transcendent Child, Families on the Fault Line, Just Friends,* and *Intimate Strangers.*

D. Travers Scott is a novelist and short story writer. He has written *Execution, Texas: 1987* and edited *Strategic Sex: Why They Won't Keep It in the Bedroom.*

Laura Sells is an assistant professor in the Communication Studies department at Louisiana State University. She is co-author (with Lynda Haas, and Elizabeth Bell) of *From Mouse to Mermaid: The Politics of Film, Gender, and Culture.*

Corinne Squire is Reader in Social Sciences at the University of East London, and Codirector of the Centre for Narrative Research. Her research interests are in subjectivity and popular culture, and in HIV, identity, and citizenship.

Mercedes E. Steedman teaches in the Department of Sociology and Anthropology of Laurentian University. In addition to co-editing *Who's On Top: The Politics of Heterosexuality,* she has published *Angels of the Workplace: Women and the Construction of Gender Relations in the Canadian Clothing Industry, 1890–1940.*

John Stoltenberg is the author of *End of Manhood: Parables of Sex and Selfhood, Refusing to Be a Man: Essays on Social Justice,* and *What Makes Pornography "Sexy"?*

Luci Tapahonso is the author of five books of Native American poetry and short stories, including *Blue Horses Rush In, Navajo ABC: A Dineh Alphabet Book,* and *Saanii Dahataal: The Women Are Singing.*

Nicholas Townsend is the author of *The Package Deal: Marriage, Work, and Fatherhood in Men's Lives.* He is Assistant Professor of Anthropology at Brown University.

Mary Douglas Vavrus is a member of the graduate faculty of the Feminist Studies program at the University of Minnesota and is the author of *Postfeminist News: Political Women in Media Culture.*

Rebecca Walker is co-founder of the Third Wave Foundation, the only national, activist, philanthropic organization for young women aged 15–30. In addition to editing *Telling the Truth and the Changing Face of Feminism,* she is the author of *Black, White, and Jewish: Autobiography of a Shifting Self.*

Abu-Lughod, Lila, "Is There a Muslim Sexuality? Changing Constructions of Sexuality in Egyptian Bedouin Weddings," from *Gender in Cross-Cultural Perspective,* 3rd ed., edited by Brettell & Sargent, copyright © 1993. Reprinted by permission of Pearson Education, Inc., Upper Saddle River, NJ.

Afkhami, Mahnaz, "Empathy Among Women on a Global Scale," from *Women in Post-Revolutionary Iran: A Feminist Perspective,* by Mahnaz Afkhami. Reprinted by permission of I.B. Tauris & Co. Ltd.

al-Idlibi, Ulfat, "The Women's Baths." Reprinted with the permission of Wesleyan University Press.

Allen, Kim, "The 3rd WWWave: Who We Are, and Why We Need to Speak." Reprinted with the permission of The 3rd WWWave. Copyright 1997 by Kim Allen.

Chesler, Phyllis, "Letters to a Young Feminist on Sex and Reproductive Freedom." Reprinted with the permission of Four Walls Eight Windows. Copyright 1997 Phyllis Chesler.

Davis, Eisa, "Sexism and the Art of Feminist Hip-Hop Maintenance."

Davis-Floyd, Robbie E., "Gender and Ritual: Giving Birth the American Way." Printed with permission from the Dunham Literary, Inc., New York, NY. Used by permission of Robbie E. Davis-Floyd.

Enloe, Cynthia, "The Globetrotting Sneaker." Reprinted by permission of *Ms. Magazine,* © 1995.

Friedman, Ellen G., and Corinne Squire, "Family." From *Morality USA,* Minneapolis: University of Minnesota Press, 1998. Reprinted with permission from the authors.

Hill, Anita F., "Sexual Harassment: The Nature of the Beast." From Anita F. Hill, "Sexual Harassment: The Nature of the Beast," 65 Southern California Law Review, 1145-1148(1992). Reprinted with the permission of the Southern California Law Review.

Hochschild, Arlie Russell, and Ann Machung, "The Second Shift: Working Parents and the Revolution at Home." From *The Second Shift* by Arlie Hochschild and Ann Machung. Copyright © 1989 by Arlie Russell Hochschild. Used by permission of Viking Penguin, a division of Penguin Group (USA) Inc.

hooks, bell, "Witnessing the Death of Love: She Hears Him Tell the Woman That He Will Kill Her . . . " From *Bone Black: Memories of Girlhood* by bell hooks. Copyright © 1996 by Gloria Watkins. Reprinted by permission of Henry Holt and Company, LLC.

Hughes, Donna M., "The Internet and the Global Prostitution Industry." Reprinted with the permission of Donna M. Hughes.